Keatley

Winthropping

KEATLEY'S
WINTHROPPING
Finding the 'here' in 'where'

Prof. David Keatley, PhD

Published by ReBSA Publications, Australia
First Edition Published: July 2024
Paperback ISBN: 978-0-6489214-3-1

Please note this book is written for educational purposes and is not to be used as legal advice or review. All comments and statements used in this book are the Author's opinion or those of named sources. Statements and cases are given for illustrative purposes and should not be interpreted as critique of legal process or outcomes nor used as precedent for legal process. The Author retains the rights to change any part of this book. Further training should be undertaken before attempting to use these lessons in an applied setting. Cases are used for example purposes and no comment on the process or outcome of cases is intended.

DEDICATION

I dedicate this book to the victims, and the families, friends, and loved ones who are left behind.

Regrettably, this book focuses primarily on the offenders. Sadly, it feels as though the victims become a byline in their own storyline. As much as I dislike this, it is necessary, as the focus is on the offenders' motives, cognitions, and geographical behaviors. I can only hope the outcome is worthwhile. I do not claim to have the answers, but perhaps together we can take steps towards the truth.

To the living we owe respect,
To the dead, we owe only the truth.

CONTENTS

Acknowledgements

This is always the hardest section of any book for me to write. Let me say from the start, the names of those who need acknowledging would and should fill an entire book. I can only hope my gratitude to you was made clear at the time, and that you know I still feel an insurmountable debt of gratitude.

Of course, my utmost thanks go to The Vidocq Society. I am honored, humbled, and grateful to be a full VSM. The work The Vidocq Society does is exemplary. The dedication and professionalism the members show to the cases we are tasked with working ensures that I am constantly learning and developing. To the Post-Presentation Work Group (PPWG), which I am co-chair of, I owe further thanks. It is always a pleasure, honor, and humbling experience to work cases with you all. Thanks also to the other task forces, Detectives, and investigation teams I have worked with over the years. Rest assured, all of our cases remain locked in my brain, not in these pages.

I would also like to thank Karsten Bettels, leader of the ICCAP. Karsten's tireless dedication, hard-work, and commitment to helping students and working on cases is inspiring. Furthermore, Karsten has been one of the biggest supporters of my approach to Winthropping. I am forever indebted to your support and eagerness, Karsten. We will solve those cases, I know it. I also thank the students who have participated in the various ICCAPs throughout the years. Several in particular have stood out as being exemplary.

To my co-authors on various papers that we have published on this topic. Prof. Chris O'Donnell – you have been a friend and mentor for years. I would not be here if not for you. Prof. David Clarke, my lecturer, supervisor, collaborator, colleague, and more importantly, friend. My entire career is indebted to you, I hope to one day earn it. Dr Brendan Chapman, thank you for your constant pushing to improve my methods and develop my understanding of forensic science.

Of course, many more students of mine are worthy of praise than I can fit into this book. I thank you for the consults you have provided me with. To all my other research and postgraduate students, and those in the various ICCAPs, Major Crimes Review, and formerly in Cold Case Review, you all deserve individual praise. My apologies for not naming everyone, here. Thanks also to Elizabeth Gourlay, who once again has provided a brilliant cover worth favorably judging – I can only hope the content of the book lives up to it.

Now to the personal ones. This is the first book I have written wherein I cannot thank my mum in the normal way. I still cannot believe you're gone mum. I've written a whole book on finding the missing, but you've gone to a place I can never bring you back from. I would trade everything I have for one more day with you. I miss you.

To my dad, who I know can never read this. I hope this works somehow. I hope you know how much I respect you. Our nightly chats about cold cases have inspired me for years. In another timeline, I think of you as a detective, and that world would have far fewer unsolved cases. For a man with failing eyes, you see everything and have one of the keenest minds I have known.

To Stacey and Paul. Ok, first, here's what most people do not realize – how many times I have texted you both asking for the American translation of my English words. So, thanks for the constant Americanisation of my words (I left that one in for you).

To Tara, my wife, my love, my life. Truly the greatest find I have ever found and the only waypoint I'll ever need or want. None of this would be possible without your constant support, encouragement, and guidance. Thank you.

And finally, to *you*. Yes, You. My readers. You have picked up a book with a title many of you will not know much about. You have taken a step towards learning something new. You are the kind of people the world needs more of. The inquisitive type, the eager type, the open type, the good type. I only hope this book provides you with the questions you require if not the answers you desire.

To all: We will never stop the evil in this world. We cannot stop the tide of missing persons and murders. Within our power, though, I believe, is the chance to give one last gift to the missing and those left behind, to show all is not lost. Together, if we work hard, persevere in the face of adversity, ignore the allure of pessimism, and keep moving forward, we will find the answers. I know it. And I can think of no greater calling.

Preface

Before we begin, it is worth putting some things into context. I would not want anyone misunderstanding the intention of this book or the line of research and development it represents. First, the name. *Keatley's* Winthropping was chosen not for ego nor for fame (I try to avoid the public eye and attention as much as I can). Instead, it is my humble way of saying, "I have attempted to understand and redevelop what Winthropping is."

Alongside various colleagues, I have been attempting to redevelop the original Winthropping method. Now, I need your help. From where we started to where we are, now, I think we have made significant progress. There is a possibility, however, that as we continue to develop our version, we may move further from the original. This may offer us new innovations; but at the risk of misrepresenting the original version.

I could have called it *Keatley and colleagues'* Winthropping – but then who are the *and colleagues*? There have been numerous. Also, while I am leading the research, is it fair to throw their names collectively into the firing line? The standard academic 'et al.' also seemed cumbersome. *Keatley et al.'s* Winthropping suffers the same issues. So, I have opted to place my name before it, therein if anyone feels that my version of Winthropping is incorrect, the fault lies with me. So be it.

I am, of course, indebted to many academics – outlined in the acknowledgements and beyond. I will say again, though, that Prof. Chris O'Donnell, Prof. David Clarke, and Dr. Brendan Chapman have been very helpful in the (re)development of this version of Winthropping. I am indebted to their help and insights.

Language/Terms

My next *a priori mea culpa* involves language and terms. Please allow me to apologize unreservedly from the start if any language or any use of terminology in this book offends you. When I first started assisting in criminal investigations, I was at times equally dismayed at some of the language I heard. "How," I thought "can these people proclaim to care for the dead, when they speak about them in that way?" I was, it is fair to say, naïve. The detectives and investigators I have been fortunate enough to work with care deeply. They simply hide the scars behind a bandage of humor. They try to muffle the screams of ghosts with the sounds of jokes. I understand that it is not appropriate in the wider public eye. I know how it appears to the outside world. I have also seen my fair share of the horrors that these investigators have. I have heard the ghosts screaming and the felt the pain of desperation, the iced grip of a case going cold. If my language appears anything less than respectful, then I apologize.

Rest assured, any jokes or light humor in this book will be primarily self-focused. Beyond that, I have been told I sometimes slip into "police speak," which I believe means I use terms that police find acceptable, but the wider world do not. Here are some examples, said to help you understand, *not* to offend. "Dumpsite" to me is a regular term indicating the place a body/victim/item/trophy was put. There are obviously various ways a body can be placed, hidden, buried, or left, but 'dumpsite' loosely covers them all. It is 2 syllables. Done. It is convenient, concise, and expedient. I am aware that '*body deposition site*' is the preferred term. This is where my two lives abut.

In my role as an academic, a teacher, a lecturer, I understand sensitivities and always attempt to ensure my students and audiences are not offended. I do not want to cause offense. When I work with police, however, our feelings are secondary to progressing a case with efficiency. "Give me the meat and potatoes," is a phrase I have heard all-too-often. Essentially, stop flapping your gums and give me something of substance, succinctly. I can already feel my police friends reading this preface and probably feeling tempted to skip it – feel free to. For my non-police audience, please accept my apologies. If I use the term 'dumped' or 'dumpsite' in this book, it does not reflect a lack of concern or care for the victim. I assure you the same is true of police if you catch them using the term.

Next, *Missing person* (4 syllables) or *MisPer* (2 syllables – though I can sometimes drawl it into about 1.5). The point, again, is that I appreciate that the utmost care and concern should be taken when talking about someone missing, and potentially worse. My heart breaks for you. But I also have a job to do. Please allow me to just use a term that is more expedient and gets us on to the next important piece of information quicker.

I am not, of course, suggesting that we adopt this relaxed attitude to all words, terms, and language. I appreciate how contentious language and labelling is. Again, in this book I have not used a single term, label, or statement with the intention of being derogatory – unless in reference to myself. I have tried to proof-read out every instance of potential misinterpretation that could lead to someone being offended. But language is personal. I cannot ensure that a reader will not find offense if they go looking. Please remain aware of the fact though that while you are looking for offense, I am looking for MisPers and dumpsites.

The cases herein

Managing expectations is something I am always keen to do early. From the start, therefore, let me make it clear that the purpose of this book is not to provide in-depth biographies of famous, infamous, or relatively unknown murderers. Of course, the life history and lived experiences of offenders is important in order to understand their crimes. That said, I wanted to keep this book brief. Inflating the page count by providing information that is not germane to understanding Keatley's Winthropping seemed redundant. Therefore, do not be surprised when you see a chapter on Ted Bundy, for example, that only spans a few pages. My students will revolt! A few pages on everyone's favorite serial killer?! Whole books have been written about Bundy. While that is true, first, it means repeating it here seems unnecessary, and second most of the information about Bundy's life is not pertinent to our focus on Keatley's Winthropping. You just get the meat and potatoes. If you want the trimmings, rest assured a reading list is provided in chapters and at the end.

Next, cases are chosen for specific reasons. Often, a case is outlined to show you certain facets or features of Keatley's Winthropping more clearly. That said, I have not provided a full geographic analysis of each case in every detail. It would end up being very repetitive. The aim is that by the time you finish this book, you have multiple cases that you can reflect on and draw from when considering others.

During the writing of this book, several people kindly offered me more cases to add. Some I gratefully included. This process, I must admit, is a driving force of writing this book. I am keen to get this re-developed method out there, into the wider domain. I am sure that many more people have many more cases that have either directly used Winthropping (e.g., Napper) or have a case wherein Winthropping could be used. I have little doubt that in about a year or two's time, I shall be writing a second edition with twice the number of cases. I look forward to the collaboration with people who suggest cases and insights.

Which brings me to the inevitable next point. I have not

included every case that you know. I am sure that readers will be disappointed to find out "*that famous case*" is not included. I am equally sure readers can name myriad other cases that you feel should really have been added. I offer some apologies, but again remind you all that this is part of the reason for publishing this – to form those collaborative links. I am sorry if you feel a case that really should have been included is not. Simply let me know. I shall include it and where appropriate offer my written thanks to whomever provided it, if you want. Hopefully, the 30 or so cases in this book offer enough foundation that there is something in Keatley's Winthropping worth pursuing. When applied to missing persons, no-body homicides, and deposition site profiling it may offer new insights. Will another 30 cases change the approach? Possibly. But that is the nature of science – to constantly question, revise, improve, and progress.

"What about-ery"

A further point I wish to consider is the "*what about…*" or "*have you considered…*" questions and comments. Recently, I attended a brilliant conference, 'Behaviour Analysis.' The focus of the conference is on all manner of topics related to security, threat detection, and criminal behavioral analysis. While I was there, I was fortunate enough to sit at a table with two security experts from a large shopping mall in USA. They were kind enough to show interest in my new book, this one you are currently reading. But of what use is Keatley's Winthropping to them? I did ask if anyone had ever hidden a body in their shopping center. But no.

That, of course, is not the only application of this approach. Indeed, as you will soon learn, Winthropping was originally developed to find clandestine caches. Now, we are moving towards a behavior that may be more relevant to my newfound friends. I explained to them the basics, but before I could reveal my 'ah-ha' moment, they already struck upon it. "Have you considered using Keatley's Winthropping to help in bomb threat situations?" Luckily, I had, and therein a great conversation ensued.

These meeting-of-minds opportunities are what I love most about the field I now work in. Everyone has the same goal, the shared motivation, and the combined work ethic to improve our security, safety, and detection approaches. The point I wish to make, here, is that if while reading this you have a similar "what about" moment, then please do feel free to get in touch. I am always more than happy to soundboard ideas. So, while the majority of this book is about missing persons, no-body, and located-body homicides, know that the method can and has been used across a wider range of areas.

The Black Swan

I imagine it will be less than a week before I receive my first message, email, or review suggesting I have missed a case that makes one of my conclusions untenable. "*You said killers don't do X, but I think you'll find that so-and-so did*" or something less kindly worded. "*This so-called expert doesn't even know the case of Y, that clearly refutes his assertion about Z.*" I am not going to say here that you are wrong. I am going to say you have probably misunderstood my aims for this book. And given I am writing this here, you have probably just skimmed it, found the one case you know more about (it won't be hard*) and then flexed your superior knowledge. Well done. Really. Well done. Good for you for knowing a lot about the case. I am happy to edit, revise, and update my work to account for better information. Please let me know and I shall gratefully receive the information and rectify the book as soon as possible.

*It won't be hard to know more about these cases, because for the most part, the cases herein are not cases I have worked. These cases are proxies for cases I have worked. I cannot and will not reveal information about cases I have assisted on. I just won't do it. So, how do I write an entire book on a new method I have developed for cases I have all the known information for but cannot tell you anything about? The only option is to try and use public-domain cases.

This means that I have collected as much information as I can from as many resources as I can. But it does not mean I am an expert on these cases. Not even close. That's the key point I want to make clear, though. I am not writing this book to show you I am an expert in Bundy or Birnie, Ridgway or Meirhofer. I am writing this book to give an introduction to my approach to Winthropping. I have provided over 30 cases to give you a general overview and insight.

I will say throughout that for Keatley's Winthropping to be most effective, we need to know as much as possible about the case. We may not know everything, but the more we know, the better, clearer, and more accurate the Keatley's Winthropping profile we can build. But even in real-world cases I assist on, I am not naïve enough to think we have either all the details or only truthful, accurate details. Even in police files, omissions hide, and errors arise.

We know this. We work with this. And that is why no single tool should be taken as 100% valid (not even DNA). So, if you find an error in a case, remember, that it is unlikely to be wholly damning because the Keatley's Winthropping profile takes information from multiple sources. It builds upon various angles, insights, and investigative leads. And then, when we have collected, collated, and considered as much as we can. Well, even then, we should not wholly rely on Keatley's Winthropping or believe it to be infallible. It is a tool, to be used with caution and alongside every other tool in the toolbox.

Going backwards

As the famous quotation goes, it is always easier to connect the dots working backwards. When I tell people about some of the cases in this book, I often hear, "yeah, it's obvious when you know where the body is." Too true. But let us take a moment to think about what is being said in that statement. The outcome location, the body deposition site, or the clandestine cache site is 'obvious' when we know it. I often agree. The point I want to consider is whether we can use that to our advantage. Here are a couple of ways I think this criticism can be turned into a strength.

First, it would be entirely useless for my purposes to have a book filled with unsolved locations and ongoing no-body homicides. I need to show you how my approach to Winthropping could work. Therefore, I need to show you solved cases and re-analyze them with my approach. Along the way, we can learn and develop it, together. At the end of the book, you'll find a chapter on missing persons and no-body homicides. What? Still unsolved? Even with this method I've created and put my name on? Yes. Because I am not saying that I have solved the unsolvable. My hope is that you learn enough about Keatley's Winthropping throughout the preceding chapters, that by the time the unsolved cases come along we are better prepared to consider them.

Second, if we really do think that discovery sites are 'obvious,' then let's use that. This is how I mean. When I am talking to investigators about a missing person or no-body homicide case, they typically have several potential locations.

These locations are based on multiple sources of information, evidence, and profiling tools. One 'trick' I do is to presume the body or cache is in a location they have chosen. Imagine the case thus solved. Now, in this hypothetical situation, can we look at that location and say, "well, it's obvious." If we can – owing to various sources of information, profiling, evidence etc. then we have strengthened our case for that being the real location. Often, though, when running this thought trial through matrices (see Chapter 32), I am met with rather blank expressions and uncertainty. Perhaps it is not so obvious. Of course, let's not remove it entirely, but let's move on to site 2 and see if it becomes more "obvious." In this way, certain sites can become elevated.

But then, the inevitable. We strike out. We go, we explore, we survey, we sniff, we dig, we find nothing. No magic wand, no silver bullets. In this situation, it's time to review our hypotheses, evidence, and geographical profiles. It is not time to give up. The first thing I consider is, if all our background information and hypotheses are sound, perhaps there is a location version '1.b.' that fits the specifications in every dimension but is simply somewhere else (nearby). Each misstep may still take us a step forward, even if we stumble.

The fallacy of the Texas Sharpshooter

In the ol' Western days, there was a Texas Cowboy known throughout the lands for his sharpshooter skills. For those military trained or shooting afficionados, I know that '*Expert*' would be a better sobriquet here, but bear with me. The sharpshooter was renowned for hitting bullseyes on every shot. What a mythical legend. He never missed.

The only problem was no-one had ever seen him shoot. Sure,

they could see his handiwork afterwards, but they never saw him actually shoot. I am, of course, narrating a well-known fallacy in the hope it sticks in your mind. The fallacy is about how we may look for clusters and patterns, while ignoring differences and randomness.

I am going to try to avoid this fallacy throughout the book. It is hard to avoid, though. I am purposefully looking for patterns in chaos. It is hard to ensure we are finding only the true patterns, while ignoring the false positives. That is why we must be vigilant, push back, and constantly remind ourselves to re-analyze our results, even (and perhaps especially) if we are correct.

Here is what I mean. We may look at a case and use Keatley's Winthropping to help us understand it. I want to ensure that we are not drawing bullseyes around the location and pretending we got there through our analyses. That is why you will constantly see me repeat warnings about the effectiveness of my approach to Winthropping. I want to ensure the theories, models, analyses, approaches, and arguments I am putting forward work. I have to use solved cases to show you how it all works. But do not lose your skepticism. I do not want to be seen to be simply drawing rings around my theories to make it seem as though I am accurate. I want to actually improve the accuracy of our work.

Indeed, this is the main reason for this book. To work with other experts in the various related fields and disciplines. Let us improve our sights, narrow our vision, and improve the approach such that we can more accurately find the hidden locations.

It is time to begin…

I apologize if this preface seems overly defensive or pessimistic. Experience tells me that both positions are required. I have been on the receiving end of enough criticism to know that it is important to defend my position *a priori*. That is not to say I am defensive. Quite the contrary. I welcome criticism and the opportunity to develop my methods. That said, I also see people wanting my approach to Winthropping to be the silver bullet or magic wand for their case. It is not.

The hardest part of writing this book is knowing that I will fall short of readers' hopes and expectations. I don't have the answers. I won't be able to point at a map and tell you, "Look here!" to find your missing person, loved one, cache, or clandestine location. At best, I'll barely have a suggestion – and even that, only after a lot of questions and discussion. So, what is the point of this book? To introduce you all to a method that I think can prove extremely effective. It may not be there, yet, but I hope that if enough people learn about it, use it, apply and develop it then we may get to the next step together…

So, with all that said, let's move on from this and take our first step…

OUR FIRST STEP

1. Where are they?

This is one of several haunting questions that we face when investigating missing persons (MisPer) cases. *Where are they?* Attempting to solve a crime, when you cannot be certain a crime has even occurred, is one of the most challenging tasks. Even if we are fairly certain a crime has occurred, even if we have evidence to suggest the victim is deceased, we might still be faced with the mystery of where they are located. I have been a part of many investigations in which a suspect has admitted to killing a victim, but still will not explicitly reveal what he did with the body. In these cases, especially, I hear the haunting bell tolling, the bereaved family calling: *Where are they?*

This question is often met with a less-than-helpful response, "*they could be anywhere*." While this is perhaps logically true, evidence suggests that is it not practically true. Indeed, in many cases, the victim is found somewhere that is both predictable and intuitive. I strongly encourage investigators to avoid the siren song defeatist trap of believing a victim could be dumped *anywhere*. In fairness to investigators, while they may say "anywhere," they are often quick to designate high priority areas for ground, water, and aerial searches. The focus of this book is on helping to narrow those search areas further, and perhaps elevate some so that they can be seen more clearly.

Sometimes, however, we know where the body is. We find the victim. In these cases, the investigation changes focus. Now, we are not profiling *where* are they, but *why* are they here? One of the earliest cases I was asked to review involved a missing young girl. I'd like to introduce you to Mary (not her real name). Mary was a sweet kid. Life dealt her a bad hand, so she took it and shook it with a smile. The type of defiance I've only ever seen in children who face adversity without realizing they deserve so much better. Yes, it's safe to say Mary is a ghost that haunts me. On brighter days, I sometimes imagine her playing in the park, like she did one summer's day. Laughing with her friends. Carefree. Alive. Then, missing. And as the day turned to dusk, the call came in.

My daughter is missing. Horror writers cannot depict a more chilling experience. *Where is she?* We did not know. *Who took her*? We were not entirely sure. The only known witnesses with her before she went missing were her equally young friends. Understandably, and through no fault of their own, they did not provide us with any verifiable leads. Canvassing of the neighborhood also offered nothing. It was, as the saying often goes, as though she disappeared into thin air. She was gone. Until she wasn't.

You see, when I first came to little Mary's short story, I already knew the ending. Sadly. Mary had been found barely a mile from where she was taken from. Bringing loved ones back from the ether certainly helps an investigation, it does provide some answers, but sometimes they're to questions you wish you did not have to ask. I knew the outcome of Mary's story because Mary had sadly been found. Sadly, because she was found – deceased.

Mary, the girl who never had the chance to grow up was dumped on an overgrown bank of a swamp. A swamp. Discarded like trash. I don't like using tabloid-terms like 'monster' or 'evil,' but it is hard to think of Mary without those words hauntingly swirling around her. So, if Mary wants to haunt me, who am I to tell her to disappear. Truthfully, I don't want her to go missing. Not again. Not like the last time. In some way, I feel she's safe if she's with me. We found her. We found the 'where.' Now, we owed her only the truth. We needed to find the 'why' and then hopefully the who.

At the time I was asked to assist on this case, I had no idea what Winthropping was, but looking back, it turns out I was attempting something naively similar. Let me explain. I am not from America. I do not know most of the towns, cities, or states that I am asked to assist in. To overcome this limitation, I often turn to various maps to orientate myself. I did this in Mary's case. As it turned out, the location Mary was left made no sense to me. Mary was found 1 mile from where she was taken, in a westerly direction. But the same distance to the north was a much larger, much wilder swampland area. I wagered that if she were left by or in this swampland, we might still be looking for her until this very day. Detectives with historic experience of the locale agreed.

To add to this incongruity, where Mary was found was right behind and below a row of high-build houses. It would be risky to take a child there, dead or alive. Why, then, had the suspect decided to leave her there? And this is how the question shifted, from where is she, to why was she left there? And the answer to both of these questions became the basis of a whole area of investigation that I was about to discover and re-develop.

Winthropping

It is worth saying from the outset that little is known, in the public domain, about the original Winthropping. There are relatively few publications on the method and Freedom of Information applications have been largely met with neither confirmation nor denial of the existence and use of the method. This was my first stumbling point when I was trying to learn about it. From the scant information available, we know that it was developed in the 1970s, to help tackle the Irish Republican Army (IRA) troubles. Winthrop, a Royal Engineer officer, attempted to predict where individuals would hide weapons caches.

Before we continue, it is worth remembering that many of the great advances in Forensic Psychology and Criminology have come not from viewing criminals as monsters or evil specters, but instead as everyday humans. It is often hard to do. In this more human frame, however, we can map their cognitions and actions as deviations from regular, everyday thoughts and actions. Essentially, a criminal's thoughts and actions are underpinned by the same cognitive structures and processes as you and I have. When we attempt to understand criminals by applying our common sense, intuition, and thought processes onto theirs, we often make important steps forward.

That is not to say we are always accurate, but who better to understand a human than another human? This, I believe, was a strong underpinning for what Winthrop suggested: to understand where a criminal would hide a cache, let us imagine where *we* would hide that cache.

That, in its most basic terms, is the essence of Winthropping. We must put ourselves in the position of the offender or criminal and imagine what we would do. I know, I know. It seems almost ridiculously simplistic. When I first mention this method to investigators, I am often met with skepticism. That is perhaps fair. But remember, criminals are not cyborgs. They are not aliens. They are not monsters. They are humans. They are making decisions using similar processes to us.

Nowadays, I often hear investigators turning to Artificial Intelligence (AI) to help crack crimes. This may prove very effective in some applications, but we should be careful with its deployment, use, and interpretation. I opine: what happened to good ol' fashioned *human* intelligence? Instead of attempting to build a computer machine or program to mimic and map human behavior, why can we not use our own pre-existing, exquisitely complex and extremely powerful computer: our brains. If I were attempting to build a tower of academic knowledge, why not build it atop the mountain of human experiential expertise rather than setting the foundations from the ground and hoping to one day see over the hill of human knowledge?

This is not to naively say that our intuitions or gut feelings are always accurate. Far from it. But even our inaccuracies can be turned into important learning experiences. In many ways, the worst mistakes are the ones we do not learn from. Bear that in mind as we progress. You will learn of investigations that made mistakes. It is easy for us, now, in the warmth of wherever we are reading this to condemn from the position of hindsight. That is not the point. The point is to learn. Where did the investigators get it right? Where did they falter? How can we improve moving forwards? If you want a method that is 100% accurate, turn to science fiction. Evidence is often open to interpretation.

Back to Winthropping. Further research showed that the approach has also been used in other military areas. Several publications outlined the approach that I have stated here. The two in particular that I have read show the use of Winthropping in site exploration and bomb discovery. Both articles are very brief and provide few explanatory details.

One of the publications on the Winthropping approach I have found provides a good summary for us. Beware, it takes a bit of cognitive ability to put yourself in the mind of an enemy. Imagine you are the enemy. You must, as the enemy, find an ambush or attack point. Once you find a suitable location, scan the nearby area for where you would stash a weapons cache.

The chosen location must be hidden – because otherwise it may easily be found. It must be accessible, so that you or your comrades can get to it quickly enough to use in an ambush. It must also be somewhere that is locatable. There's no point hiding it in a place your own colleagues cannot find – you may also need to direct your colleagues to the location. Now, consider where in the area near the ambush site meets these criteria. Found it? Good, now switch back to your own mind and go and look there. Variations of this approach have been effective in locating clandestine sites and weapons caches.

A further key reference I came upon was a poster outlining the method, but again with relatively few practical details. The next step forwards, therefore, was to take a step backwards, and reverse engineer *how* Winthropping works. Also, while Winthropping appeared to be focused on military settings and caches, could I redevelop it for missing persons and homicide cases? There are a small handful of research publications and master's theses that provide some groundwork for this possibility. I applaud the authors and hope that this book helps us all find our way.

I note, here, that the following is not necessarily a reflection or true account of Winthrop's original formulation. Alongside several researchers, I have been attempting to develop a working procedure, based on theories, research, and practical applications that may underpin and explain what I think Winthropping is. I may have made mistakes. Those mistakes should land squarely on my shoulders. In order to ensure that readers know this, I have taken to affixing my name before it: *Keatley's* Winthropping. This is done solely to ensure that if I have made a mistake along the way, or inaccurately re-developed the method, then the limitation reflects my approach, not Winthrop's original version.

I note that some authors refer to Winthropping as 'feature focused searches' or 'reference point searching'. Both of these have intuitive appeal, given what we know of Winthropping. While there are only a few publications mentioning Winthrop and Winthropping, there are fewer that appear to use these other terms. Therefore, for consistency in the literature, and as deference to the creator, I have opted to maintain the use of his name. To ensure that any deviation to the approach is not held against, him, I have used mine as the first point of reference.

2. Keatley's Winthropping

Some of you may wonder why I am so keen to deconstruct and then reconstruct Winthropping rather than just get on with having a go at using it. Is it just academic curiosity? A form of navel-gazing? No. It is important to understand the framework of a method, so that we can then discover how to develop and strengthen it. Indeed, a more recent development of Keatley's Winthropping has been to focus on integrating forensic linguistics. This tentative development is something that is possible because I developed the framework on which to attach linguistics. But I am getting ahead of myself, let me first explain the foundational theories that I believe are important to understand to gain the most out of my Winthropping approach.

Criminological Approaches

Rational Choice Theory

Perhaps the most obvious place to begin is with the decision making that an offender engages in when deciding to move a cache, item, trophy, or body. Of course, not every offender moves a body. But, for those that do, some form of decision making takes place. Here, we can turn to Rational Choice Theory (RCT) to help us. RCT outlines the weighing-up that criminals perform when determining a course of action. Most criminals, especially those who decide to move a body, must weigh up the pros and cons of such an action.

Of course, not all actions are the outcome of a clearly considered weighing-up process. This also becomes part of the later profiling that we may turn to. Originally, Winthrop appears to have focused on deliberative decision making for hiding caches or explosives. This is certainly true of some offenders. Cognitive Psychologists will tell us that decision making can also be more impulsive, less planned. This is true, too. The movement of a body, however, involves some thought process (otherwise the victim would simply be left where they were killed – which is also a decision). Therefore, the choice to move a body in the first instance and the location chosen is where Keatley's Winthropping aligns with the original version.

We are barely one paragraph in and already the ease of "*just pretend you're a criminal and consider where you would hide a body*" becomes much more nuanced. We must consider our own expertise and biases and try to align them more closely with the suspect (if known) or a range of suspects (if not). We must profile ourselves and our biases as carefully as we attempt to profile the offender.

Let us take a case in which the suspect has admitted to the murder and dumping of a body but refuses to guide us to the location. In this instance, we may profile the suspect and then attempt to put ourselves in his shoes, with his biases and beliefs. Of course, we may still not be 100% accurate, but do not let inaccuracy be the enemy of progress. Every time we are wrong, feed that back into the decision-making system. What led us to that location? What tenets might be altered to improve our accuracy? Did our bias affect the process? If we are wrong, let us learn. I do not know of a single forensic method that is 100% accurate 100% of the time.

Now, let us come at this from the other end: a body has been found. In the case of Mary, outlined previously, we found her. We knew the *where,* now we had to consider the *why*. Here, again, Keatley's Winthropping can be useful. Recently, my colleague, Prof. Christopher O'Donnell and I considered Winthropping as a profiling tool for these types of crimes. If we know where a deposition site is, we may effectively work backwards to consider what type of offender might choose that location. This is the *why* of Keatley's Winthropping. This is such an important avenue of investigation that it will have several chapters devoted to it later.

For now, a brief overview will suffice. In Mary's case we do not believe the murder was planned. But she was moved? So, we have a potentially impulsive crime with a considered deposition site. Or was it random?

The location was not random. Few locations are ever truly 'random' – they may only appear that way if we are unsure of the meaning or pattern. Here's an example of randomness: "110618." Sorry, I lied. While 110618 may look entirely random at first, it is not. It is the date I moved to Australia (11th June 2018). Sorry to any American readers that are offended by that date construction. The point is this. Once you decipher the code and know the why, you can see the pattern of what previously appeared random.

This is why I am keen to apply my Winthropping to solved cases, too. They provide valuable learning opportunities. When you have found the body, consider the *why* of the choice. In Mary's case, the deposition site made no sense from a purely rational perspective. Here are some brief considerations that will be explored more later. First, why leave Mary on the bank of the swamp – where she would easily be found? A few feet into the swamp, which had debris that could have been used to weigh her small body down, and we may never have found her. Perhaps entering the swamp would have been noticeable by someone the offender lived with. More importantly, why choose the swamp she was found? An equal distance to the north was a much larger swamp – one less frequented by locals. Exploration of *why* the site was chosen has proven to be very effective in narrowing the suspect list. The seemingly apparent irrationality of the location required us to consider the why. Why would the offender choose this location? As it turned out, it was not a random choice. The reason for choosing it, once understood, has helped us move the case forward.

Routine Activity Theory

Another classic criminological approach that can help us to understand Keatley's Winthropping is the concept of Routine Activity Theory (RAT). The classic RAT model outlines that for crime to occur, three conditions are necessary:

1) A likely offender
2) A suitable target
3) The absence of a capable guardian

These can be drawn in a Venn diagram, showing the interconnection between them.

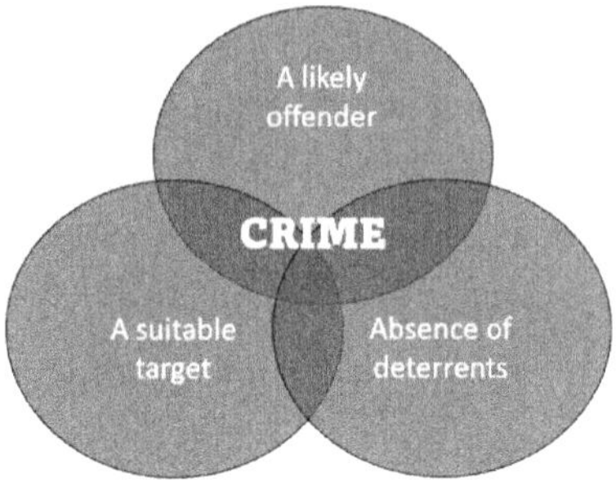

This model has been applied to various crimes, from fraud and cybercrimes to robbery and theft, to sexual assault and homicides. It's a mainstay of classical criminology. Here is my adaptation of it, for the purposes of helping us to understand how Winthropping may work.

First, of course, we need an offender. Without an offender there is no cache or clandestine grave. This is straightforward enough. Next, the 'suitable target' needs a slight tweak to help us. Typically, in criminology it refers to a suitable 'victim.' In Keatley's Winthropping, I would suggest a suitable target is a geographical location that is suitable. What defines the suitability of a target location? Several factors and features, which we will cover. In many cases, the suitability stems from the offender's routine lifestyle. We will return to this in the next section when we talk about Crime Geometry and Geographical Profiling.

Finally, the absence of a capable guardian typically means the absence of security (people, systems, and surveillance) or police. These are all still relevant in Keatley's Winthropping, but I would suggest a slight modification. Instead of simply focusing on guardians, we should extend it to include any 'deterrents' that will push or repel an offender away from a location. When deciding upon a suitable site, a criminal may be mindful of threats to detection – both at the time of using the site and in terms of future discovery. The offender's routine knowledge and expertise may help them to know such sites and either travel towards or away from them. The absence of deterrents will mean they continue moving towards a site. Also, as we will see in the later serial killer section, offenders may return to a site feeling more confident in using it if it has not been discovered.

Crime Script Sequencing ~ Timelines

My research has shown that mapping the temporal patterns of offenders' behaviors may help us plot their geographic pathways. As much as some people might like to think of themselves as unique snowflakes, or spontaneous adventurers, the reality is that we are more uniform than unique. We are more structured than spontaneous. In everyday life, we follow regular patterns. It is easier for us to do what we previously did than create a whole new track to tread every day.

The classic example of this is restaurants. When we enter an eating establishment we have not previously been to, we seldom fall on the floor crying because of the overwhelming novelty. Instead, we look for clues that help us to successfully guide our behavior. This concept will underpin a lot of Keatley's Winthropping – looking for features in the landscape that guide us. Back in the restaurant, we may look for a staff member at the door to take us to a table. If none are there, we typically walk to a table. Few of us stand at the door for hours waiting for service if none is coming. We may also look at the décor and type of establishment to find cues.

Once at the table, if a numbering system seems to be in use, this is another clue that we are meant to go to the bar to place our orders. We do not sit at the table for hours awaiting service. Of course, breakdowns in the script may occur. What if there are no numbers clearly visible at the table? Perhaps we are given them once we place an order? Or should we wait to see if we are attended to? Again, a scan of the local landscape – the restaurant – may give us guidance. Is there a member of staff patrolling the tables? Maybe that's an indicator. Criminals do the same mentally and physically when searching for a suitable deposition site to use.

Few of us ever stop to consider this process. Usually, we are too hungry to care. The point is that we can navigate new landscapes by referring to previous, similar ones. The same, I contend, is true for criminals' deposition sites or clandestine cache locations. The apparent similarity in scripts and sequences of behavior can give us insight into their patterns and thoughts. What stood out to them? What was salient? What are they basing their actions on? Again, *why*? If we can begin to map the patterns of an offender's crime script sequence, then perhaps we can trace their locations. Perhaps we can begin to generalize about the usual landmarks and features that criminals use. A lot has been done in this area, already, and my approach to Winthropping seeks to integrate it.

Crime Pattern Theory and Crime Geometry

So far, we have discussed the criminal psychology of decision making in relation to site choice. Next, we shall move more towards the criminal geographical profiling approaches. Before we begin, there are some key terms to know, as they will help us to think about landscapes and mental representations.

- ***Awareness spaces***
  - These are areas or spaces that can be defined as locations that a person has at least a small or minimal threshold of knowledge about (even without visiting). These are areas wherein

someone might feel they are aware of the general location or area without direct experience, knowledge, or activity in.

- ***Activity spaces***
  - These are areas in which people perform (regular) activities, such as attending work, school, shops, entertainment, or socializing. Their home living area also falls within an activity space. In these areas the individual frequently visits and interacts with people or the environment itself. These spaces may also contain leisure activities – including hiking, walking, and nature viewing.

- ***Comfort zones***
  - The area in which a person operates with relative comfort, owing to their awareness and activity within proximity to the area. Many classic geographical profiling studies have shown clear patterns that place centers of gravity around where someone lives.

- ***Anchor points***
  - Activity spaces may also be anchor points, of varying levels. Someone's home, for example, is an anchor point around which they are fixated, as if on a leash or line. Like a boat anchored to a point, certain points in a person's geographical landscape can act as anchors to keep them close. These anchor points are like 'attractors' – keeping the individual nearby. As will be seen in many of the serial killers and single-victim

killers, later, their home is typically central in their areas of activity. They therefore perform their crimes in their *comfort zone*.

- Criminals also typically exhibit *distance decay* – reduced likelihood of offending further away from anchor points (i.e., their home). Though this is not fixed and can be affected by a range of individual difference variables.
- Note, as we saw previously, I also look for deterrents or 'repellers.' These are locations, features, factors, or areas that may repel people from approaching or using then (e.g., neighborhood watch areas, proximity to police departments, highly visible areas).

➢ ***Buffer zones***

- These zones are the areas around a point, in which the offender is unlikely to conduct criminal acts. This is often around an offender's home. While we know many offenders operate in close proximity to their home, few commit crime at home.
- An important point that I am still developing in my Winthropping approach is the difference between those offenders that move a body far from home and those that move a body within the home area (i.e., from the bedroom to the basement). Further consideration of the difference between these offenders will be given later.

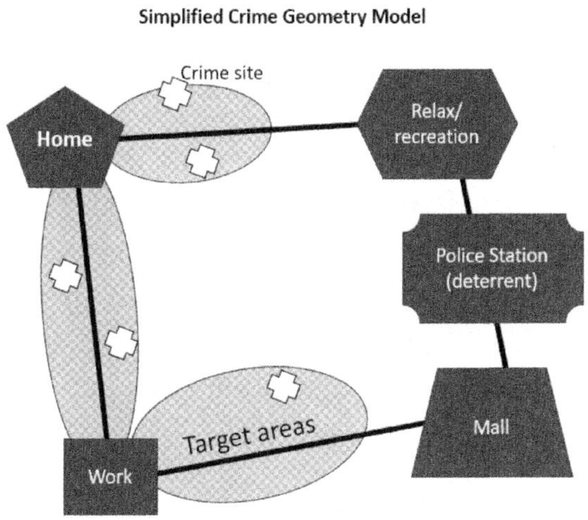

- ***Convex Hulls***
  - Take the previous figure. This is a geographical representation of an individual's map. Several areas of awareness and activity can be seen. If we imagine each of these points as being on a map, then we can connect the outer most parameter by a series of lines that create a polygon or *convex hull*. Of course, there is a 'buffer zone' around areas, such that the polygon may lay further out than some points, but connecting the activity dots provides an initial area for investigations. The convex hull contains all of the known spaces that an individual uses and knows. Many individuals may not have an inner map that directly relates to the convex hull (see Chapter 4 for more on mental maps). And investigators may not know all activity spaces. That is why this method is only as good as the data and interpretation thereof.

Psychological Approaches

Salience

Take a look around you. Go on, observe your surroundings. I imagine there are myriad things around you that you can see. Now, in a moment, I'm going to ask you to close your eyes and think about what is around you. The task is to see what 'pops out.' What stands out? Go ahead, close your eyes and spend a minute trying to recall what you saw.

Welcome back.

Now, of all the many things surrounding you, what stood out to you? What came to your mind first? For me, it was the computer screens on my desk, followed by my guitar, and from there it was the picture I recently hung on the wall. We must be careful here to disambiguate that which we noticed from that which we recall. We may have noticed a lot more than we can recall. I am sure if I were doing a memory test, I could remember many more of the items in my room. That is not the point, here. Instead, I want to show you how we are *cognitive misers* – we opt for easy mental routes and decision making. We reserve our cognitive resources whenever possible. We are also likely to pay attention to certain things, for different reasons.

The computer screens stood out to me, because I have been staring at them for so long. My guitar stands out because I listen to music as I write, and it makes me want to play. My picture is big and new and stands out given its novelty. Simple explanations of course, but with important implications for my Winthropping.

I am going to suggest that as we navigate our worlds, both mentally and physically, we perform similar cognitive processes. Sometimes these processes are explicit. We may reflect on why a new sign has been put up. It stands out as being new and potentially important. Or these processes may be implicit or subconscious. Consider the number of times you have driven home and have no real memory of the drive. Standing in your driveway, you cannot remember much of the drive at all. It is likely because you were on a form of autopilot. But that autopilot was still reacting to features in the environment. This is why I think random is never truly random. We are guided and influenced even if we are not conscious of it occurring.

My point is this: certain features of your environment may be more salient than others. They may stick in your mind or stand out more than others. You may not even be aware of it at the time. The cover of this book depicts exactly what I mean. The crossing trees literally formed an 'X' (marks the spot). I obviously took that photograph knowing it would make for a good book cover one day – and here we are. I am not suggesting that criminals navigate their world searching for similar crossed trees. I am suggesting that other features of their journeys may have salient features.

One factor to remember alongside salience is *permanence*. A feature is not useful for re-locating a site if it is not stable or permanent. A stick on the ground is likely to be moved or rot quickly. A large tree stump, however, may last longer. Natural contours, hills, mounds, and larger trees (especially those with peculiar features) are likely to endure. Broken walls and decayed buildings or ruins may also be salient. Countless case studies have shown that individuals orient and navigate through features in their environment. The longer lasting the feature, the better it is.

Next, I have provided several images, edited to make a point of how certain features of the environment may 'stand out' (be salient) and act as (afford) navigational purposes.

Clearly, my photo editing skills are a limitation. Hopefully you can see the point I am aiming at. Natural features of the environment can act as waypoints. They may stand out. When you begin to notice these, you cannot stop noticing them. The skill is then to prioritize them. Perhaps consider the relationship (sequence) between them. That is the art of Keatley's Winthropping.

Take the picture above and below of a rock in the forest. Perhaps some features 'stand out' or stick in one's mind. It is enduring and relatively unique. It stands out, whether we realize it or not. It makes for a perfect place to stash a cache (possibly nearby if not directly at or under the feature).

In the two images below, I am attempting to show how certain features of the environment may not 'stand out' to the untrained or unobservant eye. However, they may be more salient for those wishing to track their locations or hide a body or cache nearby if not in the tree stump – as one killer did in England. Our skill is to notice them, categorize, analyze, prioritize, or dismiss them.

What makes something salient? That is the big question that my research colleague, Prof. Chris O'Donnell and I are trying to clarify more clearly. My intuition is that there will never be a definitive, universal answer. What stands out to me may be irrelevant to you. I like looking for oddly shaped trees, you may prefer looking for rock formations, someone else may focus on broken walls or derelict structures. I do believe that we can train ourselves to be attentive to salient features, though. Indeed, in some recent research, Prof. O'Donnell and I surveyed a large group of individuals who have trained themselves in hiding-and-seeking caches. We noted some clear patterns and preferences in the groups who hide-and-seek caches.

Searching for salient features may also offer us two more insights into our cases. First, if we can begin to 'profile' an offender's preferences for salience, we may be able to track their further crimes. Later, in the serial killer section, we will see how killers use deposition sites with similar salient features (hillsides, rivers). We will also see how several independent serial killers used the same locations as other serial killers. I posit that this may be influenced by the same salient, stand-out features.

The second way that salience may be important is in the newest use of Keatley's Winthropping that I have been involved in: missing persons (MisPer) tracking. The salient point in MisPer cases was this: what would the missing person focus on in their journey? In one case, in particular, a child appeared to have wandered off, rather unexpectedly. My question was: what might the child have seen on their journey that may have influenced their route? What features along the path they wandered might encourage (attract) them, or push (repel) them away? Imagine if we knew the child loved animals – might signs of animals encourage them closer to explore? What if we found the child was afraid of water? Then, it is unlikely they would walk along a riverbank or follow signs to it. In the same way an offender may be deterred from a salient "Neighborhood Watch" or "Surveillance Cameras in Operation" sign, so too may the missing person be repelled from certain salient features of their environment.

I appreciate this seems obvious, but we are building a more complex profile. Let us add as much 'obvious' as we can to this complexity, rather than remote guesswork and naïve intuition. The hope is that the complexity creates a more complete picture.

Affordances

While we are discussing salient features of the environment, it is worth considering the meaning that individuals attach to objects or features. Affordance is the way in which a person interacts with their environment. Their interaction is based on an interpretation of an object's properties and the operators use of that object. That's a word salad, I know. Here is an easier way to understand it: when you see an object or item in your environment, you may have an intuition about how to use it. That intuition may be based on similar experiences with similar objects in the past. Or it may be something about the object that implies its use. In this way, objects can be designed to facilitate your use of them. Let us turn on to the easy example of switches.

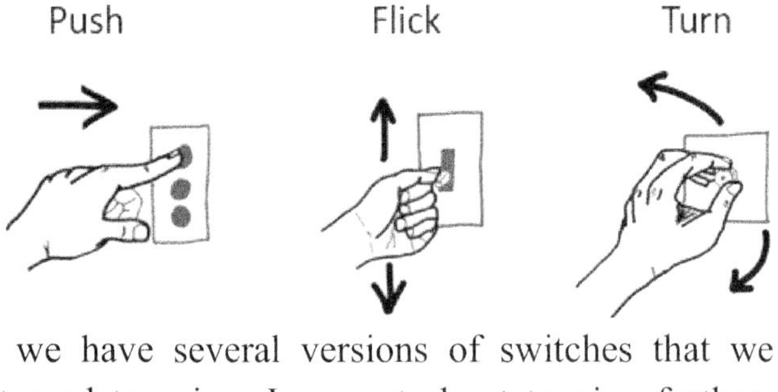

Here, we have several versions of switches that we are all accustomed to using. I am not about to give further detailed instructions for each switch or button, because experience will already tell you how to use them. This is an area of cognitive psychology with some rather fun examples (if you're into that kind of thing). For the interested reader, search "Norman doors" and you can see some good and bad examples of door handles.

The point is this, we can intuit how to use certain well-designed objects by their structure or shape. They are created purposefully to provide us with an indication of how they are to be used. A door with a flat pad on it incurs the perception we should *push* on that pad. A door with a handle to grip suggests a *pull* is required. Affordances can facilitate our actions, interactions, and allow us to progress even without our conscious awareness.

If certain human-made objects can be designed to give affordances that the user infers, perhaps nature can provide similar optic and cognitive indications. If we accept this conceptually, then we may ask what type of objects in the natural environment can give an affordance of guidance? Does a tree bending in a particular way, or a rock formation not only stand out as salient, but then afford us a navigational tool?

There is a slight nuance that is worth considering. An object can be salient but not provide much affordance. An example is a hand-written note posted to a wall. This is likely salient, especially if it has colorful writing or images. Similarly, a garishly colored candy wrapper may be salient in a rural environment. While both are salient, they are not useful in terms of affordance for navigation.

This is where permanence becomes important, too. The hand-written note will likely fall apart in the next rainfall, the discarded wrapper will blow away. This is important from a Keatley's Winthropping perspective because we are not just looking for salient features, but also those features that are likely to provide navigational stationarity and permanence. We will see later that many serial killers can return to their clandestine sites many years after their crimes. Whatever waypoints or landmarks they are using must surely be permanent enough to afford them this opportunity.

Theory of Mind

Imagine the scene: there is a box in front of you that has the word "Chocolates" written clearly on it. I ask you what you think is inside. Chocolates, right? Simple. I open the box to show you that, actually, there's a bunch of pens and pencils inside. Sorry. Then, I close the box back up. Once it's closed and reset, your friend walks in on this fantastical scene. I ask you: what will your friend think is inside the box? Most likely, you will answer, "Chocolates." Though you know pens and pencils are actually inside, you can suspend your own knowledge to appreciate what they will think – based on your previous state of mis-understanding. This is what is referred to as "Theory of Mind" (ToM) – the ability to understand others' points of view, lived experiences, knowledge, and awareness and that they may be different to our own.

I suggest that offenders progress through a similar process when deciding on a site to leave a body, cache, or other items. Part of the decision-making process is to understand what investigators will be looking for. Let me put it simply. A killer attempting to hide a body in the center of a city is unlikely to successfully hide it for long. Leaving a victim in their home is also unlikely to keep the body hidden for long unless additional steps are taken – like burying the body under the patio or stairs. Lone-actor terrorists typically place their bombs near, but not directly in the middle of busy throughfares. The aim is to maximize damage while minimizing the risk of being thwarted.

Some offenders will attempt to understand the thought processes and position of investigators. Those criminals that can do this effectively can very likely keep a body or cache hidden for longer. Therefore, when analyzing scenes, part of the imagination process is to consider what you would do to thwart you. You need a place that is relatively easy to access and exit, but that is not so easy to be spontaneously disrupted or found.

We, of course, as investigators, must attempt to reverse this process back on to the offender. Can we attempt to put ourselves in their mental-shoes and consider what their considerations were? If we can, perhaps we can narrow our search parameters. We might consider, for example, if the offender is well-versed in forensics and criminal psychology. Does the offender have a heightened level of forensic awareness? This may mean that they have taken additional steps to avoid detection – perhaps burning the body or placing them in (running) water. Or perhaps the salient feature you are searching around is a landmark indicating "nearby." Consider whether the salient feature is directional.

Remember, this isn't a TV moment. There's no grand reveal. You are going to make mistakes. Do not give up so easily. If you had a good reason to look in a location, reconsider your parameters. We will see later how detectives are often correct about the features, the salience, affordance, and ToM but just chose the wrong place that had them.

While a clever and cunning criminal may create a more frustrating search for the victim, they may also be providing us with additional clues. Organized killers are harder to catch because of their meticulous planning but knowing that the crime has been meticulously planned provides us with useful information, too.

Memory

Perhaps the most obvious of the cognitive issues related to returning to geographical locations is if the individual can remember them. On multiple levels, memory, including how we encode objects, routes, landmarks, and pathways is an important part of Keatley's Winthropping. Most people, if asked, will meekly admit to having a rather poor memory. Of course, there are individual differences, but overall, we all forget things. This is important when we are trying to put ourselves in the position of the offender. What might they choose to focus on and use? Salience may be more than what 'stands out' in the environment, it may also be what stands out in their minds/memories. Later, we will hear from Gary Ridgway, an infamous serial killer who, realizing the limits of his memory, used various methods to decrease the need to memorize multiple areas.

In multiple cases, we will see proximity of deposition sites to activity spaces. This is understandable not only from a routine activity perspective, but also for the fact that well-worn paths are memorable. Remember that forgotten drive home from work? It's likely because you have done it so often that you can do it without remembering the details. If you have a suspect, then to put yourself in their shoes, try to put yourself in their lives. Walk and drive their paths. Learn their spatial memories. That is the difference, I think, between someone scoffing at the 'put yourself in their shoes' simplicity, and someone really attempting to understand their suspect.

Some important things to remember when thinking about memory. First, humans are not machines. We cannot remember everything on a journey. We are, however, relatively predictable and cognitive misers. We repeat patterns of behavior that have previously been successful. Therefore, if you are tracking an individual, aside from tracking them, track their choices, their decision points, and their choice of features. What are they using as memory aids? What is their memory profile, if you like. This may help you to locate the next one. For example, if the individual seems to use rock formations, then prioritize those. If the offender appears to use combinations of roads and trees, then this is likely a feature they will continue to use, so please be mindful of it.

Of course, be wary of awareness, too. If the offender becomes aware of your tracking them, this will affect their behavior. It is called the Hawthorne Effect, and you should remember it. Humans will change their behavior if they become aware of being studied or evaluated. This is true in other contexts, too. Have you seen someone acting suspiciously? Did you decide to follow them? Did you elevate them as a person of interest, perhaps to a suspect? Did you follow them more closely? Did you not think your increased surveillance might be contributing to their anxiety? Innocent people get nervous around security and police, too. It's a feedback loop. Remember that.

Next, there is good research to show that the more features a person remembers, the longer they come to believe their journey was. This makes intuitive sense. If I tell you I travelled from A to B and saw a bridge on the way, it sounds relatively straightforward. You have no idea how far that is, of course, but you would not be surprised to hear it was not far and did not take long. Now, imagine I told you I went from point A, via A1, A2, A3, A4, A5, A6 (*you get the idea*) to B. Now, it seems a lot longer. The same is true for memory. If you are interviewing a person and the route, they relate to you has multiple waypoints or landmarks, there is a good chance they will overestimate the distance. This is not necessarily a case of them lying or even being deceptive, it is just a quirk of memory. So, when they say something like "I did/didn't walk far to drop the body/cache," be aware of their memory bias.

Randomness

Last night I rolled a die six times. I noted the outcomes for you. Below are two sequences of outcomes. Your task is to predict which is the real one.

Sequence A: *1, 2, 3, 4, 5, 6*
or
Sequence B: *3, 2, 4, 2, 1, 5*

Humans like to believe we are all unique. The fact that we all believe that is what makes us predictable. The fact we're so predictable surely makes us somewhat less unique. In reality, we are all much more alike than we might like to admit. This is an important point to understand and accept, but not overdo. First, the fact we are all so similar is why we can perform Keatley's Winthropping. We can imagine what others imagine. I am not suggesting we are always 100% accurate. I am suggesting we are currently better than any machine I know of. Who or what better to understand a human than another human?

We must, of course, recognize our limitations. We cannot reach perfect prediction. We must always see differing angles, different perspectives. This is why Keatley's Winthropping works best when teams work on it – each with their own contribution. Teamwork is even better if structured, using clear frameworks to frame and develop divergent ideas. This is especially true if the person you are trying to use Keatley's Winthropping on is neurodivergent. It is always essential to seek out specialists who have experience and expertise.

The next way in which randomness is important is that we,

as humans, are relatively poor at performing it. Going back to how this subsection began, who thought that Sequence B was more likely? If you did, then do not worry, most people do. We see a regular pattern in the first sequence and so are convinced it is not random. The truth is you have as much chance of rolling the first sequence as the second. If you do not believe me, you can waste your time trying to prove it with a die.

The fact we cannot easily recognize randomness is an important understanding in Keatley's Winthropping. Because it means that nor can the people we are trying to track or understand. It means that those who are attempting to hide something from us, be it a body, a trophy, or a cache may attempt to appear random. They may even believe they have been random. But their attempts to be random, if carefully understood, can also catch them out.

A more common expression of this is seen in staged crime scenes. I have studied and worked on a number of equivocal deaths. Equivocal death is a fancy way of saying, we don't really know what happened, it could be a suicide or homicide (or some bizarre alternative sequence). Real crimes do not always fit neatly into a script. There is not always a clear pattern and sequential pathway in crimes. Believe me, I wrote the book on *Pathways in Crime*. When we see a scene, therefore, that seems almost too sequentially perfect, alarm bells begin sounding.

Criminals will sometimes attempt to thwart an investigation by making the scene appear less random. They might throw in stereotypical behaviors that they think fit what a scene should look like. They are essentially trying to direct you to the conclusion they want you to draw. Like a stage director guiding you to the interpretation they desire, a criminal staging a scene does not want to leave anything up to imagination. They remove randomness that we would naturally expect. Many crimes scenes are messy. The fact we have so many equivocal deaths is testament to the fact that human behavior and the real scenes we create are seldom straightforward.

Sometimes, in a desperate attempt to throw-off investigations, criminals will attempt to create randomness. They will throw in nonsense (verbally or in terms of physical evidence). Again, being mindful of this is important. Always, though, we have to push back on ourselves. We cannot let our hubris dictate our hypothesis. As bad as criminals are at understanding randomness, we can be equally bad. Pushback on our hypotheses is essential to ensure we have not suffered from a confirmation bias.

Finally, as a teaser for future developments. I am currently researching the link between staging and Keatley's Winthropping. I think there are going to be links between the types and styles of staging that offenders perform and where the bodies are hidden. In fact, some cases later in this book will point towards that likelihood. Emergency calls, for example, can form a seemingly great way to misdirect an investigation from the start. We might wonder why an offender wants to lead the charge in this way – is the body closer to home or a known location? Time, and careful research, will tell.

Satisficing

We started with a definition of Winthropping that seemed so easy: *just imagine you are the person, put yourself in their position, and then consider what you would do*. Now, all these pages later, it probably feels a lot less clear. Do not worry. If you are feeling overwhelmed, then this part may help you. You see, I do not think that humans are masterminds or computers with infinite capacity to weigh odds and calculate plans. Without a coffee, I can barely operate my shoelaces let alone consider intricate criminal pathways. The realization that humans are not all-powerful computers is not new. Indeed, most humans attempt to simply '*satisfy*' their needs to reach a goal in a '*sufficing*' way. Putting those two words together in a portmanteau, you get *satisficing.*

When attempting to deal with a complex or difficult decision, humans may attempt to reach a satisfactory or sufficient outcome as easily as possible. We are cognitive misers whenever possible. Of course, some of us enjoy the mental arithmetic and gymnastics necessary to strategize and overcome complex tasks. Most of us, however, will opt for an easy solution whenever possible – especially when under stress, duress, and pressure. The satisficing approach is more likely to occur in situations of increased stress and cognitive load.

We have all experienced one of 'those days.' We wake up a little later than we'd like, a little less rested than we'd wish. We arrive at work to find an angry boss, a demanding colleague, and a lack of time for a coffee and break. The day spirals from there. We finally make it through, somehow, and return home. Our loved one, quite innocently but nonetheless lethally, approaches us with an otherwise easy question, *what would you like to eat?* Our ability to manage our emotions, to make decisions effectively, to restrain ourselves, has gone. Our fuse has burnt out to the bomb. We are cognitively depleted. We explode.

Now, imagine another situation: the criminal who has committed a crime, and is now faced with attempting to remove the body from the scene. The pressures mount quickly. They likely have multiple factors and threats racing through their mind. This cognitively loads up on them. At this stage, are we really expecting them to operate as a supercomputer, able to pass through the various stages of Keatley's Winthropping without issue? Clearly not.

While all of this may seem obvious, here, it is worth bearing in mind when attempting to run through Keatley's Winthropping in a case. While our analyses could and perhaps should take time and consideration, we must always be cognizant of the fact that the criminal in the moment will likely have been operating via satisficing.

Furthermore, we humans operate within a limitation of *bounded rationality*. There is only so much processing we can compute; only so many equations we can balance; only so many levels of I-think-he-thinks-I-think-he-thinks iterations. Again, the average and most common criminal is not some Hollywood mastermind, but instead a relatively plain and otherwise normal thinker – criminal proclivities aside.

Profiling

I am keen to avoid the term profiling in proximity or association with myself. I am *not* a profiler. I have no issues with profilers, they can be extremely useful. I simply do not like the term being used for me. I am aware it has been used to describe me; I know some investigators use the term for me. I just want to make it clear that I do not consider myself a profiler and try to avoid the use of it in connection to me.

That said, I have a lot of respect for good profilers and for the various types of profiling. In terms of my approach to Winthropping, profiling is essential. I am speaking primarily of psychological profiling and geographical profiling. These are extremely broad approaches to understanding criminal behavior, and I imagine my readers will know how many books, papers, guides, shows, seminars, lectures, and podcasts there are on these topics. It feels like every time I load up YouTube or my podcast app, I am met with a dozen more self-proclaimed expert profilers. In truth, I listen to them all. Why not? Who am I to ignore someone without giving them a fair chance. There are some great ones out there, too.

The point for Keatley's Winthropping is this: to better understand a criminal's mind, we need to psychologically profile them. Are they outgoing? Are they a narcissist? Are they controlling? All of these factors, and more, may influence their choice on body deposition sites. I am not suggesting we listen to a psychological profile and nothing else, but why would we not add it into our analyses?

Similarly, considering this book is more about geographical locations, of course we should listen to geographical profilers. In many cases, geographical profiling is extremely effective in narrowing search areas and locating caches and body deposition sites. I am not suggesting that my approach to Winthropping means we no longer need geographical profilers. Far from it. I am suggesting that we combine our approaches. I am keen to collaborate. I am certain that there are superstar profilers out there who will read this book and add to it. Please, let's work together. If you do read this, and you see an area you can provide input into, then please do.

I think I have covered the core and essential profiling elements in the development of Winthropping that I have created. I am not naïve enough to consider myself an expert in all areas, so please take this section as a 'catch-all' for profiling. In real, applied cases, I welcome profilers being part of the conversations. I am fortunate enough to work in some very highly esteemed task forces that have professional profilers in their core team. I constantly learn from them.

Ground Searches

In this book, I have chosen to omit the formal ground search practices, line searches, dog searches, and aerial or drone remote sensing approaches. These are all, of course, invaluable approaches that could and should be used when investigating a missing person or no-body homicide. Alongside this, soil and site suitability studies are also important. There are a number of experts in the field, many of whom have real-world homicide investigation experience. They have also developed a very nice Red-Amber-Green (RAG) approach to highlighting those areas that are more likely to be used for burying caches or bodies. References for these researchers can be found in the recommended reading/bibliography list at the end of this book.

My view is that we should all work collectively, in all ways, always. One method alone seldom stands up to the task. One tool will not build a house or a case. In this respect, while some authors have suggested that Winthropping approaches may or even should come later in the search strategy, I think it is valuable to gain these insights from the start. Why delay an expert opinion? The Winthropping expert will need time to develop their understanding and map the landmarks and likelihood of locations. Why wait for this? It takes some time to develop a Keatley's Winthropping profile. Why not allow that process to begin from the start? If the profile is wrong, then better to learn that along the way – the feedback from being wrong will help to improve the process as the investigation continues.

Of course, decisions like this are contextual and at the discretion of the Search and Rescue leader, the detective, investigator, or Senior Investigating Officer (SIO) involved. Expectation management is key throughout. This is no magic trick. Sometimes it appears to work impressively well, other times it is hard to find a trace to track. This is true of many forensic methods and profiles. The outcome of a Keatley's Winthropping profile is a suggestion, to be evaluated as much, if not more critically than any other investigative lead.

Consider it like this. If you were using a satellite navigation system in your car, and it said, "turn left," you would not immediately swerve to the left without consideration. Surely, you would check the lanes were clear, the timing was correct, the suggestion was safe. The same is true of Keatley's Winthropping. It is a suggestion. If you feel unsure about the direction it is leading you, this becomes the basis for a discussion. Maybe your gut feeling, or uneasiness is a key bit of information that can develop the profile. Maybe.

The key is to talk about it… speaking of speaking…

3. Forensic Linguistics

Finding the 'here' in 'where'

And so, finally, we come to the subtitle of the book. As I am sure anyone that knows me will agree, I am a bit strange. One of my many quirks is that I enjoy words. I enjoy the way people use, abuse, and misuse them. I enjoy considering what people say, compared and contrasted to what I hear, and what I think they mean. It will come as no surprise to most, therefore, that I have integrated forensic linguistics into my Winthropping approach.

Before I proceed, let me try and jump a hurdle that people often try to trip me on when I mention 'forensic linguistics.' There are some experts who would prefer I do not use the term. To them, what I do is not 'forensic linguistics' – it is a form of content or statement analysis. I do not particularly want to take on this argument. I shall simply say that I study crime (forensics) and the use of language (linguistics) in it. It seems pretty straight forward that 'crime language' is better known as forensic linguistics.

If you feel that forensic linguistics is something that should be reserved for other approaches, methods, and analyses, then I respect your views, but I am afraid I shall keep using the term. I do not consider myself a 'linguist' (or a 'forensic' for that matter). I do hope that even if you detest my misuse of the term, you can put that aside and continue along this journey with me.

Also, for those interested, I have written an entire book on investigative deception detection. Over half of that handbook was dedicated to statement analysis or forensic linguistics – whichever term offends you less. The aim here is not to repeat the information. Instead, I shall focus on a few key parts that I think are relevant to Keatley's Winthropping. My general approach to all my work is to consider my methods and analyses as tools in a toolbox (oh, I also have a book called 'The Timeline Toolkit' – OK, sales pitch over). We may use our tools in different formations to build our case. Some of my most exciting breakthroughs have come from adapting, combining, or crowbarring methods together. I raise this not to boast, but to encourage readers to join me, help me, work with me. Let's build this project together.

Forensic Linguistics

Leakage

When you were younger, did you ever have someone tell you to say "toast" repeatedly, quickly. If not, do it now, as quick as you can, say "toast" 50 times. Go! Toast, toast, toast, toast…

Now, what goes in a toaster?

If you said 'toast' then do not worry, most people do. There is an easy explanation for this. You have got 'toast' on the mind. Because you said 'toast' so often, it is quite literally at the front of your mind and on the tip of your tongue. It is what psychologists call "*primed.*" You are ready, or primed, to say it. Of course, we both know that bread goes in a toaster, but 'toast' is so readily available, and so closely linked to bread and the whole toasting process, that we slip-up and say it. Next, it is story time, I hope you're sitting comfortably…

One morning, a man loses control and stabs his wife. He sees the blade as he stabs her, he sees the blood flow as he removes it from the stab wound. He sees the stab wound. He has stabbed her to death. He goes to work, attempting to remain calm, neutral, normal, on the outside. Inside, he knows. He knows he has stabbed her. He gets to work, still seeing the blood from the stab wound in his mind. He stabbed her. His colleagues ask how his weekend was. His weekend? He stabbed his wife, that's how it was. By midday, the panic is really setting in. He is close to chucking a sick-leave and going home. Around and around his mind, the same spiraling thought, "I *stabbed* her."

Then, his cell phone rings. Yep. It's the police. They are at his house. How did they know? Who could have found his wife? His wife he stabbed to death. He knows he must go home now. He knows that because the officer is telling him to come straight home.

The entire drive, every stop light, every corner, all he can think is that he stabbed his wife.

When he finally arrives home, he sees the flashing lights of his impending imprisonment. He parks his car as a police officer approaches him. The question is inevitable, "*do you know what happened*?" His response is equally predictable.

I'll take a stab at it.

What is on our minds will come out through our lips, in one way or another. We cannot help it or ourselves. It simple leaks out. We must bear this in mind when we are listening to suspects speak to us. What are they telling us? Not what are we hearing, what are they saying? Are they coherent? Listen closely in case of a meaning hidden there within their words? In short, can we find the 'here' in 'where'? Sometimes, it's not even as subtle as I have suggested here.

Leakage can be words that denote the actual location of the victim. In Section 3 you will see multiple cases wherein the offender quite literally tells you where the victim is. If we listen closely to what a person says, not what we hear and interpret, I believe we will find many more of these cases. In the few months I have been collecting these cases, my database has grown substantially. Next, in my research, I want to explore how to identify these types of verbal and nonverbal leaks more successfully.

Temporal Lacunae

Despite Hollywood portrayals, most criminals will avoid lying to you. The cognitive demand of creating a lie that is possible, plausible, and consistent is difficult. Added to this is the fact that a criminal must try to tell a lie that you cannot easily disprove. In my experience, a verifiable lie from a suspect can often be more damning than an admission – which could later be retracted. A verifiable lie can catch a suspect off-guard when exposed. It can ruin their entire story, timeline, and lifetime. And they know this. So, they try to avoid this. Instead, suspects will use strategies to avoid outright lying to us. The first relevant one is through simply missing time.

Rather than create an entire fictional timeline, it is much easier to simply omit portions. Leaving out information is cognitively less demanding and harder for investigators to catch. Let us imagine that a criminal, after he left work, went to the local mall, and sexually assaulted a victim in the toilets. Here are two example statements he may tell us.

1) *Last night, after work, I went to the mall to buy groceries and then I went to the gas station to fill-up and then I came home, and I stayed at home for the rest of the night.*
2) *Last night, after work, went mall, then basically came straight home and stayed there for the rest of the night.*

Seen in sequence like this, the point is clear. But the real point is that in an interview of the suspect, you will likely only hear the latter. Why? Because it is less cognitively demanding for the suspect. Less from them and less for you. It provides you with fewer avenues of investigation. There are fewer chances to catch them out. In the first version, you could turn to questions about the groceries, for example. You could ask the suspect, what they bought, how much it cost etc. From one tiny statement, a whole new fiction must be woven. These small questions can loom large for the defendant. That's a big risk for our creative suspect.

In the second version, the suspect attempts to skip over this. Also, because we are all used to hearing statements with missing time, we typically let it pass by – because it is cognitively easier for us to just carry on. In an interview, you must stop, consider what you heard, what is missing, and what needs to be asked. Sorry, I know it is a lot, but you will get better at it when you start to listen for it. When a suspect tries to push you over a temporal text bridge, from one time point to the next, do not go easily. Stop and see what is flowing in the time between the before and then after.

In case it is not obvious, let us delve into statement 2 a little further, to explore what is missing. Question: what did the suspect do at the mall? Obviously, as he's the suspect we suspect he sexually assaulted the victim. What does "basically" mean?

Focusing in on statement 2, we have no idea what he did at the mall. This missing time is bridged over by the word '*then.*' We call this a 'temporal lacuna.' A time gap. They are very effective because as we hear the suspect speak, we follow. Before our brains can engage with the fact the suspect just admitted to being at the mall, he has already moved on to home. The moment passed in the blink of a word.

It seems so clear when it is written and slowly dissected. I see these statements pass-by in interviews so often. If you hear particular words (e.g., *then, next, after*) that skip or bridge over time, you should mark it out. Make a note. Return to it. Make the suspect slow to a crawl. Learn every step they took. It will take longer; it will give more. Better to do one longer interview correctly, than a shorter one insufficiently. For those who have read my other book on deception, well done for spotting the many other indicators of deception.

What does this have to do with Keatley's Winthropping? Well, if people can linguistically skip time in their verbal or written statements, can they do it mentally in their maps? I say yes. I have some evidence for it, too. In the next chapter on mental maps, I'll show you some examples. But here is an extra one for you as a peace offering for spending so long on language.

A few years ago, I was asked to help on a cold case involving a murdered young woman. Her body was found in a disused parking lot. Although she was found in this parking lot, investigators did not believe she was killed there. Evidence pointed to a house she was seen at earlier in the night where a party had occurred.

It was not a large house party, but enough people were there to keep police busy pinballing between statements. The victim was also in attendance at the start of the night. Then, like so many others, she appears to have disappeared. What happened remains a mystery to most. One thing stood out to me. Everyone at the party was resolute in the fact they did not go upstairs at any point. Even when pushed, it was like there were a repellant. Every single partygoer avoided any mention of the upstairs floor. I am incredulous that none of them used the toilet in all that time – the only one being on the second floor. No matter the push or prompt, when asked, they outright denied that they went up there. *Why*?

It is not the fact that partygoers simply stated they did not go up there. It is the fact that if you read their statements, you would never even know there was a second floor. It was very obvious that it existed though – given the staircase just off the entrance to the living room. The beer bottles and glasses were also a clue. No Keatley's Winthropping *toast*crumb analysis needed here. If you have forensic evidence, you can obviously follow that. I was interested, however, on why the partygoers were so keen to avoid mentioning upstairs.

Perhaps it was nothing. Perhaps none of them did venture up there. An indicator is just an indicator. It does not always show intention or mean deception. But, given there was forensic evidence to suggest the victim met her demise upstairs. I was intrigued about people attempting to avoid the spatial area as they would avoid a time. A Spatial Lacuna if you like.

If you are interviewing a suspect and the case involves geographical locations, then look for where there are no bullet holes. Yes, friends, it is time for that plane again. If you know this story, then feel free to skip to the spontaneous negation section and feel deservedly smug. For everyone else, it's hi*story* time.

In the second world war, bombers were returning to American airbases riddled with bullet holes. The story goes that the American military obviously wanted to save its assets about as much as the aircrew wanted to save their… you get the idea. The issue, of course, was that the planes could not simply be fitted with thick armor plating all over. The weight would be too much and resources too few. The military decided to run some analyses.

The returning planes were checked for bullet holes, and a composite sketch created. The sketch indicated where the planes were being shot. A representation of the sketch can be seen below. As you will see, there was a very clear pattern of where the enemy appeared to be targeting when shooting at the American bombers.

Look for where there are no bullet holes.

Of course, appearances can be deceptive. A mathematician had another view about the planes. Abraham Wald told the military they were wrong. Dead wrong. Wald, in a moment of clarity allegedly said the following, "Look for where there are no bullet holes."

The planes making it back and being entered on to the sketch, Abraham allegedly said, are the planes that are making it back. This is known as survivorship bias. We are seeing the planes that, even having been shot, can still make the flight back to safety. The message was clear: if you want to see more planes returning, defend the areas we do not see any bullet holes. When these areas are being shot, the plane does not return.

I appreciate this story has been retold so many times, including a lot by me, that it is probably now a very distant echo of the original. But I love it. It is printed on my office wall. It is saved on my phone. It is on my mind throughout every case I work. Look for where there are no bullet holes.

We are trained to look at what we see, to observe and analyze what is shown and spoken. It is much harder to analyze what is not there, but therein lies the potential blueprint for a breakthrough. We will return to this in the next chapter regarding sketch maps. I am convinced. No. I know that looking at what is missing is vital when trying to find the location of what or who is missing.

Spontaneous Negation

Another common form of deception is the spontaneous negation. I have heard deceptive suspects use this technique many times. It is an attempt to do more explicitly what the temporal (or spatial) lacuna does: avoidance. Rather than lie, suspects will attempt to skip over sensitive or criminal times. Rather than be questioned about something, deceptive people will try to deny any insinuation of it, ahead of time. Consider the following statement.

> Question: *What did you do last night?*
> Answer: *I went to my friend's house, but I never went to the mall.*

Note, the suspect was not asked about what he did not do or where he never went. Anything worded in the negative is always sensitive. Look at it another way, the suspect could recite a lengthy list, many thousands of actions long, about what he did not do. Instead, he has chosen to tell us about one thing in particular. What is on the mind, remember, will leak out the mouth.

The aim of a spontaneous negation, of course, is to stop you from asking anything more about that topic. It also allows the suspect a cognitively easy response, "*I've already told you; I never went there.*" This, by the way, is called a performative or referral response, and is a skillful way of avoiding lying. Because, technically, the suspect is telling the truth. He *did* already tell us he never went there. Be mindful of this in the interviews and written statements of your suspects.

Also, be mindful of how spontaneous negations translate into a person's geographical maps. A suspect may attempt to delete or distort parts of their verbal and spatial map to avoid it ever existing. Perhaps this is innocent, perhaps it is a place they have never been to, or perhaps it is geographical deception and distortion. This is where local expertise is vital. This is where we need someone who knows the area and knows how it may be viewed by locals. Do not rely solely on current software and geographic information systems (GIS) to save you. Nothing beats a local with lived experience for that lived experience expertise to help guide us. So, if you're ready, let's leave language for now and start drawing our next step.

4. Mental Maps

So far, we have discussed what the original Winthropping may have been. Then, what my colleagues and I have tried to reverse engineer. From there, we took a swerve into linguistics. Now, I would like to start moving towards a more applied approach of how we may use Keatley's Winthropping. Not too much farther from here, we will see some real-world criminals who provide some concrete cases. The first step on this pathway is with the last step my colleague, Professor Chris O'Donnell, and I have taken into the world of Winthropping.

When we talk about geographical locations – places we know and travel to, we can form a mental representation of them. If we plot them in our minds, we form a mental map. If I tell you to think about where you live, you can most likely find and imagine it in your mind. If you were to take an aerial view of it, you could probably imagine, to some degree, the surrounding roads, lanes, features, landmarks.

Next, imagine if I asked you to mentally travel your journey from home to work or the local shops. I am not expecting you to provide me an exact copy of your journey, to scale. I imagine you will imagine the basics. Perhaps the main roads and turnings. Leaving artistic or cartography skills aside, if I asked you to now draw a picture of your mental map, you would be able to. In fact, let's do it. I will leave the rest of this page blank. Sorry if you feel this is wasting paper, but if you use it well, it will not be a waste, I promise. Go on, draw a map from your home to a location you know well (shops, work, leisure center). Take your time, add some landmarks so that someone else could follow your map.

YOUR MENTAL MAP

Did you do it? It really will help if you do. Go on, I've given you permission to write or scribble in this book. Have at it. Just remember, if you sell this book, it's probably best to scribble over the map!

Ok, now let us consider what you included and, perhaps more importantly, excluded. You are not, as far as I know and hope, a criminal that has hidden a body, a cache, or trophies. That said, the way you mentally represent the geographical landscape of your awareness and activity spaces is likely similar to the psychological process that offenders use. We are all humans.

I appreciate in academic circles this is often referred to as sketch maps, but I prefer to keep the focus on the psychological understanding that sketch maps may afford us. The focus of Keatley's Winthropping is about how offenders mentally see, think, represent, and remember their worlds and routes. In turn, following their mental processes, we may begin to recreate their mental maps.

Remember when I said that your mental map would not be 100% accurate or to scale. You have undoubtedly left some things out. But you have also included specific waypoints or features. Indeed, even the scaling can be important. Did you place your house at the center? Did you put some waypoints closer together than other waypoints? Does this reflect how you view them? Is that a spatial proximity or a psychological proximity? Rather than critiquing your mapping skills, I am intrigued about *why* you represent your mental landscape in the way you do.

My point is: what can an offender's sketch map tell us about their inner mental map? I have in my possession a growing database of offenders' hand-drawn maps. Finding them has become somewhat of a hobby – which is a nice way to say obsession. I am keen to see how offenders represent their mental maps when they draw their sketch maps. I am eager to look at the patterns in both what they include and what they *exclude*. To explain why both are important, I want you to indulge me in a little trip down my memory lane.

Many years ago, I lived in Liverpool, UK. It is a vibrant city, with interesting people. My job there was great. I had the most amazing students. I lived by a place near the beach, which I ran along daily. Beyond the beauty of the shoreline, there was another feature that stands out in my mind. At the end of the beach was a large wall of rocks. I am not a good runner, so those rocks became a goal to race toward and then run away from. Life should have been great. Sadly, it was rocky. It was awful. I spent much of my time in Liverpool dreaming of leaving. I will not get into the reasons why, but I will say that part of my coping mechanism was that daily run to the rocks. That wall of rocks symbolized a wall I needed to overcome. It became so enshrined in my coping mechanism that I made myself a promise. I would not touch the rocks until I could be sure to leave Liverpool. Daily, I would run at those rocks with all my strength, desperate to touch them – and signify I was leaving. Months went by with this daily race-to-the-rocks ritual. I cannot proclaim it makes sense, but it is what it was. I can still imagine those rocks now.

Then, one day, I got offered a job in another city. My time in Liverpool was officially at an end. After months of running at the rocks in all manner of weathers, I finally reached my goal and, on that run, I reached out and touched the rocks. It was a very big moment for me.

Why am I telling you this?

I want you to consider two sketch maps I have drawn of my home and the beach in Liverpool. Before you look, take a moment to think what is the one thing you expect to see on the map? After all I have taught you so far, and all I have said right here, what are you expecting on that map?

The rocks.

Obvious, right? Now, before I show you the two pictures, let me explain two scenarios. In one scenario, I have buried a body somewhere in the map, and I don't mind telling you where it is. Let's imagine you have caught me, I have confessed, and I am simply showing you where the body is. I have not put an 'X' on the map, but I have drawn the location so I can point to it in the interview room. I'm just that helpful. You're welcome.

In the other scenario, I am attempting to avoid showing you where I hid the body. I'm denying the crime entirely and though I have to draw a map, I don't want to let it be known I buried the body in the rocks. In this version, I still need to provide a sketch map. I need to make it realistic, including my home and surrounding areas. But I do not want you to know where the body is. My options are limited. Do I draw the location and simply not point to it? Or do I take a more common deceptive approach and omit the area entirely?

Sketch Map 1

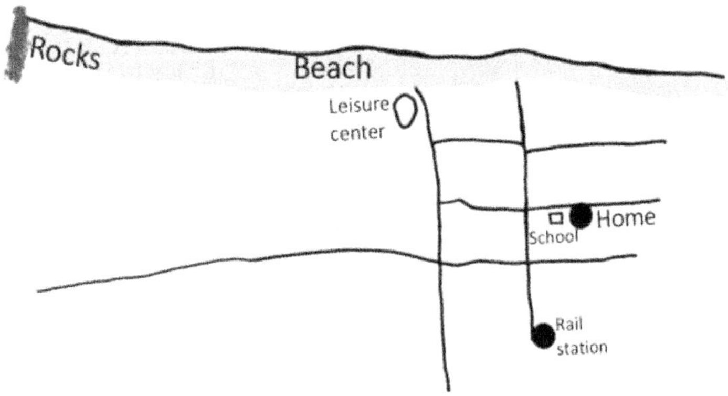

Sketch Map 2

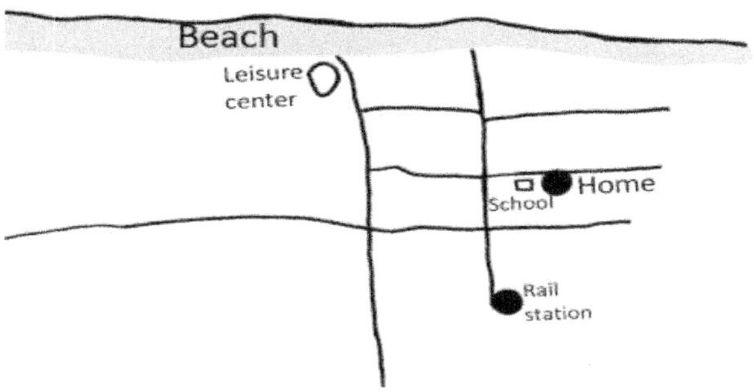

I appreciate this may seem like a relatively obvious task. But I have seen this in real-life, in a real offender's map. The offender spoke at length about a particular place they frequently visited. Again, and again it spontaneously came up. Then, when they provided a sketch map, it was omitted. In the place where the location was, I drew a red flag in my mind.

Also, let us see what I have included in the map and what you may discern about me. A leisure center may tell you about my fitness or hobbies. It may indicate I can carry a body a certain distance. The rail station may indicate I commute – if so, where else is in my geographical awareness?

As we have seen, offenders may speak freely, and they may make verbal leaks. They may tell us more than they realize. In the build-up to my Liverpool sketch maps, I told you about a location (the rocks) that stood-out to me. I repeated it multiple times – to make it as vivid in your mind as it was in mine. When it came to drawing the maps, in the situation that I wanted to hide the location, I deliberately left them off the map.

If I were being particularly sneaky, I could have added information about a different direction entirely. Perhaps this would be too obvious, though. Removing the rocks might not raise your awareness, removing the sea entirely might. These are the additional steps we must consider when doing Keatley's Winthropping. The omission of information is a common way individuals attempt to deceive, and it has a long history in cartography and forensic linguistics (see Chapter 3).

Investigative Sketch Maps

This book is not about interviewing or information elicitation processes. I would be remiss, however, to not point out that some exceptionally talented academics have been investigating sketch map creation to facilitate and improve memory. Coral Dando, Fiona Gabbert, and Lorraine Hope, amongst others, have shown that individuals who created a sketch map showed improved memory recall, without additional errors. I am not suggesting every investigator now asks their suspects to draw a map, but I am suggesting: why not? Alongside other approaches and methods, it may help trigger memories and offer new insights.

From experiences and reviews I have done, I have seen detectives use computer software, geographic information software (GIS), and good old Google Maps in interviews. This is perhaps better than nothing; however, I wonder if it allows some suspects the chance to fabricate truthful sounding paths based on what they are seeing, not what they are remembering. For example, if I knew I drove down Road A, then I have a memory for that. In an interview, attempting to concoct an entirely different route may be difficult. I would have to access my internal map of the area and seamlessly create a new route.

If someone were to show me a map, it would be easier to pick an alternative route. It also offers me the chance to fill the silence. "Stop there a second," or "that doesn't seem quite right, can you scroll back?" These types of statements buy time, allowing me to keep building a fictitious route while the investigator tackles the computer system. When drawing a sketch map, however, any pause in my drawing is obvious.

Of course, the sketch map alone is not enough. No silver bullets, here, either. Further research by Wartmann and Purves in 2017 showed that a simple sketch map produced 74 different feature types across a sample of 19 participants. Essentially, participants in the study suggested 74 different features and landscape waypoints in their maps. That's a sizeable amount. However, when participants were asked to *verbally* explain and outline the map with spoken language, 156 landscape categories emerged.

The point here is that the sketch map may form the basis of further information elicitation. That should be the aim, after all, of interviews. Deception detection may look good in the movies, but in real life, we should use it as an investigative, information elicitation approach. Perhaps my rock-less sketch would have thrown you off the scent, but a follow-up verbal interview may have left me between a rock and a hard place.

Cartographic Deception

When I was researching how individuals create and draw their mental maps, I came across an excellent book that had an almost-too-perfect title: *How to lie with maps* by Mark Monmonier. I cannot recommend it highly enough. It provides some great insights into the history of map making (cartography) and the many ways that maps can be manipulated to misrepresent features of the landscape, or outright lie about them.

Innocent mistakes can of course occur. For example, the American Automobile Association lost Seattle in the 1960s. Sorry Seattle. Or like how the Canadian government omitted

Ottawa from an airplane map in a brochure for British tourists. Oops. Other mistakes are purposeful but playful. For example, cartographers created fictitious places like "Goblu" and "Beatosu" in Michigan. These completely fictitious places echoed the chant for the football teams ("Go Blues") and the rivalry with Ohio State University ("Beat OSU").

Finally, mistakes may be deliberate and for less playful reasons. Cartographers used to purposefully draw "trap streets" on their maps in order to catch-out would-be copiers of their maps. Some map makers would purposefully put in a completely fictitious street to trap anyone copying their map and trying to re-sell it. This may sound ingenious but think about how it may affect an investigation. Imagine if you were asked to review a case, and the suspect said they used a route (that did exist), but you noticed a much more direct (but fictitious) route. Would you question the suspect about why they did not take it? Would you be suspicious if the suspect said they did not even know that street existed? This is why local experience is essential.

And then, of course, we come to the military maps that were deliberately designed to thwart enemy intelligence. This practice became especially prevalent during the cold war, when army bases, silos, and important infrastructure were deliberately omitted or changed on maps. This may seem unimportant for police investigations, but what if we think a body may be buried on a military base? Later in this book, we will see this in the case of Suzy Lamplugh. Suzy was reported missing in 1986 and an army barracks has since been searched for her remains. Imagine if an old, distorted map were used to outline the search parameter. Again, do not underestimate the importance of experiential expertise.

What is the relevance of all of this? There are several points worth considering. First, there is a growing trend in criminal cases to use Open-Source Intelligence (OSINT) when attempting to map historic places. Google Earth and related modern technology provides a great opportunity for fast tracking, but it is sometimes limited when attempting to look at historic maps. Though you can see snapshots of the past, I have known and have personal experience of trawling old maps to get a better and clearer understanding. This is only as good, however, as the map of the time was. These historical maps are open to the many biases that Monmonier outlines.

Some readers might think these mistakes are easy to spot and not a major concern. So, if you are still not convinced, here's another fun fact. It took about two years for cartographers to realize that 'Mount Richard' in Boulder, Colorado did not actually exist, even though it was on the map. It was most likely the cartographer Richard Ciacci's attempt at immortality. While this may seem like a 'cheeky' bit of fun, it can prove problematic. Let us imagine we are investigating a case from the 1970s in Boulder, Colorado. Google Earth is not of much help, so we turn to older versions of maps. Now, Mount Richard may seem like a landmark worthy of highlighting. It would fit quite well into the Keatley's Winthropping approach – a huge mountain is a salient, permanent waypoint. But it is entirely fictitious. The question becomes: how many other maps carry these playful, purposeful, yet no less problematic pranks?

Time matters. I know that more than most, having written two books on analyzing it. Monmonier raises another way in which time matters for maps. We take for granted that a map printed in 2007, for example, has information that is correct and up-to-date as of 2007. This is a generous hope. Consider whether you really believe that in 2007 the cartographers of the map went out and re-surveyed the entire landscape to ensure that every square mile was 100% accurate. I am not going to suggest they did not, but we have already seen how long some errors or mischievous pranks can persist in a map. I am sure the bigger named map makers take more care of their maps. But what about the ones who copy parts of maps? That was why trap streets were first included in maps – to catch copiers. How many maps have cut-and-paste errors?

Even if we take the generous step of assuming maps are correct at the time of drawing, another issue arises: time. The time between drawing the map and it being approved, printed, and published can sometimes create a long enough lag that the manmade landscape changes once more. I currently reside in Perth, Western Australia. It sometimes seems like the city grows so quickly that when I leave and come back after only a week, it feels new. This is perhaps great for the economy and residents, but it is a nightmare for tracking roads, lanes, highways and byways and all of the detail we might need if considering offenders' movements.

Where does this leave us with Keatley's Winthropping? Well, it is not the end of the road. As long as we remain aware that historical maps may be inaccurate, we can proceed with caution. This is also where I believe there is no substitute for lived experience. Time to take another trip with me down memory lane.

Years ago, I was talking with detectives about two murders that had occurred. They dated back to the 1980s, so online maps were limited in what they could tell me. I took the OSINT route. I found old maps, travel guides, routes, phone books, newspaper clippings – anything that might provide either a map or some indication of roads. I rather naively wanted to show my ingenuity to the detectives. I wanted to show them I could find information that was not low-hanging fruit.

I spent several days re-creating maps based on a range of sources. I am by no means a cartographer, but I felt rather proud of my drawing, replete with details, sources, and information. After about a week, I returned to the detectives, like a school child eager to show their homework. I began my mini presentation, "*The victim was taken from* [name omitted] *street, which is parallel to* …" I could not even finish my sentence before the detective chimed in with the parallel street, and then proceeded to tell me about all the streets and shops around it.

While I had been busy burying myself in historic artefacts, I had a living record right there. This is the power of having lived in the area, the experiential expertise. This cannot be quickly learned or trained. This is why I always tell my students when they ask how to make it to be a Major Crimes Detective quickly: don't. You cannot rush knowledge; you cannot cheat real, lived experience. We will hear this echoed in so many of the cases we are about to explore.

And with that, here endeth the background lessons. It's time to take our next step, into the world of real crimes.

CASE STUDIES

5. Overview

Typically, most of my time researching and assisting with criminal investigations focuses on the suspect(s). In many of the cases I work, the victim is deceased, and while victimology is vital to understanding the complexity of the case, the identity of the suspect is what we need to solve it. That said, I am always slightly disappointed when I read a book, and the focus is solely on the suspect. It seems sad to me, in ways, that everyone knows the name Ted Bundy, yet most would struggle to name his victims. Hollywood A-listers now portray serial killers, while the victims are but a means to a technicolor end.

That said, I am afraid this section of the book will be devoted almost solely to the perpetrators themselves. Keatley's Winthropping is focused on the mindset, motivations, and machinations of the person you are trying to track – and in criminal cases that is the suspect. It would be misleading or erroneous, however, to think that victimology is not important. Far from it. The intersection between suspect and victim is an integral part to building the profile.

Was the victim in a place that they frequented often? This may tell us whether the perpetrator was stalking the victim. Did the victim participate or work in a position that made her a more accessible victim? This might tell us about activity spaces and routine activities. For example, a serial killer may simply target sex workers, and thus the choice of victim is a secondary decision from the initial choice to attack people in that line of work.

There are multiple angles, approaches, and pathways to understanding human behavior and decision making. This is also true in terms of deposition sites. If the victim is known to the offender, this may affect the choice of deposition site. If the victim has fewer social connections, then their being found is less of a risk for identification and backtracking to the perpetrator.

We must remain vigilant, however, to not turn our perpetrators into supercomputers or supervillains. Remember *satisficing*. Just because we know the life history and circumstances of the victim, it does not necessarily mean that the suspect did. It is easy to create 'just so' narratives to explain the origin of the behaviors. We then fall into a whole range of other biases that make these stories seem more fitting and more accurate. At each point of the Keatley's Winthropping profile construction, we must consider how likely or realistic it is to reflect the position of the offender.

In this way, my Winthropping approach will always be structured by science, and colored by art. We may strive to use data and statistics to narrow our radars and improve our vision. The reality is that humans are too chaotic to ever be accurately predicted for long. Our profile may well have been very accurate, but "alas!" the world conspired to make it wrong. Let me explain this with an anecdote I have long dined-out on.

Many years ago, at a conference, I listened to an undercover cop telling us about a stakeout he had been involved in. A well-known and trusted source (informant) had tipped his team off to a large drug trade occurring. The officer and his team set-up close-by. Unfortunately for the team, 'close-by' happened to be in a rather smelly swamp. The police also had to set-up early to avoid being seen. Hours they spent in that fly-filled stinkfest. And then… No. Trade. Occurred.

The officer returned to his office with a few apology cakes to bake and beers to buy. The informant returned, suggesting he did not know why the trade had not occurred, but promised it would the next week. Back to the swamp they slumped. This time: success.

When the drug seller was brought in for questioning, the officer finally raised the issue of why the previous transaction had not occurred. The suspect, once overcoming his bewilderment that the officer even knew about it simply said, "my car broke down, so I couldn't get there." As simple as that.

For all the profiling, information and intelligence, a simple fact of life broke all the pathways down. This is apt to happen even to the best of profiles. The answer is not to throw profiling (or informants!) in the bin. The answer is not to give up on the endeavor because one strike seems to strike-out. Know this: you will make mistakes with Keatley's Winthropping. You will be inaccurate sometimes, especially at the beginning.

Think of Keatley's Winthropping as a skill like any other. Would you expect to read a book on baseball and get the home-run winning hit? Would you read a book on cooking and create a Michelin star masterpiece? Of course not. It is a skill to practice. The same is true, here.

But, as we progress and practice, we improve. Our accuracy increases. The search areas narrow. And hopefully, we can provide some small solace for the families of victims: bringing them home.

The Cases

I. Serial Killers

1. Gary RIDGWAY
2. Theodore BUNDY
3. Ivan MILAT
4. Christopher HALLIWELL
5. Hadden CLARK
6. Stephen WRIGHT
7. David MEIRHOFER
8. Robert NAPPER
9. The BIRNIES
10. Herbert MULLIN vs Ed KEMPER
    LISK and John BITTROLFF

II. Single-homicide cases

1. Michael SAMS
2. Gerard BADEN-CLAY
3. Michael ATKINS*
4. Christhean RIVERA
5. Robert BROWN
6. Mark REDWINE
7. Brett Peter COWAN
8. Ben BLAKELEY
9. Munawar TOHA
10. Tahreen Zeus RANA
11. Wendi DAVIDSON

III. Linguistic Leaks

1. Karen MATTHEWS
2. Ian STEWART
3. Samantha WOHLFORD
4. Chris WATTS
5. Scott PETERSON

6. James WORLEY
7. Sahara ERVIN

IV. The MisPers

1. Susannah LAMPLUGH
2. Vivienne CAMERON
3. Sarah SPIERS
4. Tegan LANE

CASE STUDIES I

The Serial Killers

6. Gary RIDGWAY

Gary Ridgway, often better known as "The Green River Killer," was charged for over 40 separate murders, committed in the 1980s and 1990s. Ridgway earned his name owing to the similar locations of many of his victims. Ridgway is by no means a unique or special serial killer in terms of returning to sites he was familiar with and putting the bodies in close proximity. Indeed, most of the serial killers covered in this book exhibited similar preferences – two even appeared to argue over the same deposition sites! What makes Ridgway an important start to this case study section of the book is his own words about why he chose his deposition sites.

Ridgway was a prolific serial killer by most standards and metrics. Though charged for an already high number, he is suspected and even claims to have killed many more. We need not speculate here on his absolute number, instead, let us focus on the ones we do know about. At his trial, Ridgway proclaimed to not have a good memory for his victims' faces. This is perhaps not surprising, given the passing of time, or the disregard he had for his victims. It may also be a memory issue that many of us face. So, we should perhaps not jump to calling Ridgway a monster based on this admission. I highlight this only to remind readers that calling a killer a monster may undermine our attempts to understand them.

I appreciate that the pain that killers cause can make those suffering want to vent their hurt. I am nowhere near qualified enough to wade into the psychotherapy of this issue. I will simply say that as investigators and researchers we should remain detached. We should also not give way to the temptation of defeatism. It can sometimes feel easy to simply proclaim we do not know, or may never know, because the suspect is a monster or 'crazy.' In missing person (MisPer) and no-body homicide cases, I often hear investigators say, "they could be anywhere." This is simply not true.

Let me be facetious for a moment to prove a point. Imagine someone has been abducted and murdered from your local area. Now, you could say, "they could be anywhere." So, I ask you this: could they (realistically) be in outer space? Could they be in the secure bunker of the White House? Clearly, no. The point I am making is this: they could not be "anywhere." Now that we agree on that, let us see how much further we can narrow the search parameters. How many more places can we decrease in likelihood, and how many might we escalate? Do not give up because the area involves a large forest, do not simply throw your arms up, sweep a wide arc over a large map, and say "anywhere." We can do better. We must.

Let us return to Ridgway for a better example of what I am trying to show you. Ridgway owned a vehicle. He lived in the USA. After his murders, he could have driven his vehicle and hidden the body anywhere within the over 3 million square miles that makes up the USA. If he dared cross some borders, he'd have Canada and South America to choose from too. So, in theory his victims could, in a sense, be anywhere in North and South America. The fact is, they were not. In fact, Ridgway followed the pattern of so many offenders: he mostly attacked close to home and while he moved his victims, he still remained relatively close to home and known, frequented locations for the majority of his victims.

While Ridgway was unable to remember his victims' faces, he had developed a method of remembering their locations. Indeed, his reason for placing bodies close together, in what he called "clusters," was so that he could keep track of them.

> *"... I wanted to keep track of all the women I killed... I liked to drive by the clusters around the country and think about the women I placed there. I usually used a landmark to remember a cluster and the women I placed there."*

Of course, I am not naïve enough to suggest that this is some bizarre technique beyond the scope of most people's everyday experience. We have all likely done similar memory tricks. I park my car in a large carpark. The first thing I do is look for a landmark or feature, so that I can find it again. When navigating a new city, I take account of several buildings, street corners, or landmarks such that I can find my way around. Ridgway was simply using a similar method, albeit for a much more macabre reason.

The fact that Ridgway so clearly outlines the basic tenets of Keatley's Winthropping makes him an ideal place to begin. Ridgway exhibits several classic geographic profiling points. His 'journey to crime' (JTC) and distance decay were relatively standard – only a few miles from his home and activity zones. In fact, his home was found in the statistically most likely place, according to several statistical programs. Similarly, his body deposition sites were relatively close to his home, with his home being central and in the area of highest probability according to several statistics.

What is more important, in terms of my Winthropping approach, is not just that he used areas close to home. But in addition, we are considering *why* these locations? Well, the locations are within Ridgway's areas of activity – close to home meant he knew the areas well. His crime and body deposition sites are in close relation to his activity zones. This means he would have felt comfortable in them. The areas are accessible, allowing for quick entry and exit. The landmarks were relatively stable, allowing for re-finding of the clusters. The bodies were not left in wide open areas, but some level of detection avoidance was deployed. His use of similar areas for many of the bodies was also not by chance. It showed a preference in his decision-making routines. From here, we might consider what other locations he would choose.

Ridgway did change his locations. Though he is referred to as The Green River Killer, he actually had several cluster locations. Remember, people are not static. Decision making is affected by our investigations, too. Call it the Heisenberg Uncertainty Principle of the Hawthrone Effect if you want. We are not ghosts when we investigate, we shine a light that offenders may try to move out of.

The fact Ridgway changed locations indicates his growing awareness that he may be caught, thus his need to move further from the initial locations. Even when he changed locations, he could not be completely random. A recurring pattern was the proximity of bodies to rivers. Remember, Ridgway could choose anywhere in the USA to move his bodies. Instead, he chose somewhere close by (likely for practical as well as psychological reasons). Beyond that, even while behaving with forensics and detection awareness in mind, he still fell into predictable patterns.

Once caught, Ridgway was able to lead detectives to the

locations of his victims. Video footage shows how desolate these various locations seemed. To the unknowing eye, they were overgrown woodland and river areas. We might naively believe that they were 'random' and chosen to be invisible. We know better now. In footage of Ridgway directing detectives to the locations, Ridgway can be heard naming landmarks on the route. This gives an insight into his mental map and process. Remember, the verbal map provides many more details. If it is on the mind, it will likely come out the mouth. Let your suspects speak.

To Ridgway, even years after the crime, he could remember the pathway quite clearly. He did this because his pathways were plotted using landmarks that stood out to him. The task for us is to learn his landmarks, and then see how many others might use a similar process.

7. Ted BUNDY

For whatever reason, Theodore "Ted" Bundy is perhaps the most famous serial killer. Certainly, if my students' essays are any barometer of awareness, he's the most famous. Interestingly, Ted Bundy, once caught, would later help Robert Keppel in understanding Ridgway (see Chapter 6). Bundy eventually confessed to multiple murders, committed across multiple states, in the 1970s. One of the difficulties in properly profiling Bundy is that his absolute number of victims is unknown – which also means we do not exactly know who his first victims were. Nevertheless, Bundy provides us with some support and insights for my Winthropping approach.

As with Ridgway, Bundy had access to a vehicle. Indeed, several of Bundy's victims were manipulated through a ruse that Bundy used involving his car. Once the victim was overpowered and put in the car, Bundy had the option of transporting them anywhere in the USA. We also know that Bundy travelled around the USA, so he was not located solely in one state for his entire life. Therefore, the proximity of some of his victims requires some explanation.

While entire books have been written about Bundy, I must

admit to being rather bored of hearing about him – perhaps the burnout of having to read hundreds of essays about him. So, my apologies if you are hoping for a longer biography of Bundy. I can recommend several books, but I am keen to just get to the Keatley's Winthropping aspects. So, let's look at some of Bundy's victims.

On February 1, 1974, Bundy broke into Lynda Ann Healy's apartment and proceeded to beat her unconscious and carry her away. Bundy stated he drove Healy to a secluded location, where he raped and murdered her. He then moved and attempted to hide her body.

On April 17, 1974, Bundy appears to have used a ruse involving a sling on his arm to lure and then overpower Susan Elaine Rancourt. Rancourt was on her way back to her dorm when she appeared to disappear. In reality, Bundy had taken her. A few weeks later, May 6, Roberta Kathleen Parks was on her way to have coffee with friends when Bundy claimed he saw her and persuaded her to go to a bar with him. Bundy then claimed, after alleging that she willingly got into his car, he tied her up, gagged her, and drove her back to Washington – attacking her multiple times on the route. Then, on June 1, Brenda Carol Ball disappeared after leaving a Tavern. Witnesses claimed to have seen Ball talking to a 'brown haired man with his arm in a sling.' Bundy claims he and Ball had consensual sex at his home before he strangled her. Forensic pathology would later question this account.

Therefore, between February and June 1974, four separate victims were taken by Bundy. With the entirety of the USA providing possible body deposition sites for each of the victims, where did he choose to put them? In an area he knew well: Taylor Mountain. Bundy, like so many others, was predictable, not random.

Bundy knew Taylor Mountain well because he had often

hiked various trails there. From a general geographical profiling perspective, this makes sense. He knew the area well – it fits within his awareness space and activity spaces. He would have felt comfortable in this area. I believe we can take this profile a step further by looking at the deposition sites through a Keatley's Winthropping perspective. Before we do, however, perhaps some readers will need more convincing that Bundy did have patterns across his different body deposition sites.

If Taylor Mountain were the only time that Bundy appeared to cluster or group his victims in close proximity, we might have to admit that even in randomness, patterns can emerge. Humans are seldom so random. The victims found at Issaquah further show that Bundy was more predictable than random.

In June 1974, Georgeann Hawkins was abducted from the University district of Seattle. Bundy claimed to have knocked her unconscious and strangled her. In July 1974, Bundy abducted Janice Anne Ott and Denise Naslund from Lake Sammamish. In September 1974, a grouse hunter discovered the remains of Ott and Naslund near a service road in Issaquah (2 miles east of Lake Sammamish State Park). More remains at this site were later identified as belonging to Hawkins. The question for us is why Bundy chose the same location. According to Keppel, who was on-scene in 1974, the entire hillside was engulfed in thick nettles, bushes, and grass. The tree cover and foliage were so dense that the forest floor was very dark, even in daylight. Leaving aside possible hyperbole, it is easy to imagine such a wild location. Indeed, such a location has obvious benefits for an offender. Let's apply a Keatley's Winthropping lens to this scene that Keppel has drawn for us.

Being so hidden means that an offender can find and return to a site with relatively small chances of being casually observed. The site, therefore, passes the rational choice equation. Of course, before the offender can use and return to the site, he first must access it. Here is where an entire forest area can be reduced to some key features. These features are not unique to Bundy's pathways.

First, the location of the bodies was in close proximity to a pebble-covered road. Note: not a main road. But a route that could be travelled by humans. This is similar to the Taylor Mountain locations. This is also a benefit from a risk-benefit analysis. The offender does not want to physically carry the body vast distances – especially over inhospitable environments. From personal experience having run studies using life-size, life-weight (70kg) mannequins, people do not want to carry them too far from a car. So, again, when plotting likely areas for body deposition sites, the interior of a heavy woodland area is a lot less likely. Most offenders want to get in, remove the body from their car, and get out, quickly.

Car access is preferable to get close to the body deposition site. From there, a 'beaten path' but not main throughfare provides reduced through-flow risk, while maintaining a relatively easier passage. Finally, from here, the final site is often just to the side by only a few feet. That way, the body is still not on the pathway. Typically, landmarks are used to designate the final location, as we saw with Ridgway and the same can be seen in proximity to Bundy's body deposition sites.

Criminal consistency

Taking a step back, we can see that Bundy re-used similar ruses in his approach and overpowering of his victims. By pretending to be injured, with his arm in a sling, Bundy was able to appear more harmless and had a reason for asking his victims for help. Bundy is by no means the first or only serial killer to use a ruse, but the fact that he used it so often helps inform us about his style. He has a pattern, and his pattern was to re-use behavior sequences that had been successful. The ruse worked multiple times, so he kept using it. This mentality, what some psychologists may call habit or using a crime script, supports what we then see in his choice of body deposition sites. Rather than attempt to appear random, Bundy simply stuck to what he knew, what he had previously done, and what had worked. So much for randomness and a criminal mastermind worthy of hundreds of student essays. Bundy turns out to be relatively mundane and predictable.

From follow-up interviews and confessions, we know that Bundy also returned to his clandestine sites. This, again, is not unique to Bundy. Ridgway confessed to returning to his clusters. It may well be that the presence of a cluster indicates an increased likelihood of the perpetrator returning. Perhaps the increased number of victims increases the 'attraction' of the site. This is more likely to be the case if the bodies have not been found (i.e., no deterrent/repeller present).

8. Ivan MILAT

Lest anyone suspect that I am only going to comment on American serial killers, let us turn our attention to where I currently call home: Australia. Perhaps one of the most infamous serial killers in Australian history is Ivan Milat. Milat's crimes are often referred to as 'The Belanglo Backpacker Murders.' This is because Milat targeted (mostly foreign) backpackers in New South Wales (NSW) and left them in Belanglo State Forest. Between 1989 and 1993, seven people in relation to Milat were reported missing; though it would take some years for investigators to link the missing and murdered to Milat. After extensive police investigations, Milat was convicted in 1996, though he never confessed to the crimes.

Before we continue, I need to give readers who are unacquainted with the 'land down undah' a little geography lesson. Bear with me on this, I promise it will be relevant in the end. When I first moved to Australia, I wanted to buy a motorbike in Perth, Western Australia. No such luck. Over east, however, New South Wales (where Sydney is) had lots of options. I made the seemingly easy choice: I'd simply buy a motorbike in Sydney and then enjoy a nice ride back to Perth.

There were many more options of bikes in Sydney, and then the added benefit of a nice ride back to Perth. A double-win, or so I thought.

When I mentioned this to an Australian colleague, he laughed out loud. Actually. Out. Loud. He told me before I invested some money on a motorbike, I should spend some time on Google Maps. It turns out Sydney to Perth is just a thin slice under 2,500 miles (approximately 4,000km). For my American readers, it's not too dissimilar to the drive from Boston, MA to Salt Lake City, UT, only a lot less scenic. For my UK readers, imagine Edinburgh to London *and back*, 3 times. The point I am making is this: Australia is big. It's really big. If you already knew this, then I apologize for the redundancy. Experience tells me, though, that while people intuitively know "it's big," the scale is sometimes lost on them. Another important fact of Australia is that there's not a lot going on in the middle. In central Australia, there are miles and miles of desolate desert.

Why am I giving you this geography lesson? Well, because you need to know that there is a vast expanse of relatively unused landscape in Australia. If you were going to get rid of a body, you'd certainly have a large area of possible locations. So, when we see clusters emerging, we must be able to provide an explanation for this – which, of course, we can. Further, we need to remember this the next time a person is missing, or we are investigating a no-body homicide and are tempted to utter the "*they could be anywhere*" mantra.

Back to Milat and his series of murders. While missing persons (MisPer) reports are nothing new, a cluster of them in the late 1980s and early 1990s raised suspicions. Then, in September 1992, two hikers discovered a partially concealed corpse in Belanglo State Forest. Once police and forensics had arrived, it did not take them long to discover a second body, approximately 30m (100ft) from the first. Dental records confirmed they were the bodies of Caroline Clarke and Joanne Walters, two British backpackers who were last seen in April 1992. Caroline had been shot multiple times, and police formed a hypothesis on why so many shots had been fired.

A year later, October 1993, a local man discovered more bones in Belanglo State Forest. Police investigation of the scene resulted in the bodies of Deborah Everist and James Gibson being found. They had been missing since December 1989. While the geographic location linked the crimes, the style of attack was different. Gibson had suffered multiple stab wounds from a large knife, puncturing his heart, lungs, and severing his spine. Everist was beaten and showed indicators of knife wounds.

The final three victims, Simone Schmidl, Gabor Neugebauer, and Anja Habschied were found soon after. These victims showed indications of stab wounds (Schmidl) and having been shot (Neugebauer). Habschied and Neugebauer were found in shallow graves approximately 50m (160ft) apart. Habschied had been decapitated. All victims were found near trails. This gave investigators their first indication that they were dealing with a serial killer. Beware. As we will see in a later chapter, we should not jump to the conclusion that multiple bodies in the same location are always the work of one offender.

Remember how big Australia is? Even if we were to be more conservative and only focus on New South Wales – the state that the abductions and murders occurred – NSW is approximately 309,130 square miles (~801, 150km^2). Within that state there are multiple forests, national parks, rivers, lakes, and an entire coast with which to hide bodies in clandestine graves. Milat would not need to have driven for long to be somewhere even more remote than Belanglo State Forest. Nor would Milat need to have driven far to find a different forest that *afforded* the same benefits.

Of course, by now, if you have read the chapters in order,

Milat's behavior is not only understandable, but it is also almost predictable. That is why I will not spend too long profiling the scene. Indeed, it fits within a Keatley's Winthropping profile.

First, Milat had extensive knowledge of the area. Belanglo State Forest lies just off of Hume Highway (Route 31) in NSW. Milat knew the highway well, having worked with the Department of Roads on the highway for some time. We also know that Hume Highway was a hunting grounds for Milat, as he was convicted of abducting two women and raping one of them in 1971. Later, we will see how roads may link another serial killer to their victims.

When police finally came to arrest Milat, they found a number of hunting weapons in his house, and his relative's house. A large sword was found in his mother's house, which police postulated was the weapon used to decapitate Habschied. Police also found several guns, including a pistol, two shotguns, a rifle, and a crossbow. Knives and blades were also located. Interestingly, one of the weapons, the Ruger .22 rifle, was found in a crawlspace in Milat's home. Remember, Winthropping began as a method to find hidden caches. It can therefore be used to locate suspect's weapons caches. If you are searching a suspect's home or attempting to find hidden caches, Keatley's Winthropping can be very effective.

Police also found a number of potential 'trophies' taken from the victims. Simone's canteen and Caroline's camera were found at Milat's home. Whether he took these purely as 'trophies' or 'souvenirs' is unclear, but he certainly had them. While they were relatively open and on display, a Keatley's Winthropping search could and perhaps should be used to find such items at other locations.

The reason I have speech-marked souvenir and trophies is because Milat also had two sleeping bags, belonging to Simone and Deborah. It is unclear, therefore, the motivation for taking items. It may be that they served both a tokenistic trophy memento of the offending and a practical purpose. In either case, Milat was not the first nor the last offender to take and keep victims' possessions. I wonder how many more offenders have taken how many more items that have been missed owing to the lack of a (Keatley's) Winthropping search.

That Milat took items, kept them, and did not do a great job of hiding them is consistent with his body deposition site choices. The campfire found between Caroline and Joanne indicates that Milat returned to the sites. This fits with his taking items to relive the offenses. The fact that the bodies were relatively easy to re-locate, situated just off of fire routes and paths, is also consistent with Keatley's Winthropping. Belanglo State Forest is approximately 3,800 hectares, and yet several of the bodies were placed in very close proximity to each other.

The point is this: if we stop allowing our inner monologue to convince us that victims could be anywhere, instead we might begin to see the patterns that emerge. From there, we might begin to profile the offender. We should ask not only "*why here?*" but also "*what features brought the offender here?*" This may help with further cases.

9. Christopher HALLIWELL

If you have made it this far, then I shall reward you with some trophies as well as more bodies. As we just saw, some serial killers take and keep items from their victims. The taking of items, or souvenirs, or trophies is well-documented across several well-known serial killers. What interests me more, here, than the psychological reasons for taking a trophy, is what the offender does with it afterwards. We know that some will 'gift' the trophy to a loved one. Ivan Milat, who we just saw in Chapter 8, was known to take trophies and keep them at home. But what of the killers that are not so brazen? The ones that may hide trophies in clandestine locations? I raise this to remind readers that Winthropping began with searching for clandestine cache locations. I have adapted it to focus on MisPer and NBH cases, and scene profiling. Readers should remember it can be used whenever we are trying to locate or profile a site. Let's look at the case of Christopher Halliwell, to learn more.

On March 19, 2011, Sian Emma O'Callaghan was last seen at 02:52 on CCTV exiting a nightclub in Swindon, UK. Her boyfriend, unaware of her situation, sent her a message at 03:24. Later cellphone tracking appeared to show her cell phone was in

Savernake Forest, some 12 miles away from the nightclub she was last seen leaving. A large-scale public and police search of the forest commenced on March 22, though later investigation would call into question the geographic accuracy of this initial location. Allow me to re-raise the reminder that technology is great but not infallible.

Once the certainty of Savernake Forest was called into question, police were once more left with the uncertainty of where exactly Sian may have been taken. The cell tracking still placed her cell phone (and thus potentially her) in the area.

Stephen Fulcher, the Senior Investigating Officer (SIO), decided that he would employ some Winthropping-esque techniques of his own. With his expertise and local knowledge, Fulcher focused on Barbury Castle as a possible location. This makes sense from both a forensic, criminological, and Keatley's Winthropping perspective. Barbury Castle was close to where Sian was last seen. It is easily accessible, and a salient, permanent 'feature' that would stand out in an offender's mind. Lest anyone is misled: if you are currently imagining some looming stone castle with parapets and banners, I shall spoil this image. Barbary Castle is in effect a mound of earth, or 'secluded hillfort.'

Fulcher further hypothesized that Sian may have been dumped down one of the small trenches that surround the mound. In this respect, Fulcher had the right Winthropping idea, just the wrong location. This will happen to you, too. Please do not be disheartened when it does. There is valuable learning to be done. And remember, of all the places in all of the UK that Fulcher could have Winthropped his way towards, he chose somewhere in close proximity and with similar features to the actual body deposition site. I believe that given his skill and insight, if he continued profiling in this way, he would have eventually found Sian. He was righter than he realized. But, as it turned out, he did not need to profile potential sites any further.

Examination of the CCTV footage had led investigators to identify the car that Sian had entered after leaving the nightclub, and from there, through some painstaking tracking, police had finally found their suspect: Christopher Halliwell. In proper police vernacular, Halliwell immediately became a TIE subject (Trace, Interview, and Eliminate). I shall skip over several of the next parts of the investigation, and we will regroup after Halliwell had been stopped by police for initial questioning.

Police had detained Halliwell in a supermarket (shopping store) parking lot. They enacted a brief series of questions in the parking lot, to which Halliwell made it clear he wanted to go to the police station. This is where Fulcher decided to attempt something. Fulcher knew the likelihood of obtaining a full confession was unlikely once Halliwell returned to the police station. Weighing up that Sian may be alive somewhere, and only kept alive through Halliwell's returning to her, Fulcher knew he had to try everything he could to get the information he needed. That is why Fulcher ordered the police officers to instead take Halliwell to Barbury Castle.

Fulcher was still operating on the hunch that this is where Halliwell had taken and possibly left Sian. I will not go into the legalities or even moralities of whether Fulcher's actions were correct or not. That is for others to decide and live with. I will say that I can understand Fulcher's actions. Let me tell you how this story ends and then you can decide.

Fulcher arrived at Barbury Castle and began questioning Halliwell. After some questions and pauses, and some encouragement of doing the right thing, it appears Fulcher got through to him. Halliwell agreed to lead Fulcher and the officers to Sian's body. She was not at Barbury Castle. The actual body deposition site was near the White Horse in Uffington, Oxfordshire. Look it up. It's a clear 'feature' in the landscape.

Fulcher, in his autobiography of the case, suggests that where Sian was, was not a place he would ever have found. I am not sure if this is modesty or not, but I will say that I think though Fulcher was wrong about Barbury Castle, if he had kept along the same path, he would have eventually come to the correct location.

Fulcher outlines some salient landmarks and features of the route that Halliwell took them. A farm with various outbuildings served as enough of a landmark for Fulcher to mention it. Farther along a remote country lane, just beyond a grass verge, was a steep drop. Halliwell indicted he had pushed Sian down there. Note the repeated salient features that are emerging across our cases: isolated, accessible, salient landmarks. In this particular case, we have a natural decline. Given enough time, and the similarities between where Fulcher originally thought and where Sian actually was, would Fulcher have zeroed in on this location? Perhaps. I think with a little more training in Keatley's Winthropping, the odds increase favorably.

The story does not end here. What happened next is where the real controversy begins. Having found Sian, it was time to take Halliwell back to the station for a formal interview and legal processing. But Halliwell had not finished. Halliwell indicated he wanted to talk more with Fulcher. The outcome of this conversation was a lot of strife for Fulcher's career, to say the least. But also, through this talk, Fulcher found another body. The body was of a young woman who had been missing for years.

Fulcher, following Halliwell's directions, took the investigators on a longer drive to a very remote field near a remote village, Eastlich, UK. If I could be generous in believing that Fulcher may eventually have found Sian, I can make no such allowances for this other victim. The field was, to the untrained eye (and perhaps even a well-trained one), completely vacant of any features. Fulcher describes it as 40 acres, covered by reddish clay, but without trees. It was to this otherwise vacant, plain field that Halliwell took detectives. Once at the field, Halliwell led the investigators across the field to *exactly* where he had buried another victim, Becky Godden-Edwards.

While this is an incredible story, and I highly recommend reading Fulcher's autobiography, *Catching a serial killer*, this is not the end of the story for us. Halliwell does indeed provide us with some interesting examples and learning points for Keatley's Winthropping.

For example, the fact that Halliwell was able to re-locate a body in an otherwise bare field is worth consideration. I have seen the field and there are some potential landmarks and waypoints that I believe Halliwell could have used. I would be interested to see whether these align with what Halliwell actually spoke about and used on the journey.

Do not worry, I did not forget. I began this chapter with talk of trophies, so let us return to that topic. Halliwell was known to keep trophies of his victims. Indeed, investigations showed that Halliwell used a pond as a 'trophy store.' Current estimates are that there are approximately 60 items of women's clothing around the pond. Who they belong to and how many more victims Halliwell may have is not yet known. I believe Keatley's Winthropping may once again be useful here.

Halliwell's body deposition sites were not as random as they appeared. His trophy cache site was also not random. Halliwell utilized a naturally occurring feature (a pond) to provide an affordance for something else – a landmark to re-find a location of personal importance. If we put together all that we know of Halliwell, alongside what we have learned from other offenders, I believe we could find much more.

10. Hadden CLARK

My pathway to Hadden Clark was dissimilar to the previous cases. While I have studied, researched, and taught about the other serial killers for many years; Clark was different. Clark, I needed to know about. I needed to know about Clark because I needed to inculpate or exculpate him in a case I was helping with. Before anyone asks or tries to work it out: no. I will not divulge the case nor any details of it, for obvious reasons.

I also want to make it clear that I do not go 'serial killer hunting' when I work on cases. There is a truism I have found when looking into cold case homicides and it is this: *it is always a serial killer, and it is never a serial killer*. What I mean is that any time you are investigating an unsolved homicide, especially in the USA, there is more than likely going to be at least one serial killer who was operating in close temporal and geographical proximity to your case. It is easy to think, if only for a moment, therefore, that your case is one of their victims. That is why the offender in your case can always seem to be a serial killer. In my experience, this has so seldom been the case. That is why I was not rushing to pin the victim on the killer, Clark. But pushback is always necessary, perhaps this was the case wherein it was a serial killer – hence my focusing on Clark.

I also know that some readers will take umbrage with Clark being listed in the serial killer section when he only has 2 confirmed kills. First: that is the new definition of serial killer, according to the Federal Bureau of Investigation (FBI). Second: the definition of serial killer is not the main point of this book. So, let's move on and look at why Clark is in this book.

Hadden Clark was originally arrested for the murder of Laura Houghteling, in 1992. Clark had recently begun working as a gardener for Laura's mother, in Bethesda, Maryland. While Clark appeared to like Laura's mother, there was some animosity between him and Laura. Then, there was an argument between Laura and Clark and on October 18, 1992, Clark broke into the Houghteling home and stabbed Laura repeatedly. Laura died from the stab wounds and suffocation. During the attack, Clark used a pillow to smother Laura. After the attack, he carried Laura in a bedsheet through a wooded area and buried her half a mile away.

Police investigation found a bloody fingerprint on a pillowcase nearby and linked this to Clark, who they later arrested. Some 8 months after killing and burying Laura, Clark was able to take investigators back to her body. By now, of course, such a remarkable feat of memory is probably unsurprising to you. Without knowing more of the case, you can probably imagine the various landmarks and affordances that Clark used to navigate his way back to the shallow grave. Perhaps some of you are thinking that 8 months is not all that long for such a horrific act. In that case…

In 1986, Michele Dorr was playing at home with her father, Carl. Carl last saw Michele walking out of the kitchen. Michele walked a few doors down the street to see if her neighbor and friend was at home. Sadly, her friend was not at home. Instead, Hadden Clark answered the door and let Michele in. What follows is not exactly clear and it took many years before Clark finally confessed to the crime. Even then, the confession only came after a prison inmate, whom Clark allegedly thought was Jesus, encouraged him to confess.

Clark initially gave police instructions on where to find Michele's clandestine grave. Even with directions, police failed to find her body in the wooded area. Let this be a lesson to all investigators – if a suspect gives you a location and you fail to find what you are looking for there, it might not mean the suspect was lying. Anecdotal conversations I have had with researchers in the field have repeatedly highlighted the difficulties in finding clandestine locations. They are hidden. They take skill to uncover. Do not give up if at first you do not succeed.

In the case of Clark, investigators took the bold step of bringing him out of prison so that he could lead them to the location, in person. Here, again, we see a little bit of Keatley's Winthropping slipping through. Also, for those who enjoy the film *The Shawshank Redemption*, which also has a beautiful Winthropping-esque moment, note the following location features. Hadden had placed Michele's body under a large and salient tree. This was clearly not enough, so, substituting a black, volcanic glass rock for a mattress, he created a feature that allowed him to directly find the grave, even after all those years.

Of course, I am not suggesting that police begin lifting every bit of roadside trash and debris in case a serial killer has hidden a body beneath it. However, let us take a step back from some of the cases we have looked at. Fulcher could have given-up after his strike-out at Barbury Castle. Clark's investigators could have given-up when they did not immediately find Michele. But Fulcher continued and found Sian in a place with similar features and affordances. What if police had considered Keatley's Winthropping when looking at the location Clark gave? Maybe then the tree and mattress form a pattern of salient affordance indicators. Maybe other locations are consistent and could lead to more discoveries.

We are not quite done with Hadden Clark. Beyond his bodies, which provide some anecdotal evidence for his ability to re-locate his clandestine sites that were clearly incognito to investigators (even with directions), Clark provides us with another trophy case. In 2000, Clark led investigators to a trophy site that contained over 200 pieces of women's jewelry. It is unlikely that this indicates Clark had over 200 victims. He was known to steal women's jewelry. What it does indicate, again, is that criminals appear to keep mental maps of their clandestine sites.

There is some speculation that Clark kept a physical map, too. Prosecutors believed a map they found in Clark's car indicated the sites of where he buried bodies. This, they suggested, led Clark to remove the body sometime after. Defense, however, suggested that the map was no more than plans to bury the remains of Clark's cremated father. Owing to what we learned in Chapter 4 on mental maps, I would be keen to see what other maps Clark had, or any maps he could or would draw of his sites.

11. Stephen WRIGHT

Over a 10-day period in late 2006, the town of Ipswich, UK, was plagued with the discovery of five women's bodies. More commonly now known as the 'Ipswich Murders,' the killer of all five women was a lone man, Stephen Wright. Wright was married at the time of his murderous series. Wright waited until his wife was busy or away to commit his night-time crimes. In reality, there is little new, novel, or shocking about Wright – beyond the number he killed in such a short span. This of course, as with all cases, is not meant to diminish the severity of the crime nor horror the victims' and their families have endured. It is more of an attempt to dispel the myth of the psychopath serial killer that lurks as some monstrous entity. The reality is often more mundane.

Wright has worked his way into this book not because he is a relatively rapid serial killer, but because of his choice in body deposition locations. They, as with others we have seen, can teach us valuable lessons about geographic decision-making. As disturbing as Wright may be, if we move beyond this to focus on his actions, we can learn something from him. Let's begin.

Gemma Adams, a 25-year-old woman was last seen outside

Freemasons Tavern, in Victora Street at 10pm on November 14. 2006. She would not be found until December 2, 2006. Tania Nicol was last seen outside Sainsbury's garage on London Road at approximately 11pm on October 30, 2006. Tania was found on December 8, 2006. The next discovery came on December 10, 2006. The body of Anneli Alderton, who was last seen on December 3, 2006, was found. Then, on December 12, 2006, two bodies were found. Annette Nicholls, who had been missing since December 4, 2006, and Paula Clennell, who had been missing since December 9, 2006.

The location of the bodies, as I have suggested, is what is important for us to consider, here. The first two victims, Gemma and Tania were found relatively close to each other. This, as we have seen, is not unheard of and in fact matches what many serial killers prefer. The final three victims, however, were several miles away from the first two. This may initially confuse investigators into considering whether multiple offenders are responsible.

Changing body deposition sites is sometimes an autonomous choice on behalf of the offender. Other times, as in this case, the change in body deposition sites is a result of police involvement and investigation. Once again, we are not invisible ghosts. Our investigations cast a spotlight on the landscape, and offenders may seek to move back into the shadows to continue their series.

Wright's body deposition site choice for his first two victims was relatively straightforward. It was a location he knew. The location also provided another affordance. The stream helped to remove forensic evidence from the bodies. However, like so many other offenders, once the bodies had begun to be found, Wright realized that it was no longer safe to return to this site. That explains his choice for relocating to another area. But why choose the next area?

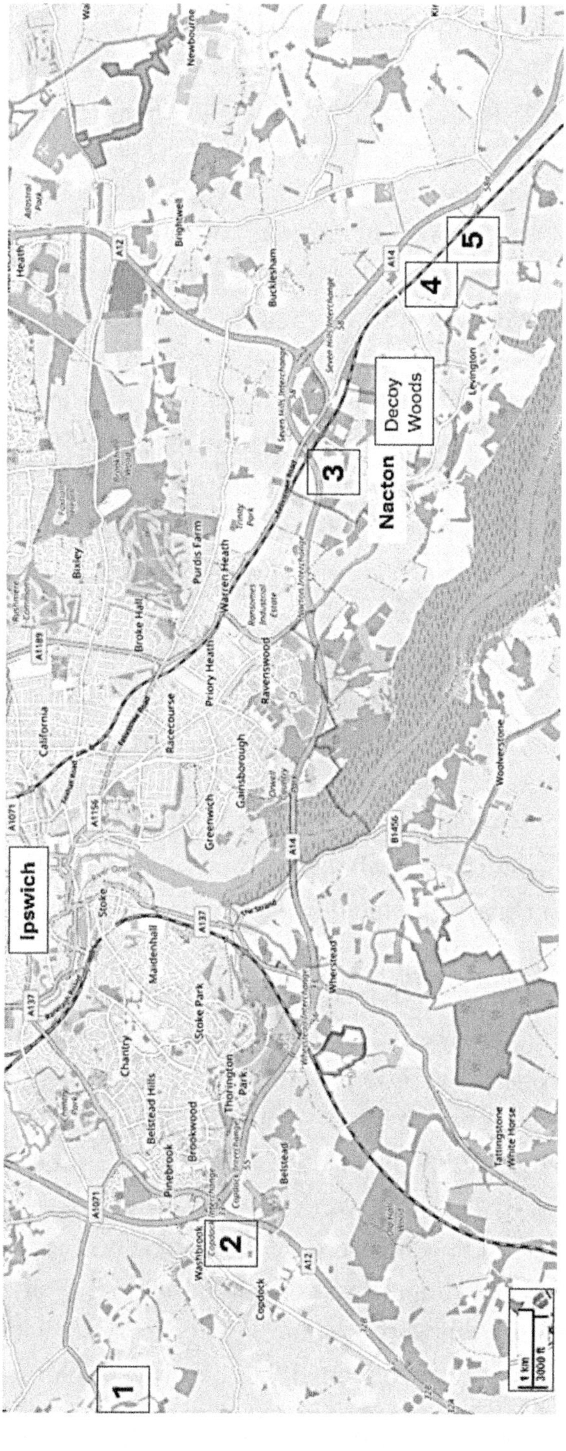
Ipswich
1
2
3
4
5
Nacton
Decoy Woods
Warren Heath
Priory Heath
Racecourse
California
Broke Hall
Ravenswood
Gainsborough
Greenwich
Maidenhall
Stoke Park
Chantry
Thorington Park
Belstead Hills
Brookwood
Pinebrook
Washbrook
Copdock
Belstead
Wherstead
Woolverstone
Levington
Bucklesham
Brightwell
Bixley
Purdis Farm
Tattingstone White Horse
A14
A12
A137
A1071
A1156
A1189
B1456

Wright owned a car. Police were acting as a repeller for the initial site, so he had to move somewhere else. But why did he choose the next location? Why not drive somewhere much further away if detection avoidance was his goal?

Nacton, the area where he left his next three victims was well-known to Wright. Again, Wright could have chosen anywhere in the UK, and he chose somewhere else he knew. He had conducted business there on several occasions and he knew the backroads very well. It was, therefore, well within his activity zones and comfort zones. When studying a local map of the area, I also could not help but notice "Decoy Woods" nearby. For those that do not know, a decoy wood was created as a method of catching ducks. In terms of semantics, I wonder whether it provided an association for Wright – perhaps a decoy from his crime series.

The next affordance this area gave is an interesting one in terms of profiling and localizing zones. One of the reasons Wright preferred the locations he did is because of the layout of the roads.

Many people may intuitively think that windy, twisty roads allow for more concealment. A bend either side of you means that no-one can see exactly what you are doing, right? This bears some intuitive sense and appeal, but it is the opposite to what Wright considered. In fact, he found the long straight roads more of an attractor. The reason is relatively straightforward when we stop to consider it. A long straight road, at night, allowed him to see vehicles coming from a long distance away. If he saw the dim glow of headlights, he knew to delay his process of leaving a body. If the horizon were dark for a long distance in either direction, he knew he had time to do what he needed to.

This is an important consideration that I often make to investigators who are conducting scene appreciations. If you believe the offender attended the scene overnight – in the dark –

then you must do the same. Of course, go there in the day to increase your visibility and look for evidence. However, if you want to understand the decision-making process of an offender, it is best to put yourself as close as possible into their footsteps – both geographically and temporally.

What appears clear at midday may be obscured or hidden at night. We must also be mindful of cloud cover and moonlight. I appreciate this may seem pedantic or obvious, but I have lost count of the number of times I have asked investigators how a scene looks at night and I am met with silence.

12. David MEIRHOFER

I am generally burned out with reading serial killer books. I appreciate many people are still fascinated by them. I have studied so many, however, that I am seldom shocked anymore. The fascination has given way to the repetitive mundane. This is not said to undermine the horror inflicted on the victims, the pain endured by the loved ones left behind, nor the great effort exerted by those investigating the cases. Personally, however, serial killers just do not hold as much appeal to me anymore. I prefer the lesser-known cases. Seldom do I purchase a serial killer book nowadays.

And then came *Shadow Man* by Ron Franscell. Against my usual standpoint, I purchased a copy. It is brilliant. I highly recommend it. If serial killer stories barely register an emotion with me, imagine my own surprise when I realized tears had formed by the final chapter. I will not spoil it, but the final line of the final chapter hit me. Hard. So, without ruining Franscell's book, I shall outline David Meirhofer's cases, which are important to our development of Keatley's Winthropping.

Okay, full disclosure. The reason I came upon *Shadow Man* was because I was looking into another, more recent case that occurred in Western Australia (WA), where I live. Some of you may remember it because it made international news. In October 2021, Cleo Smith, a young four-year-old, was camping with her family in northern WA. For various reasons, this case blew up. Children go missing every day around the world, sadly, but this one swept the nation and then the world. I have my theories on why, but the why is not the important part, here. The how and who are.

Cleo was taken, overnight, from a new tent she shared with her family. At some point, someone had unzipped the tent – beyond the height Cleo could have reached, and she was then taken from the tent. Cleo's sibling, mother, and stepfather said they heard nothing. Thus began an extensive search for young Cleo.

Now, for clarity, and despite what one leading newspaper suggested, I was not officially involved in the investigation of this case. Though I have been involved in multiple MisPer cases, I was at arm's length from the Cleo case. Cleo's whereabouts and who had taken her remained a mystery. For 18 days. Then, she was found. Alive and well.

Unbelievable.

What are the chances?

While I was not officially involved in this case, it did raise a lot of questions. Naturally, I was interested. The fact a child had been abducted is sadly not rare. From a tent narrows it down, but still not by much. It happens. From a tent that is unzipped and left open? Now we are reducing our cases, but still, it is not unique.

Next, came the suspect. After 18 days and intense police investigation, WA Police had found their suspect. Upon entering his house, where he had kept Cleo, they discovered a room filled with children's dolls. Again, this is not that rare. But, when we add all these not-so-rare factors together, it becomes a lot more unique. Or so I thought…

Back to the Meirhofer cases.

Susan Jaeger

On June 25, 1973, young 7-year-old Susan Jaeger was camping with her family in Missouri Headwaters State Park, near Three Forks, Montana, USA. Sometime, overnight, Susan was kidnapped from her family tent. A hole had been cut near the base of the tent through which Susan was snatched.

Sadly, Susan would not be as fortunate as Cleo. It would take nearly 11 years to confirm, but Susan was murdered. The investigation into Susan's abduction was every bit as intensive and exhaustive as Cleo's. But the rarity of Cleo's outcome was not matched in Susan's. Many hundreds of thousands of leads were followed, all seeming to lead to dead ends. All except one: David Meirhofer. But before we get to Meirhofer, himself, we first need to learn more about one of his other victims.

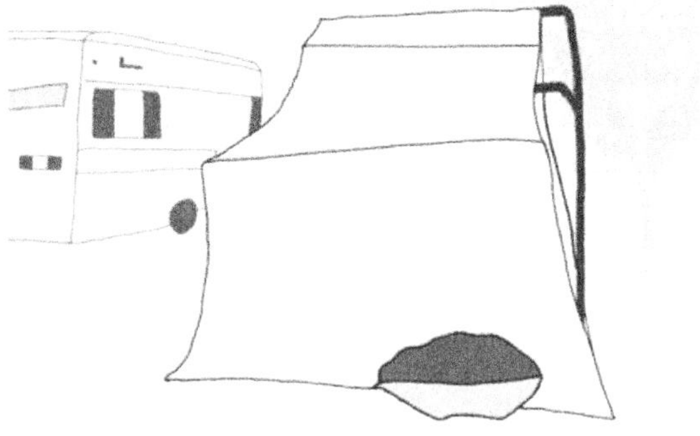

Hole cut into tent

Sandra Smallegan

On Saturday February 9, 1974, Sandra Smallegan attended a local basketball game. After the game, her parents dropped Sandra back at her apartment. But Sandra wanted to be around people, so she went to a local bar. She met up with her ex-husband at the bar and seemed to have a nice night. At just past midnight, Sandra was last seen walking out of the bar, waving to a friend as she left. As Franscell so aptly puts it, Sandra "*stepped off the curb, into the shadows*."

The search for Sandra was again intensive. It would not take police as long to find her remains, and in doing so, young Susan was also found.

The Investigation

Why does this keep happening?
Why does he keep doing this?

I know. I'm sorry. Here we are, midway through a case, and I take a side-step and begin talking about something else, seemingly unrelated. Why do I keep doing it? Simply because it is not unrelated. Keatley's Winthropping is just one small part of the richer, busier, messier, more chaotic and unpredictable nature of human behavior in an investigation. I am at no point suggesting my approach to Winthropping should be seen as a silver bullet or a magic wand. We must appreciate the wider investigation, the good and the bad.

In the current case, let us first look at the Susan Jaeger investigation. He was a small part of the *Shadow Man* book, but a suspect in the case caught my attention. *The Doll Collector* – as Franscell names him. The police had a suspect, a paroled child molester who had previously raped a little girl. In his house, he kept hundreds of dolls, most of them naked. Remember, I first came across Franscell's book because I was looking for child abductions from tents. What are the chances that in another tent-snatch case, police also happened upon a suspect who collected children's dolls? In Susan's case, this man was not guilty. This is something to remember when looking for closely-related cases. Random patterns may emerge. In fact, humans are remarkably good at finding patterns, even ones that are not there. It is called apophenia, or illusory pattern perception. We must be careful of this. Lesson over, back to Meirhofer.

Meirhofer was a suspect from the start, albeit with some 'gut instinct' pushback about the likelihood of his guilt. One of the lead investigators simply did not believe Meirhofer was their man. Gut instinct is great when it is right, but being closed-off to alternative opinion is not. I am often asked what makes a case go cold. Truthfully, the reasons are too numerous to list, but somewhere in that list near the top is the fact that someone in the investigative team closed-down lines of enquiry prematurely. Easy for me to say, in a warm, relaxed office, I know. Decisions in real-time cannot be fairly judged slowly later from afar. That said, I was relieved to see in this case that the investigator remained open to the repeated arrows pointing at Meirhofer. This openness to Meirhofer being a suspect would be tested though. You see, during the investigation, police administered a polygraph to Meirhofer, and here we have our next side-step, sorry.

The Polygraph/Interview

If you are not interested in polygraph testing and interviewing, then simply skip this section. I appreciate it is not as relevant to

Keatley's Winthropping. But polygraphs may form part of the investigation you are involved in. Depending on the perceived validity of the polygraph outcome, it may be a hurdle we have to overcome. Dismissing any evidence is risky. As risky as outright believing any piece of evidence. I know the current academic view of polygraphs is negative, at best. I am not going to wade into that war here. But this case provides such a perfect opportunity to elucidate something I have been saying for some time, that I cannot help myself but say it. Maybe the polygraph and statement analyses are only as good as the questions being asked and the answers being given. As always, review your questions and review the answers.

As we know, Meirhofer was guilty of the murder of Sandra Smallegan. He confessed to it. Lest anyone tells me confessions can be false, which they can, that was not the case here. Meirhofer supported his confession by storing body parts of Sandra in his freezer. As far as proof goes, that validates a confession in my opinion. So, Meirhofer definitely killed Sandra, let's see how he did in this polygraph interview.

According to Franscell, Meirhofer passed his polygraph interview. In real terms, that means he was declared as not showing significant indicators of guilty knowledge. How is this possible? We know he killed Sandra and yet the polygraph says he had no guilty knowledge. If we were to simply believe the polygraph, we would have had to consider Meirhofer not guilty. Or we could agree with the prevailing consensus in academic circles, that the polygraph/interview analysis is not accurate.

The reason I am bringing this up, here, in the middle of a book about my Winthropping approach is that you may one day have to overcome the hurdle of defending your Keatley's Winthropping profile in the face of results like a polygraph test.

This is a hurdle, indeed. But I think it is one that does not require a large leap of faith. Once we understand something of forensic linguistics, I think I can explain how Meirhofer passed. The step that might make you stumble over the hurdle is this: I do not think Meirhofer was deemed truthful because the test was inaccurate. I think it is because Meirhofer was being truthful (to some degree). The polygraph interview gave him a 'truthful' outcome because he was being truthful. But he also later confessed to the murder of Sandra. So, how is this possible?

In *Shadow Man* several of the questions and answers in Meirhofer's interview are given. Here they are.

> Question: Did you have anything to do with the death of Sandra Smallegan
> *Answer: I've been thinking that maybe she isn't really dead.*
>
> Question: Do you have any idea how she died?
> *Answer: I'm thinking her husband was with her until the night she was missed...*
>
> Question: Where were you on the night of February 9, 1974?
> *Answer: I was home alone. Well, I own two houses, but I only live in one*

If you know statement analysis, you are probably ahead of me, by now. For those that do not, let me explain. The first question above is relatively good – we hope that the examiner has clarified the meaning of 'to do with' and 'death.' People have mental lexicons – internal dictionaries. I may consider "to do with" in a very different sense than you. Earlier, I said I had nothing officially *to do with* the Cleo Smith case – how did you interpret that? What if your interpretation is different to my meaning? In the question posed to Meirhofer, this may be an important point of distinction. In any case, it is rendered a moot point because however we interpret it, Meirhofer's answer was truthful. Yes. Truthful.

Let us look more closely at what Meirhofer actually said. *"I've been thinking…"* this is truthful. I am sure he has been thinking. So, let's give him a 'tick' for truthfulness – or in polygraph terms, let's agree he would not display any indication of guilt. He continued, *"that maybe she isn't really dead."* The word *maybe* is a conditional term. I can think that *maybe* there are little green men on mars, or a spaghetti monster circling the moon. *Maybe* I will wake up tomorrow with the power of flight or invisibility. *Maybe* I can say anything if I couch it in the condition of maybe.

If I state something as a 'maybe,' it does not mean I believe it or that it is true. I can think that *maybe* you are reading this and jumping up-and-down with excitement. I can think it; I am in fact. I am right now thinking it. This means, that now I can say *"I've been thinking that maybe you are really jumping up-and-down."* See how that works? Me telling you what I have been *maybe* thinking, tells you nothing about any reality. Thus, no indicators of guilt in breathing, sweat, or any other verbal or nonverbal display. The results registered no guilty indicators because Meirhofer was not technically lying. I could even argue he is not being deceptive, in some senses. He is telling you *a* truth, just not the one you might think or infer.

The next question follows the same issue. Except, now, Meirhofer answers in the present. I can fully believe, at that moment, he may be thinking she was with her husband until the night she died. In fact, she was – with her ex-husband, at least. They were at the bar together. Meirhofer is being truthful here. Why does Meirhofer's analyses show he was being truthful? Because he was being truthful. There is more to Meirhofer's answer, here, but it adds nothing to the results, because it is couched in his "*thinking*." So far, we have 2-for-2 technically truthful answers, 2-for-2 times Meirhofer was being truthful, and 0-for-2 anything about reality.

The final question is trickier. Asking a suspect where they were is only as useful as the accuracy of when the crime occurred. Here, what does Meirhofer think of as 'night'? With his military background, maybe night is only night until midnight, then it is morning. Given Sandra was killed in the early morning, by this timeframe, he can answer honestly because of the framing of the question. This is a stretch, I agree, but do you at least see how important language and definitions are?

When Meirhofer replies, "*I was at home*," we infer he means that night, and perhaps all that night. We infer it, but he did not say it. "*I was at home*" is a truthful statement in itself. How does it relate to the question? We do not know. I believe Meirhofer was at home. I wonder whether he was at home all night (and morning). He does not say that, so I cannot say that for him.

In any case, Meirhofer then does a very clever trick. He adds a truthful statement, "*I own two houses, but I only live in one*." This is truthful. So, embedded in his answer is a truthful statement. This is one reason why polygraphs require only "yes" or "no" responses.

The analysis, thus, depending on how it is parsed for that response, will show truthfulness for the truthful part. That's 3-for-3 questions answered without raising any indicators of guilt or lying. In this case, the polygraph would be accurate. The fault was not in the polygraph, per se, it was in the analysis of the verbal responses. This is why statement analysts are important.

Question: did you notice the implicit spontaneous negation? I have taught you what they are. I have told you to be aware of them. Did you notice it? I ask you: how many houses does Meirhofer own? And why does he attempt to avoid one? Why the psychological distancing? There is a reason why he may have wanted investigators to not think about one of the houses.

In the end, Meirhofer may have passed his polygraph and interviews because he was technically telling the truth. In this way, the analyses back then could be seen to be accurate. It showed truthfulness, and Meirhofer was being truthful. The issue was that he was not answering what investigators thought he was. An additional explanation was provided by profilers at the time. Profilers working on the case suggested he passed because his psychopathy meant he was not emotionally reactive in the way 'normal' humans are. This means when asked a sensitive question, his pulse, breathing, and sweat showed little difference.

Whatever the explanation, I raise this only as an important reminder that we should be cautious with any piece of evidence, my Winthropping approach included. Many forensic and criminology tests and evidence are based on human interpretation, which is fraught with biases. This includes, by the way, more recent forensic evidence, including DNA. Though clearly a much more scientific and accurate approach, I am seeing increasing reports of issues in DNA interpretation.

Keatley's Winthropping is unlikely to ever compete with the accuracy of some of these tried and tested forensic analyses. However, dismissing Keatley's Winthropping because it is novel or not as accurate would not be fair, either. Especially given the issues inherent in some of the existing approaches. My advice is to view Keatley's Winthropping as just another lens to help see and build the puzzle pieces. The key is to critically review all links throughout.

Okay, lectures over, back to Meirhofer and where he moved the bodies.

Meirhofer's Body Deposition Site

Sandra's white Cortina was eventually found at Lockhart Place, an abandoned homestead near Three Forks. The Lockhart Place ranch was deserted and derelict by the time police went there looking for signs of Sandra. It did not appear on many maps. Most locals simply knew where it was. Remember the importance of local knowledge and mental maps (see Chapter 4). If you try to find Lockhart Place on Google Maps, for example, as I did when I was researching this case, it is simply not there. If you try to look through newspaper articles from the 1980s, you will find multiple directions, including opposite directions. It is simply a place that locals were likely to know, outsiders not so.

This localized knowledge is important in our Keatley's Winthropping profile. It allows us to add a "+1" to the weighting or tally for the offender being someone local. You may scoff and think that knowing the offender is local hardly helps. But consider the adult population of the entirety of the USA, any of whom could have been a suspect before we localized it. Now, we can begin to narrow that to a population of only a few hundred. That's a lot better odds in our favor.

Next, who is associated with Lockhart Place? The owner had died some years before. Though locals may know where it is, who had reason to go out there? Well, Lockhart Ranch is next to another ranch, Ralph Green's, to be exact. Ralph was not a suspect, instead he was a huge help to the investigation.

You see, Ralph had an issue around this time. Ralph contacted police and said his telephone bill seemed bizarrely large. It turned out, Meirhofer, with his military training in communications, had used Ralph's telephone line to make several calls to Susan Jaeger's family. When police responded to Ralph's complaint about his phone bill, Ralph provided a statement that serves as a perfect example of using local expertise.

Ralph knew his ranch intimately. He also knew when things were not right. Things we might miss, loomed large and salient to the man who knew his ranch so well. He noticed, for example, tire tracks that did not belong. Those tracks, he noted, were recognizable. He thought they belonged to a pick-up truck, like the one his old hired hand used to drive. His hired hand? Yes, you guessed it. Meirhofer.

Meirhofer, the person who had dated Sandra, once, and then kept hassling her for more dates. The person that knew the area around Lockhart Place very well, because he had worked around there for some time – on Ralph's ranch, for example. The person, who, according to reports from the time, also worked at Lockhart Place. The same Meirhofer, who, when police first began searching Lockhart Place, came up to investigators and gave them a woman's red blouse – claiming he had found it. The same Meirhofer who would repeatedly approach police in the local diner. Yes, it is easy to connect the dots looking backwards. But it is worth doing. It is practice, so that we might learn to connect them moving forward, in real-time, next time.

Meirhofer was initially dismissed as a cop wannabe. We now know this type of behavior is relatively common. Meirhofer's crime script was to insert himself into the investigation. It is a pattern seen in many other offenders. It correlates with his calls to the Jaeger family. The calls were likely in part to sadistically traumatize the family; and in part to continue the feeling of control over the victims and, by extension, their loved ones.

Control is a key feature in many offenders' post-crime behavior. Inserting themselves into an investigation allows the offender to try and control the investigation. It may offer a feeling of superiority, to show he is better than the officers. It may be a taunt. This may be why Meirhofer left Sandra's underwear on a post near the Lockhart farm, as a taunt that he could leave waypoints for investigators, and they still could not catch him. It may also have served as a personal waypoint, a guide to return to the site.

As it turned out, the investigators would eventually arrest Meirhofer owing to persistent and praiseworthy policing. Police analyzed the location and voice profile of a series of phone calls that Meirhofer made to taunt Susan's family. Meirhofer's own telephone behavior allowed investigators to close the net until they had him. In another eerie similarity to Cleo Smith and her abductor, it was also the use of telephones that tipped off WA police.

When investigators searched Meirhofer's home, they found frozen body parts in his freezer. Largely owing to these discoveries, he eventually confessed. He not only confessed to the murders of Susan and Sandra, but to two others, too.

Other crimes

Meirhofer confessed to shooting and killing 13-year-old Bernard Poelman, from a bridge in Three Forks, on March 19, 1967. Meirhofer also confessed to the murder of 12-year-old Michael Raney, in May 1968, again in Three Forks. In a sign of consistency, Raney was also camping at the time. A local killer, indeed. Meirhofer's cases appear to span no further than approximately a 6-mile radius.

Whenever 'odd' cases arise, and it is usually the 'odd' ones that I am called in to review, one of my first questions to investigators is always, *what other cases are in your files like this*? Solved or unsolved, I treat them equally. I am <u>not</u> suggesting that we are always hunting serial killers, but if a body is taken in a peculiar way, and abused in deliberate ways, I am aware that there may be others. In a recent case I looked into in

Australia, this line of questioning proved to open a whole new pathway to a potential suspect. In any case, while investigators of Susan's abduction were obviously aware of the similarities to Michael Raney, nothing came of it.

What could they do? That two children on a camping trip were killed (one in their tent, one abducted from it) is not enough of a lead. I would suggest that a Keatley's Winthropping approach could have helped. Remember, we can profile the locations and thus the offender. We know it is someone local. We know that they have an awareness of the area, and a close proximity to it. We know that the person has a car nearby. We know that body deposition sites in cases like this are often nearby. We know that such sites will be isolated, desolate, and likely known locally. The site will have ease of access and exit, but not have a large throughfare. It may not seem much, but this narrows down the search parameters.

By the time Meirhofer had confessed to 4 murders, it was understandable that investigators had more cases and more questions they wanted to ask Meirhofer.

Some of those questions remain to this day. Soon after Meirhofer gave his confession, he took his own life. And with him went the answers to many other questions. This case is presented here because a form of behavioral profiling preceded the discovery of evidence directly implicating Meirhofer. I think if this case occurred again, Keatley's Winthropping would more strongly point at Meirhofer much earlier. In fact, I know it would. Perhaps we could have found Susan Jaeger's remains before Sandra Smallegan's was also put there. Perhaps, perhaps, perhaps. These cold cases, even when solved, raise so many haunting questions, and so, to provide my answer to Franscell's final question…

…that is why I keep looking at these cases…

13. Robert NAPPER

The murder of Rachel Nickell, in England, UK, is taught in most undergraduate forensic psychology and criminology courses, and if it isn't, it should be. It is typically taught in relation to criminal profiling, not least because of the involvement of 'Britain's foremost criminal psychologist' – Paul Britton. Unfortunately, this is not a clear-cut case of triumph. Owing to the investigative issues in the Rachel Nickell investigation, many people are aware of her case. However, while police were building their case on their suspect for Rachel's murder, the real killer was free to kill again.

Rachel Nickell

In July 1992, Rachel was walking in Wimbledon Common, London, England, with her two-year-old son, Alex. It was, by all accounts a rather scenic Summer's Day. Wimbledon Common, on any other given day, is beautiful and enjoyed by many people. On this day, however, there was a vicious killer on Wimbledon Common at the same time as Rachel and her son.

When Rachel was found she had been viciously attacked and killed. Rachel's poor, young son, Alex, was found holding desperately to his mother's lifeless body. The scene was forensically examined to the best of the forensic scientists' abilities (remember this was 1993). No initial leads were found, and the public were demanding answers.

Given the horrendous nature of the attack, exacerbated by the presence of young Alex, the police felt increased pressure to find and arrest the perpetrator. Faced with little 'hard' physical forensic evidence, investigators turned to the relatively new profession of profiling to help with their investigation.

Paul Britton has written extensively about his involvement in this case in his book *The Jigsaw Man*. It is worth a read. The long-story-short is that Britton profiled the case and looked through the suspects. The investigators had narrowed their pool of suspects to one in particular. His name is in the public domain, but I shall call him Cuthbert. You'll see why later.

Britton was so convinced that Cuthbert was their guy that he worked with police to develop an intricate 'sting' operation. Britton's rationale was that Cuthbert fit his profile, and the chances of there being more than one perpetrator on Wimbledon Common who fit his profile were "*vanishingly small.*" A timely reminder that stats and intuition will take you only so far.

The investigators, however, hearing that their guy matched the profile and 'Britain's foremost criminal psychologist' agreed, were keen to push forward. Through the use of an undercover officer, and a series of interactions with Cuthbert, the investigators hoped that he would slip-up and reveal intimate knowledge of the crime. He never did. A judge would later throw out this investigation. An innocent man would become infamous, and that is why I omitted his real name, here.

Why am I telling you this? *Not* because I want to poke fun at Britton. Far from it. Not because I want to pretend to be any better – certainly not while I have the benefit of hindsight. I raise it because it is a stark reminder that profiles are only tools. Do not let desperation overcome skepticism. Push back, ask questions, and consider alternative hypotheses. Always. In fairness to Britton, from what I understand he attempted to ensure his information was used correctly. He was also, it is fair to say, very accurate in his profiles. His profiles did also match the real killer: Napper.

In another sad way, Britton was not entirely wrong in his profile. He says in *The Jigsaw Man* that Rachel's killer, if not caught, would kill again. Sadly, on this account, he was proven correct. The real killer did kill again.

Samantha and Jazmine Bisset

In November 1993, at her home in Plumstead, Samantha was sexually assaulted and brutally murdered. As if this were not horrific enough, her four-year-old daughter, Jazmine, was also killed. I have seen scenes that would make most people feel ill if not outright sick. So, please understand it is reasonable hyperbole when I say the scene was a nightmare. It was so awful that the police photographer had to take extended leave after documenting it. Samantha's body was eviscerated. Body parts were taken as trophies. Whoever did this, had killed before.

As you can tell, by the name of the chapter, the killer was Robert Napper. Napper's fingerprint was found at Samantha's flat, and it did not take police long to make the arrest. Then, the full story and sequence of Napper's crimes began to emerge, and with it a series of potential uses for *Winthroping*.

2 'p' or not 2 'p'

First, yes, I am relatively proud of that subheading. Second, yes. Winthroping with only one 'p' in it. That is how Alan Jackaman spells it in his book on the case, *Napper: Through a glass darkly*. When I first saw it, I panicked thinking that I had been misspelling it for years. It turns out the consensus in the literature appears to be "Winthropping," as you have seen it. Jackaman opts for the one-p version, 'Winthroping.' I must admit, I think Jackaman is likely correct. I would not expect my name to be 'Keatleyying' and there is a difference between someone 'hoping' and 'hopping.' We cannot just go around adding random letters. That said, every researcher and publication that I have seen, aside from Jackaman, uses the double-p spelling, so I do, too. I raise it here only to note that there are variations. For the sake of deference to Jackaman, I shall use the single-p spelling in this chapter.

Winthroping

So, why am I fixating on this 'Winthroping.' It is not just because it is a different spelling. It is because it was used in the Napper case. Napper, it turns out, made a series of sketches of areas and marked them. These sketches, along with *A-Z* maps with his markings in, were submitted to experts in 'Winthroping' to analyze. Napper took trophies, and investigators believed that he had made maps and notes of where some of these trophy caches were. Investigators were not naïve to the potential importance of these maps, sketches, and doodles, and so spent time analyzing them.

Plumstead Common highlighted
Winn's Common is to the right
Bisset house marked with 'X'

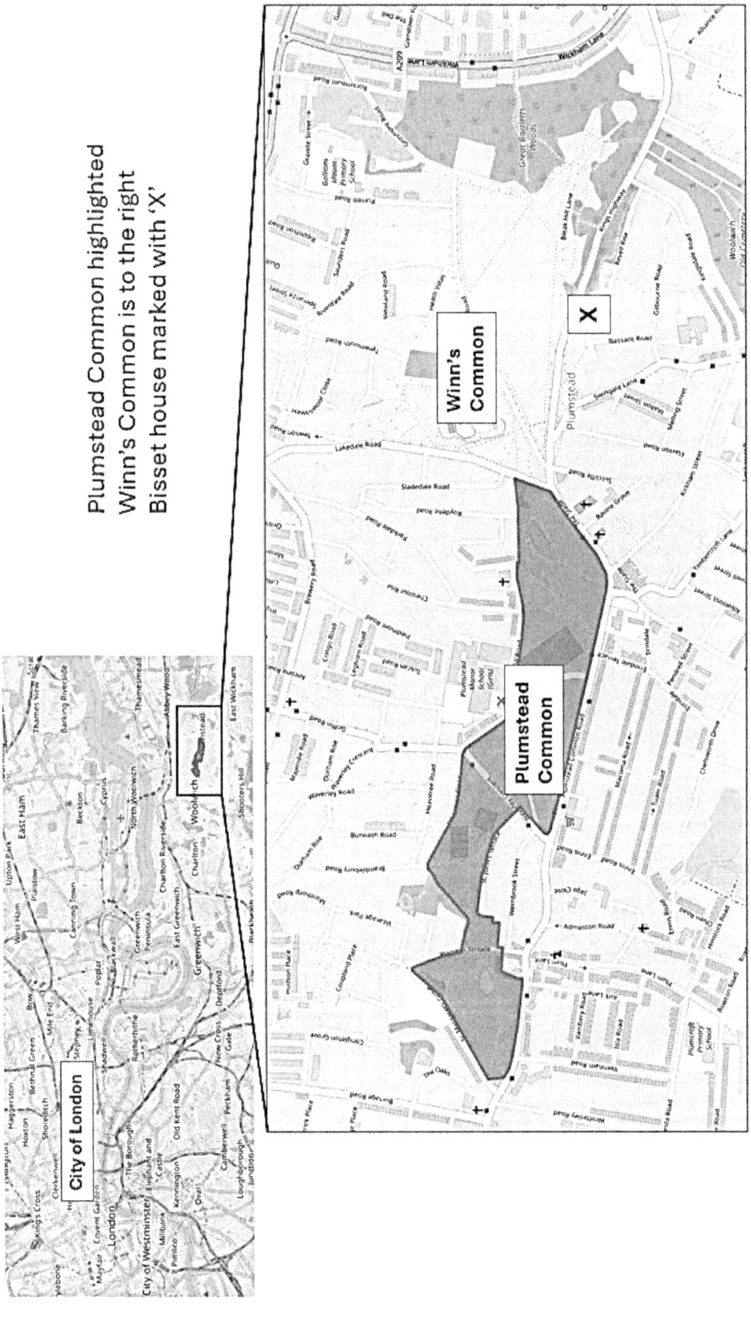

A to Z (A-Z) Maps and sketch diagrams

Jackaman provides several of Napper's sketch diagrams in his book. These can also be seen on the cover of Jackaman's book. Napper, of course, is not the only offender to draw sketch maps, but Jackaman is one of the few who notes that Winthroping was used to help analyze the sketches and the locations marked in Napper's *A-Z* maps.

Further inspection of Napper's *A-Z* maps showed that many of these markings were at locations of his known attacks. As with many violent offenders, Napper had a long history of violence that escalated into the eventual murders outlined here. For a number of years, women were sexually assaulted in an area in the Southeast of London, called the Green Chain Walk. These locations were marked in Napper's *A-Z* map.

Of additional importance for our purposes was a hand-drawn map that investigators found in Napper's house. On one particular hand-drawn map (Napper had many), Napper had marked Winn's Common and a nearby circle of birch trees. The relevance? The trees provided a viewing spot of Winn's Common and Purrett Road – where Napper's first known rape offence occurred. Napper had effectively done what Winthroping was originally designed to find. Napper had surveyed an area for an ambush/attack. He had then looked for a vantage position to surreptitiously stash something; in this case, himself.

This provided investigators with some support for their hunch that Napper was mapping his offences. Next, the investigators wanted to take the investigation a step further to see if they could uncover some of Napper's possible hiding spots.

A hidden cache

Napper was known to use knives in his sexual assault and rape attacks. When he was arrested, however, investigators could not find any of the long list of knives he had most recently bought. This led to the suspicion that he had stashed the knives somewhere in a hidden cache. This, of course, is where Winthroping is very useful. The investigators had a literal road map and a number of hand drawn maps to assist them.

In 1992, a criminal damage report was made by a young woman living off the edge of Plumstead Common. She had been in the kitchen when one of her windows was suddenly broken. It took some time before she realized someone had fired a gun and the bullet was the cause of the destruction. She called the police who attended, documented the case, but had very little to go on.

Then, in February 1993, some boys playing in the woods at Winns Common discovered a biscuit tin buried in a shallow hole. Inside was a Mauser .22 handgun. The boys, via their parents, handed their discovery to police. Police sent the gun and biscuit tin for forensic examination. The results identified the gun as being a 'match' for the bullet that had been fired at the young woman in her home.

Forensic examination of the biscuit tin also revealed something much more interesting. The biscuit tin had a palm and fingerprint that were identified as belonging to Napper. Further investigation showed the exact location of this biscuit tin cache was marked in his *A-Z*. We can only wonder what else is marked on his maps or hidden in the doodles and sketches that have yet to be discovered.

Proving a negative

This brings me nicely to another side point I would like to make. We cannot prove a negative. What do I mean by this? I mean that within Napper's drawings and *A-Z* maps there were a number of locations that were marked. In several marked locations, police investigation did not discover any crimes that had been committed there. Does this mean that the markings are random or meaningless? Possibly. Remember, we should avoid becoming a Texas Sharpshooter.

There is an alternative possibility. It may be that there was a crime that was committed at the marked location, but it was not reported. Sadly, a large number of crimes go unreported. Simply because we do not have a crime reported at the location, this does not mean a crime did not occur. I raise this only because I see many investigations going awry when a prediction or profile is made that does not appear to be supported in the files. We cannot assume every point on a map is a crime, but nor should we lose faith in a map or profile because a few do not result in 'hits.'

We should also be mindful of what we take as being misses. I recently read Charlie Hedges' excellent book, *Missing*. In it he tells of several cases he worked. One case in particular stands out with regards not finding a body. The case involved a young 19-year-old man who had gone missing near a lake. Dive teams searched the lake but appeared to find nothing. Owing to Hedges' mindful approach, he noticed that the teams had not properly searched a clump of reeds that they had previously suggested was clear. When re-searched, the man's body was found. If not for Hedges' careful and meticulous approach, would that young man still be missing? Would a dot be rendered as not relating to anything?

I have experienced personally, and via feedback from other experts in the field, the frustration of going to a known location of a known cache and not finding it. But we know it is there. It is not always easy. Before we write-off a location as being a 'miss' we should ensure we have not missed something.

A blemish on the landscape

Owing to the mounting evidence that the *A-Z* maps, doodles, and sketches held vital investigative information, increased efforts were put into searching them for more clues. All marks were indexed and highlighted for follow-up. Investigators noted that a rectangle had been placed around Isabella Plantation, which forms part of Richmond Park.

Background checks on Napper did not reveal any association or links to that area. The other marks found in the *A-Z* were mostly around Napper's activity zones – where he lived and worked. The Isabella Plantation mark, however, was harder to understand.

For those that do not know, Isabella Plantation neighbors on to Wimbledon Common. What are the chances? An *A-Z* that Napper owned, with a location clearly marked out, right next to where a vicious murder had occurred. What the investigators found next seemed even more exciting.

Careful examination of the *A-Z* showed a marking on Wimbledon Common at the exact location Rachel Nickell was attacked. According to Jackaman, it was likened to someone attempting to scrape away a part of the page. We saw in Chapters 3 and 4 that some criminals will attempt to hide their crime location by verbally or physically removing it from their report or sketch.

This had the potential to be a huge breakthrough in linking Napper to Rachel Nickell. Given the precedence of Napper marking his crimes on the *A-Z*, this would seem to fit his style.

What happened next is a prime example of great police work.

Before conclusions were jumped to, investigators decided to check other *A-Zs* published at the same time as the one they were inspecting. Remember when I say to constantly pushback and question everything. Here it is in action.

When the investigators received another copy of the same *A-Z*, printed from the same batch, they found the same mark. It was a printing blemish. Just like that, the blemish remained while the evidence disappeared. This would have been a perfect example of an offender attempting to remove a crime scene from their map. Instead, it serves as an equally important reminder to pushback on our hypotheses. While sadly not a great example of a 'spatial lacuna,' it serves as a testament to the fastidious investigative efforts of the team involved. A blemish on the map landscape, a gold star on the investigative efforts.

The heroic efforts of all the investigative team on the Napper case would eventually lead to his pleading to manslaughter charges for Samantha and Jazmine Bisset. Then, with the dogged determination that only the best cold case detectives exhibit, Napper was eventually linked through DNA to the murder of Rachel Nickell. Throughout the investigations, his *A-Z*, sketch maps, and coded scrawlings remained a specter of what other crimes, locations, and hidden caches may remain. I trust the expertise of the investigators at the time who analyzed them. I would be eager to see what else may be seen through a more modern Keatley's Winthropping lens.

In Sum

While I have known about Rachel, Samantha, Jazmine and Napper for many years, it did not originally register as relevant for this book. I came across this case relatively late in the writing of my book. In fact, this was one of the last additions I added. I thank the helpful tip-off I received via LinkedIn about this case.

This chapter is a wonderful addition to my book, and I am indebted to Alan Jackaman for writing his account of the case, and his work on it. Thanks also for the individual that recommended it (I have omitted your name in case you did not want it published). I want people to reach out to me and tell me about more cases. The more the better – they allow me to build my database, which allows me to refine my approach to Winthropping… or Winthroping

14. The BIRNIES

In 1986, Perth, Western Australia, several women were murdered at the hands of a serial killer couple, David John Birnie and Catherine Margaret Birnie. The Birnies attempted to murder a 5th victim, but through design or luck, she escaped and alerted authorities. Serial killer couples and *folie à deux* is nothing new in criminology. Indeed, while researching the Birnies, I was advised to look into the Moors Murders, too. I must draw the line somewhere, though, and so I stuck with the Australian pair.

For those interested, the Moors Murders were committed by Ian Brady and Myra Hindley in and around Manchester between 1963-1965. Brady and Hindley were another couple killings case in which victims were taken to their house, murdered, and then the Saddleworth Moor was used as the body deposition site for the victims – hence the name given to the pair. I have been informed that Brady and Hindley can be analyzed through a Winthropping lens. I have heard that Hindley attempted to lead investigators back to a body deposition site, but snow impeded her navigational abilities. I have also seen the photographs of Hindley at a deposition site. Perhaps in a future version of this book I shall include them. But as I say, I must draw a line somewhere, so let's go back to the land down under and see what the Birnies did.

The first known victim of the Birnies was Mary Neilson. Mary was a 22-year-old Psychology student at the University of Western Australia (UWA). Mary needed some tires for her car and so went to a car wrecker's shop where David Birnie worked. Likely gauging she was a student and could be manipulated into seeking a cheap deal, Birnie offered Mary a cheaper set of tires from his house. Mary agreed. When Mary visited the Birnies' Moorhouse home, she was attacked, bound, gagged, and chained to the bed. What happened next at their house does not need to be addressed in this book.

After the Birnies had repeatedly attacked Mary, they decided to take her to Gleneagle, near Albany Highway. David Birne sexually assaulted her again, before murdering her and then attempting to hide her body. It is worth noting here that before burying Mary, David Birnie stabbed her, believing that it would expedite the decomposition of her body. This is important in terms of forensic awareness attempts, as we'll discuss later.

Of course, we cannot know what pre-, peri-, and post-mortem activities a criminal performs on a victim until we find the victim. So, the stabbing of Mary to speed-up the decomposition process is irrelevant to our Winthropping approach if we have not found Mary. That said, if and when we do find Mary, if we find out she has been stabbed post-mortem, then we may bring this into our profiling. What type of person stabs a body, post-mortem? Of course, it happens. I know it does. It does not always indicate forensic awareness and detection avoidance. But sometimes it can. Surely it is worth a consideration. As we will see later, it could have provided meaningful interpretation in the current case. Sadly, though, Mary was not found before the Birnies struck again.

Susannah Candy was a 15-year-old high school student from

Nedlands, WA. Susannah was abducted while hitchhiking along Stirling Highway in Claremont (we will hear more about the infamous Claremont and another series of murders related to the area in Chapter 30). Susannah accepted a lift and entered the Birnies' car. The presence of a woman, Catherine Birnie, would likely have reduced Susannah's suspicion. Upon entering, Susannah was held at knifepoint. A similar horrific series of sexual assaults took place at the Birnies' home.

When Susannah's body was located it was in close proximity to Mary Neilson. In this sense, the Birnies are similar to so many other serial offenders – returning to a similar body deposition site. So far, we can tick the boxes for: salience, affordance, routine activity theory, rational choice theory, geographic profiling, crime geometry, and satisficing. This is not to say that every serial killer (single or couples) always uses the same sites. I am simply showing that what we observe in the data can be explained by my approach to Winthropping, and learning what was salient in the area would help track the sites.

Soon after Susannah was abducted and killed, another victim was taken. Noelene Patterson, a 31-year-old bar manager at Nedlands Golf Club ran out of fuel on her way home. She was on Canning Highway when the Birnies picked her up and took her back to their house. This murder was slightly different to the last. It appeared that David Birnie had a special interest in Noelene, and Catherine became jealous of David's additional interest in Noelene compared to the other victims.

The crime script or pattern had changed and with it the body deposition sites changed, too. Noelene was buried a short distance from the previous two victims. Of course, we would only know this once we found them. But let's imagine we are coming at this from the other end of the investigation – having found the bodies. We find two in very close proximity and one a short distance away. There are, of course, myriad reasons for this pattern. It is, however, a disfluency, an incongruency. It is a break in the pattern. Therefore, it is worth considering and then asking about. What psychologically changed to cause this break in the routine? For Noelene, the crime script and body deposition site changed. We must ask *why*?

The final murdered victim was Denise Brown, a 21-year-old who the Birnies picked-up from a bus stop on Stirling Highway. The same series of sexual assaults and attacks occurred, but the body deposition site was vastly different. Even with a small distance between them, the victims, Mary, Susannah, and Noelene were all buried to the south of the Birnies' house, in Gleneagle. Denise was taken to a site near Pinjar – far north of their house. You can guess my next question: *why*?

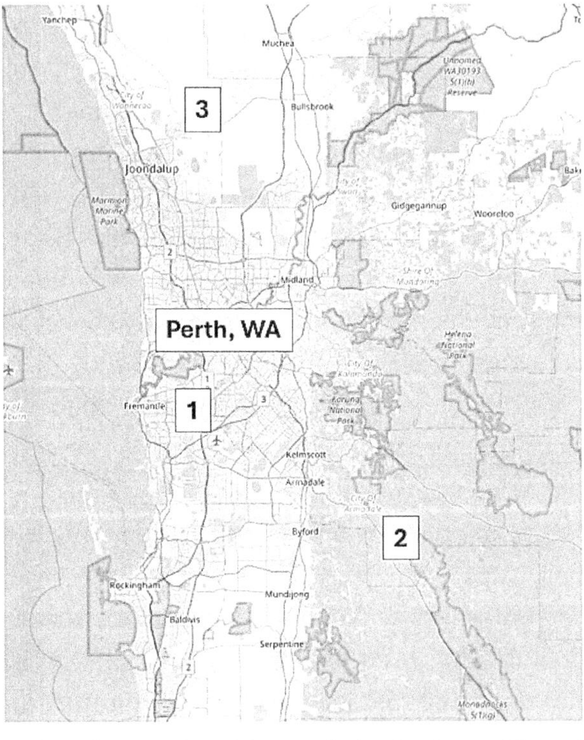

1 = Birnies' home; 2 = Gleneagle body deposition site;
3 = Pinjar body deposition site

Why indeed. If we say, "three victims taken south, and then one taken north," it may seem hard to explain. But how many times do I need to remind you that details matter? Let us be exact. Two victims taken south and buried in very close proximity. The third victim taken south but put a short distance away. And then, the fourth victim taken north. Put another way, the fourth is a continuation of a new trend – to distance the victims. Admittedly, it is not a big difference between the first two and the third victims, but it is a difference. It is a break in the sequence, a change of the script.

There may be many reasons for this. Perhaps Gleneagle became 'hot' in the Birnies' minds. Perhaps they worried that returning there was pushing their luck – after all, 3 is a crowd, so Gleneagles was getting crowded. Perhaps. I think there are other hypotheses, too.

I think Noelene was the breaking point for Catherine in many ways. We know, with hindsight, that Catherine had a different reaction to David's behavior with Noelene. This is then evidenced in the body deposition site. I think the movement north for the fourth victim is a further continuation of this separation. The Birnies were literally moving away from their cluster. It may be that Catherine did not want David returning to the body deposition site of Noelene. In this case, the northern location of Denise makes sense. Catherine may have had an additional repeller to the Gleneagle site, given Noelene was there.

Again, this is easy to quarterback on a Monday morning, so to speak. With all the facts, we can create *just so* stories all day long. I am not suggesting I am some master sleuth or profiler, here. I am suggesting that sometimes these hypothetical narrative building exercises are useful. Why not? Why not try and understand a pattern and a break in the pattern? This will not be the only case that we see an offender change the location of their body deposition site so abruptly. So, why shouldn't we take the opportunity to see what we can learn.

On that note, let us return to something else we discussed earlier. Remember when David suggested stabbing a body would expedite the decomposition process, thus perhaps reducing the likelihood of the body being found. Perhaps the movement north was another attempt to throw-off the investigators. It may be that the Birnies felt changing locations entirely would mean that Denise may not be found, or if she were that Mary, Susannah, and Noelene might not.

I find the forensic awareness/detection avoidance explanation weaker than the emotional abreaction one given previously. If the Birnies were really attempting to ensure bodies were not found, then placing the first two in such close proximity is harder to explain. Even Noelene was still relatively close. It appears the Birnies were not concerned about placing their first three victims in the same geographic area.

Something changed between Noelene and Denise. We may never know for sure what that was, but it is worth reviewing. Why? Because it is worth knowing. If we can discover why the Birnies moved body deposition site, it may help us with other cases in which we still have no-bodies for known serial killers. Put another way, what if the Birnies did not confess to Denise. Would we have found her? Would we have linked her if we did? I believe so, but it would be easier if we knew more about the geographic and psychological processes that underpin such decisions, and that is where Keatley's Winthropping can help us.

15. Herbert MULLIN vs Ed KEMPER
LISK vs John Bittrolff

While I was researching cases for the first paper that I published on the topic of Keatley's Winthropping, I stumbled upon the cases of Herbert Mullin and Ed Kemper. I am slightly wary of publishing these offenders, owing to the information being largely hearsay and without official records that I could review. Individually, Mullin and Kemper provide us with two more cases of serial killers that were able to re-locate their body deposition sites much later. This, by now, is likely getting tiresome to readers, so it is the next part that I shall focus on – their alleged argument.

Let me say from the outset, even if a scholar or officer can refute the following argument, the point still stands. The point is that if we accept that offenders progress through Keatley's Winthropping in some way when finding a site, then that means offenders have similar cognitions. After all, if we are accepting that we can engage in a form of Keatley's Winthropping when navigating our world, and criminals engage in a similar process, then surely two criminals are more likely to think in similar ways. Another way of viewing what I am trying to say is like this: the main scope of Winthropping is to put yourself in the mindset of the person you are trying to track or follow. However good we may be at doing that for a criminal, it seems intuitive that one criminal would understand another better than us. This is perhaps why Keppel listened to Bundy when investigating the Green River Killer, Ridgway (see Chapter 6).

What does all this mean? Well, something that is probably quite obvious to many scholars and practitioners: serial killers can use the same sites. It is not random, it is not 'by chance,' it is not an oddity. It is also not always the case that one is trying to emulate the other or hide their bodies as that of the other. Two criminals using the same sites is actually relatively likely, given the tenets of Keatley's Winthropping. This is what appears to have happened between Mullin and Kemper. The story goes that both criminals were locked up at the same time, at the same location, when they began to argue. The argument was about who owned the sites that they were both using.

It appears that Mullin and Kemper were both operating in the same geographical and temporal region, and both using sites that overlapped. This was not, as far as I am aware, a form of copycat killings or one killer attempting to hide their crimes by using the other's sites. It appears that both killers operated independently, and yet placed bodies in similar or same locations. This, to my mind, supports the Keatley's Winthropping approach. It is strong support of the fact that killers are making similar choices, based on similar processes, and coming to similar conclusions.

That paper was published, and I was very happy to see it out there in the world. Then, while I was researching more cases for this book, and my understanding in general, my eyes were drawn to a recent headline that outlined how Long Island police were searching the nearby woods for clues in a decades-old case, *not* tied to LISK. Let me give you a brief background for those that do not know. LISK is the Long Island Serial Killer, a serial killer who left multiple bodies along Long Island. Interested readers need only type the term into any search engine to have more documentaries and podcasts than they can hope to listen to in a year. Aside from this on-going case, there was another serial killer operating in the area, John Bittrolff. The news article outlined that police are now attempting to link another body in the Long Island area to Bittrolff, not LISK. This news has only just broke, so unless major headway is made between the time of writing and publishing, I cannot offer further updates. What I can say is this: I am not surprised that two killers operating in the same geographical and temporal regions are using the same sites, too.

CASE STUDIES II

The single-homicide cases

16. Michael SAMS

I first came across the case of Michael Sams not in relation to his own crimes, for which he was sentenced, but under the speculation that he may have been involved with another, currently unsolved crime. I am not intending to inculpate or exculpate him in the case of Susannah 'Suzy' Lamplugh – another very interesting case we shall touch on later. Instead, I will focus primarily on the crimes for which Sams was convicted of committing. First, the kidnap and murder of Julie Dart in 1991 and then the kidnap and rape of Stephanie Slater in 1992. It was also in reading about the case of Michael Sams that I found the name of someone that you'll recognize, we'll meet him later…

If you research Michael Sams, you will not have to travel far before you see a pattern emerging: railways. Sams was by no means unique in using railway tracks as an anchor for his crimes. In the 1980s, John Duffy and David Mulcahy used railway stations to navigate their crimes, earning the nickname "the railway murders." As we have seen, offenders typically stick to areas and locations they are familiar with – where they feel comfortable. Police, of course, are now very aware of this, and often look for such patterns.

Julie Dart

On July 9, 1991, Sams drove to an area known to be used by sex workers. His plan, he stated, was to kidnap a sex worker and hold her for ransom. Sams, you see, had ideas above his earnings, and was often in debt and under threat of losing his businesses and livelihood. Money, it would seem, was the primary motivation for his kidnapping.

Sams picked up Julie Dart who was in the area he had scouted. Soon after accosting her, Sams blindfolded her and took her to a warehouse he owned. Julie was then placed in a pre-made box and chained to the floor. As Sams lived with a partner at the time, he had to leave Julie alone overnight. He had rigged an alarm system that would alert him if Julie attempted to escape. With this set-up in place, all that was left were the ransom demands.

Sams forced Julie to write several letters, including one to her boyfriend, and one demanding a ransom of £140,000 (~$175,500 USD). The letters were long and detailed, and we can only imagine, if we dare, the horror Julie must have felt at being forced to write them. I will not reprint them in full here, as they are so long. Instead, I shall provide an excerpt I think is relevant to our ongoing learning. Note, the spelling and grammar is kept as in the original, and WPC is "woman police constable."

> *Next Tuesday 16 July a WPC will drive to Birmingham New Street station with the money, and await a phone call at the Mercury phone terminal in the waiting room on platform 9, she must wear a lightish blue skirt with the money in a shoulder bag.*

While there were criminal psychologists involved at the time, offering profiles and insights into the kidnapper's mind, I am more interested in his choice of locations. First, let us focus on the first location Sams chose for his ransom plan. He could pick anywhere in England. Instead, he chose a train station (Birmingham New Street), which he appeared to know well enough to direct the WPC to an exact phone.

If this were the only mention of railway-related locations, then I would agree, it is relatively meaningless. Of course, if that were the case, it is unlikely we would be focusing so heavily on Sams. So, let us turn to where he left Julie.

After he had so callously used her for his ransom plan, Sams murdered Julie with a blunt object. Several days later, Julie was left in a field in Easton, Lincolnshire. A seemingly bare field. I could show you a picture of it. I could draw you a sketch. But the field appears bare. The sketch would be of a flat field except for a tree. For those that do not know, Lincolnshire is colloquially known as the 'flatlands.' There are no prizes for guessing why. I can confirm this is true, as I grew up in Spalding, Lincolnshire. My family home is barely a stone's throw from where Julie was left. It is indeed a flat land. Flat, but not empty. As stated, there was a tree. Not much perhaps, but a feature. Another feature also appeared to be more salient to Sams.

Before we continue profiling Sams and the site, an important point needs to be made. Here we have an important distinction between Sams and so many of the serial killers we studied previously. Sams does not appear to have returned specifically to Julie's body. He never confessed to it, and I have no reason to think he did or even planned to. Does that mean that Keatley's Winthropping is not useful? I think not. Remember, 'where are they?' is only one of the questions we can answer with Keatley's Winthropping. The other question is 'why here?' So, that seemingly flat and bare field, does it have anything special about it? Well, let's turn to Sam's own words to find out. As I have previously said, let the offender speak, and listen carefully to what they tell us. The following is an exert from Sams.

> *I then... put Julie's body, still in the wheely bin, into the car, and took her south on the A1. Just south of Grantham I turned left. Then came to a T Junction, turned right. A little way along the road I spied a lonely turning on my left. There were no cars up the lane so I turned up. Removed the wheely bin and then placed the body underneath a tree and within sight of the road & lane. I did not know where I was in relation to Stoke Summit [a favourite haunt of train-spotting enthusiasts]. Nor did I know that I had placed Julie's body within 50 yards of a disused railway line.*

Please note that the excerpt is taken, with thanks, from Christopher Berry-Dee's book, *Unmasking Mr Kipper* – a book about another case that he thought Sams was possibly responsible for (see Chapter 30).

We may choose to believe Sams – that he had no idea where he was. We may consider it random chance that the person who chose a railway station to begin his ransom crime would end it by placing his victim near an abandoned railway line. We must always be willing to pushback against our human ability to see patterns. We can all succumb to seeing illusory patterns. We can see connections or meaningful patterns between random, unrelated things.

That said, some pushback to our pushback. Simply because we can see meaningless patterns, this does not mean that all patterns we see are meaningless. Too many scientists are too eager to tell experienced investigators that their gut instincts should be ignored or dismissed. I am not saying that. I am saying feel them, listen to them, but do not blindly follow them.

Also, if you think you have seen a pattern, then great. But this is one pattern. Do not stop at the first pattern you see. Explore the data or evidence further. Consider the following images.

A seemingly random assortment of dots, right?

Well, let me connect some of them for you.

Voila! A 'KILLER' emerges in our datapoints. This is good news, right? Time to stop the investigation and begin the celebration?

Perhaps not…

While we're thinking about illusions, and seeing things we logically know are not real but cannot help but see, do you see a white sphere in the center of this next image?

You know that no such sphere exists, especially on a 2D image. But our brains cannot help but see it. Let this be a reminder that we can see patterns where there are none. We can connect dots to make sense of the randomness, and if the connections we make fit with our preconceived ideas, this can lead to a *confirmation bias*. We think something is the case, we connect dots that seem to support our hunch, and thus we feel we have confirmed our suspicions… and all along, there was the alternative hypothesis lurking there. Of course, have hunches, follow leads, connect dots, make patterns make sense. But be warned. Do not become so fixated with your final picture that you draw the investigation to a close prematurely. Okay, lecture over, let's get back to Sams.

We previously found that Sams had reference points that linked him to railway lines and stations. Not quite enough for a pattern, perhaps, so let us continue our journey and meet him again when he strikes again.

Stephanie Slater

In January 1992, using a false name, Sams kidnapped his second victim, Stephanie Slater. Stephanie was working as an estate agent at the time, and it was using the ruse of viewing a house that Sams was able to lure her to a property where he attacked her, tied her up, and took her back to his workshop. Sams' crime script remained relatively similar to his previous offense. Stephanie was tied-up and placed in a wheelie-bin (like a large garbage can, for my American readers) placed on its side, which was again alarmed. Sams again demanded a ransom be paid for her safe return. The police, realizing that Sams had previously gone through with his threat to kill Julie, were aware of the increased risks. Sams, however, would not make it easy. He developed an intricate and elaborate plan to gain the money in such a way that he could not be tracked or captured.

Sams sent several letters to the police regarding his elaborate plan. Again, I will not reprint the entire series of letters here, instead, I shall make clear what you have likely already guessed: the railway line links continued. Without any provocation, Sams wrote about trains in one of his letters.

"*After 2hrs pondering & writing this on the train.*"

I see the main reason for telling the police this was to show police how much he had planned his crimes. However, the train was a leak owing to his fixation on trains. He is so familiar with this train that he refers to it as 'the' train, not 'a' train. The definite, rather than indefinite, article. This may suggest he uses 'the' train often. This fact was not lost on police, of course. I am merely highlighting it here to provide further evidence for the use of Keatley's Winthropping. Behavioral, psychological, and linguistic patterns emerge. What is on the brain leaks out of the mouth (or hand if written).

To avoid unnecessary repetition, let me tell you this: Sams would continue to make multiple railway station references throughout his letters. For example, he told police he posted a letter from Leeds Railway Station. Even if we consider this subterfuge or misdirection. Even if we consider Sams is double bluffing the police and making them believe he was in the Leeds Railway Station area when he was not. Surely, we must also ask *why* Railway Stations at all? This is the secondary stage of analyzing staging.

If we think staging has occurred, we should ask why that particular production is being produced. Not only *what* is the stage production the criminal is intending to create for us, but *why* that production? What does this tell us about his psyche? Sure, stage the scene and tell me a location you have not been, but I will still wonder why you chose that location above any others.

Let's look at this another way. If Sams were going to lie, why not go big and suggest somewhere hundreds of miles away from Leeds, like Glasgow Central Station (in Scotland – for those not aware of UK geography). Why not avoid train stations entirely?

If more evidence were needed of Sams's railway fixation, then I have more. Sams was also responsible for suspending a block of sandstone from a railway bridge in an effort to critically damage a train. While the train passed relatively unscathed, we have more datapoints all pointing us towards a fixation on trains. Indeed, the final ransom payment for Stephanie took police along several stops that included rail stations. The multi-stage path ended with a disused railway track and bridge being used to collect the money via a pulley system.

It probably comes as no surprise to hear that several newspapers at the time began referring to Sams as the 'railway nerd.' As insulting as that may seem, the 'nerd' did get away with a large ransom in a clandestine cache.

A cache. A hidden clandestine cache. It seems almost too perfect for Winthropping, right? Well, this, friends, is where we meet someone whose name should be well-known to you.

Mark Winthrop

Yes. Him. Winthrop. *The* Winthrop. The one for whom we have to thank for this entire book. He was involved in this case. You see, after Sams hid the money, police obviously wanted it back. Who better to ask to find a hidden cache than the man who developed the method for finding hidden caches? It did not take Winthrop long to deduce the same patterns we have seen above. Railway tracks became a main focus of search areas. Winthrop offered a 5-point profile to assist police in their search efforts, and I would love to say it was a complete success. What an ending that would be. But life is seldom so perfect. Police tried but did not immediately find the hidden ransom cache. Sorry.

Wait! This is not the point to throw down this book in a rage of *what a waste of my time*. Winthropping is not some magical trick. Even Winthrop appears to have not perfected Winthropping. Thus, it is not some mystical supernatural ability to find the unfindable, solve the unsolvable. No method in forensics, criminology, or psychology is. What Winthropping can do is to help narrow down search parameters. It may help us understand the criminal and perhaps help find the clandestine locations. But it will not work every time all the time.

Are you still with me? Good. You are the ones I want to speak with. The ones who will not give up at the first setback. You're the ones that will meet adversity and keep pushing forward to finish the job. You're my kind of persistent people. So, I have something for you. Ready? Winthrop was not entirely wrong. He directed police to prioritize two areas near railway tracks. First, the Dove Valley Trail (*wrong*), and second: a disused railway bed (*almost*). This second location was just a stone's throw from where Julie Dart's body had been left. Of all the places in all the UK Winthrop could have suggested, he got pretty close!

What Winthrop did not include in his profile, is what I have most recently developed to be included – forensic linguistics. Winthrop, from what is known, focused purely on his approach to Winthropping. No surprises there, really. What I have more recently been focusing on is what people say, and what they mean. I will not go into too much detail here about forensic linguistics (I have a whole book on it for those interested). I will also be covering forensic linguistics more, later, across several other cases. But here is a small taster.

Remember a few pages back, when we saw Sams' statement about where he left Julie Dart's body? He mentioned Stoke Summit. A strange thing to mention. Why mention it at all? I would suggest and will hopefully convince you later in the forensic linguistics section, that Sams mentioned Stoke Summit because he did know the area. That was his *salient* landmark. That was on his mind. When he thought about Julie, he thought about where he left her body, and he thought about that landmark. He's a trainspotting enthusiast. Of course he knew it. What was on his mind leaked out in his statement. It happened again when police interviewed him. And then, on Tuesday December 1, 1992, police found the buried cache near there.

Sams hid his money in a place he knew well, a place that felt right, likely because of its salience to him. His chosen location will come as little surprise by now: at Bridge No. 230, over the East Coast Railway near Stoke Summit.

The clandestine cache location was also close to Grantham – a town where he purchased his pet food. The location was also 1.7 miles east of where he had attempted to hide Julie's body. Railways once again loomed large in his decision-making process to hide his ransom cache.

Granted, Winthrop did not pinpoint the location exactly. But out of the entirety of the UK, he got close enough that I think we can be suitably impressed. If I may be so bold, I would suggest that by focusing more on Sams' interviews and statements we could have narrowed down the search even further. Police, of course, did find the cache. I am not suggesting that they were unaware of the importance of Sams' movements and statements. I am just offering this as tentative support for Winthropping and my addition to it.

Millgate, Millgarth, or Mill Gate

There is one more addition to the Sams case I must add. As we know, Sams sent multiple letters to the police. We also know he made several mistakes in those letters. One mistake stands out to me. In a letter sent to Police, regarding Julie's murder, Sams sent it to: "West Yorkshire Police, Millgate, Leeds." The issue is that the correct address is "West Yorkshire Police, Millgarth, Leeds." Of course, Millgate and Millgarth look and sound pretty similar. Perhaps this was an innocent mistake. It is, however, one that Sams repeated almost a year later when he sent another letter, again using "Millgate" instead of "Millgarth."

We also know that Sams thought of himself as smarter than the police, and perhaps liked to taunt them. It may come as no surprise to find that Millgate may not have been as random or trivial as it may at first seem. You see, the location of Sams' workshop, where he kept both Julie and Stephanie, was about 50 meters away from Mill Gate in Newark. Knowingly or not, tauntingly or not, Sams was using or leaking the name of a road that pointed right to him.

17. Gerard BADEN-CLAY

Time to return to the land down under. Our next case takes us to Brisbane, Queensland. It is hard for me to write about Gerard Baden-Clay without analyzing his emergency call, but interested readers can find out more about that in my other book. Instead, the focus here is on his geographical decision-making and movements.

On Friday April 20, 2012, Gerard Baden-Clay said he had woken just after 6am. His wife, he later said, was not at home when he woke up. He proceeded to have a shave and get ready for the day. Over breakfast, his daughters asked where their mother was. Baden-Clay appears to have casually informed them she had gone for a walk. Something had clearly changed in his casual demeanor and beliefs, however, as he made an emergency call at 7.15am. So began the case of Gerard Baden-Clay and the murder of his wife, Allison Baden-Clay.

Some of you, unfamiliar with the case, may have some faint recognition of the name 'Baden-Clay.' Something about it may seem familiar. Let me make the link a little easier for you: Gerard's full name is Gerard Robert Baden-Clay. Got it, yet? Keep scouting out ideas if you are not sure. Yes. He is the great-grandson of Lord Robert Baden-Powell of Scout fame in Britain. The Scouts. I would wager most children and thus adults in England know about the Scouts. I will not get into the argument of whether the American Scouts version is an offshoot or not. All we need to know here is that the Baden-Powell name is like a dynasty in Britain because of the Scouts and scouting. According to some, Gerard was immensely proud of his Scout family history. This little history lesson will be important, later, I promise. For now, let us turn to Allison and scout out what happened.

Allison Baden-Clay

While Gerard was making his call to emergency services, Allison lay dead. Of course, while police may be suspicious in the beginning, and they certainly were in this case, they had to treat the case on face value, too. This was a MisPer case, and a large-scale search ensued. While we speak of 'face value,' I cannot help but explain one of the reasons that investigators were initially suspicious of Gerard. His face.

You may have wondered why I mentioned Gerard shaving in the opening paragraph. That is because he told police that the wounds on his face were the result of his shaving. The issue was that the shaving cuts looked more like fingernail scratches than shaving cuts.

Hold up! I am not sure we should immediately disbelieve Gerard. After all, he seemed to be having quite a rough week. Further investigation would reveal he had wounds across his chest, too. Gerard also had an explanation for these. It appears the poor man had been savagely attacked by a caterpillar only the day before. I am aware of how many dangerous animals and insects Australia has; angry caterpillars seldom make the lists though.

Back to the search for Allison. Search parties tried for days to find her. Then, 10 days after Allison allegedly went missing, she was found. I realize we are still barely halfway through our case studies, but I want to see how far we have progressed. Take a breath, get ready, you are about to try Keatley's Winthropping for yourself on this case. Do not worry, I am not expecting you to get it immediately correct. It is an opportunity, however, to see how good you are getting.

Think about what you know so far regarding Gerard Baden-Clay and about Keatley's Winthropping. Remember, people are not as random as they might seem. Do not give in to the voice telling you, 'She could be anywhere.' Put yourself in Gerard's place. Think about him, his life, his world. Consider who he is, what he knows, what is salient, what is possible. He has kids, he cannot travel far. Even without knowing the precise location, which might give it away. What comes to mind first?

Did any of you think about Scouts? Yes? Good. So, let's progress with that, see where it leads us. Did any of you think about areas relating to Scouts? Maybe a Scout campsite? If you did, well done. You have pretty much just found her.

I know, I know. I can already sense the response. Some of you may feel I biased you by the information I have given you. Perhaps you feel this is trickery, "*of course we thought it was related to Scouts, you made such a big thing about Scouts, you repeated 'Scouts' in almost every line.*" You are absolutely correct, but you are also arguing my point for me.

I made Scouts a big deal to you. But Scouts was also a very big deal to Gerard! That is what was salient to him. His name. His dynasty. It seems plausible, therefore, that locations associated with Scouts would have come to his mind first in the same way they may have come to yours. Think about it, if I can influence you so easily with just a couple of paragraphs about his family name, how much would that have been on his mind at the time? His family name *is* him. It is possible that this was a factor inherent in the crime, too. Perhaps his legacy was something that caused the issues that led to this crime. And this is where integrating Keatley's Winthropping into the investigation is important. It works synergistically.

Some reports suggest that owing to Gerard's infidelity, his marriage to Allison was not in a good state. Allison had discovered his cheating in December 2011, barely a few months before she was killed. Gerard promised to Allison that he would end the affair. He did not. Then, the night before Allison went missing, he had a heated exchange with the woman he was having the affair with.

During the heated exchange, the woman told Gerard that she and Allison would be attending the same seminar the next day. This would likely have caused Gerard a high degree of emotional reaction. Anger? Fear? Frustration? Aggression? Cognitive load. Whatever the primary motivating factor, it is likely Gerard was primed and ready to explode. Though he would later declare he had a conversation with Allison on the night she went missing that was 'perfectly normal'

We know from forensic linguistic analysis that the conversation was unlikely to be 'perfectly normal.' The word 'normal' is often used to convince readers or listeners. We do not feel the need to label everyday normal situations as 'normal' – because we would forever be doing it. Deceptive, guilty people use it to convince us that a situation, which was abnormal, was normal. Children's stories use this linguistic device, too. When a story starts, "it was a normal day…" most children are alerted to something special about to occur.

The addition of 'perfectly' is also unnecessary. Unnecessary additional words should be analyzed. Why the need to further persuade us of the normality, neigh, 'perfect' normality of the conversation? You know what a 'perfectly normal' conversation is called? A conversation.

As it turned out, Allison would never attend that seminar. Was the seminar something that was on his mind? Was it a motivating factor in the crime? We may never know for certain, but it seems plausible. It may also explain why Gerard felt the need to mention it during the emergency call.

The night Allison died, Gerard faced a dilemma. After the tense phone call Gerard had with his secret affair, he knew Allison was about to find out everything. If Allison attended the conference, it is almost certain she would have met the other woman in Gerard's life. Then, she would likely have found out his secret affair was continuing. Sources suggest that Allison had previously told Gerard that if she left him, she would take the kids with her.

To clarify, if Allison went to the seminar, she would have met the other woman. If she met the other woman, and found out about the ongoing affair, Allison would have left him. When Allison left him, she would take the kids, his kids, his legacy. It seems possible, at least, to suggest that Gerard would have had his family name, his legacy, and his honor as salient thoughts in the hours before Allison went missing. With these things in mind, he killed Allison. With these things still in mind, Gerard was then faced with the task of figuring out where to hide her body.

Gerard had the entirety of the state of Queensland and Australia to move Allison. Though he had kids, he could have formed a ruse to take a few days away. He was certainly adept at creating false narratives and living lies. Instead of taking the opportunity to hide her somewhere in the vastness of the Australian outback, he chose somewhere much closer to home. Allison was found by a canoeist at Kholo Creek, approximately 8 miles (13 km) from where she lived with Gerard.

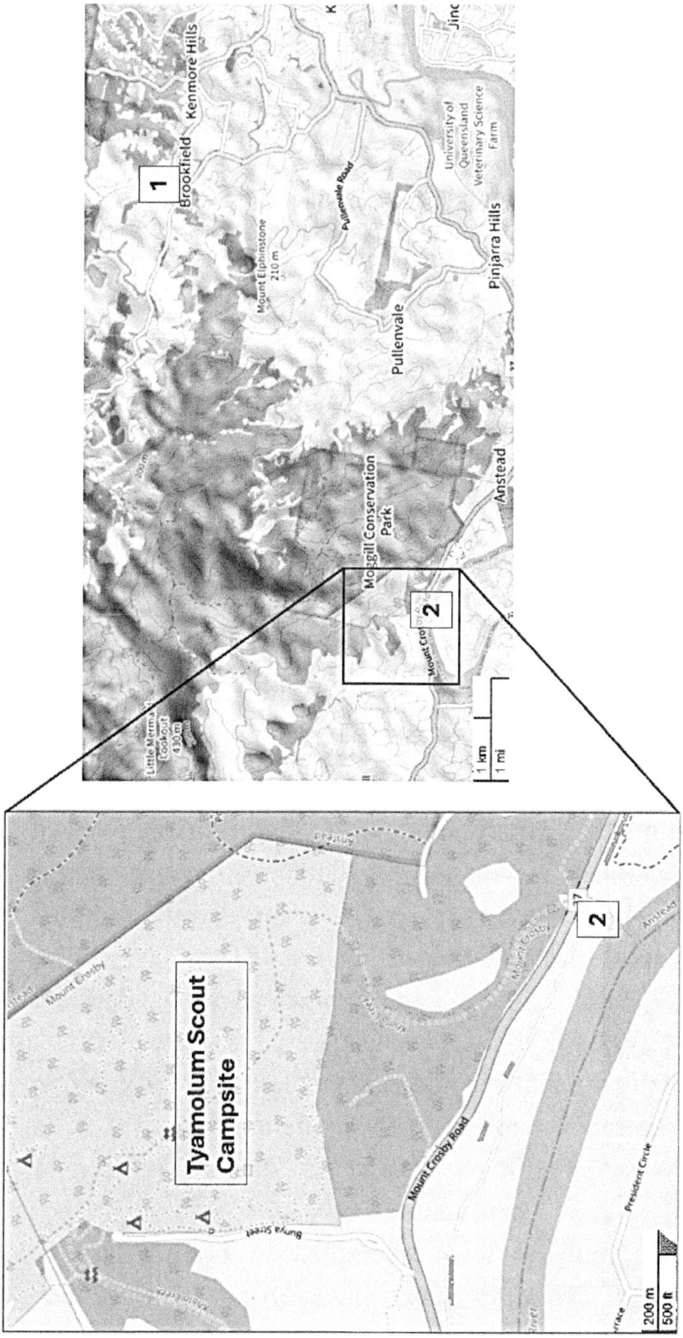

1 = Baden-Clay house; 2 = body deposition site

If we were to draw a circle around the Baden-Clay home with a radius of 8miles, there are still many, many places that Allison could have been moved to and hidden. So, we must keep returning to the question: why there? Of all the places available to him in the immediate, equal vicinity, he chose this location. And when we zoom in, we perhaps find our reason why. The location Allison was found in was very close to Tyamolum Scout Campsite. A Scout Campsite. I do not see this as random or chance.

Gerard would later claim that this was not an area he was familiar with – a spatial lacuna? He appears to have attempted to distance himself from the location by claiming he did not know it. Some evidence suggests he did know the area, as he owned properties nearby. I also find it hard to believe that someone as proud of their heritage as Gerard was would not know a Scout Camp a mere 8 miles away from his house.

Despite my earlier argument that his scouting legacy would influence his decision-making process, I could possibly accept it was not as explicit and overt as I have suggested here. Let me put it another way, I could accept that in the moment of panic, having killed his wife, he needed to think of somewhere to move her body, and the first place that came to mind was the nearby campsite with a river running next to it. This may have happened almost automatically – without much conscious deliberation. In this way, I could accept it was perhaps not a clear, reasoned, explicitly thought-out and deliberate decision-making process.

Whatever the mental pathway he took to arrive at the Scout Campsite, I find it predictable that this was a place he chose, given what we know about him.

Other authors have attempted to provide psychological profiles of Gerard. Of course, these are useful and while I do not personally create many psychological profiles, I do take them into account when attempting to develop a profile in my

Winthropping approach. If a clinical/forensic psychologist forms a profile of an offender, then parts of it may help with our profiling of where the person may travel and what they may do.

For those interested in this case, there is an excellent psychological review of it by Cheryl Critchley and Dr Helen McGrath, in their book *Why did they do it? Inside the minds of Australia's most unlikely killers*. In their book, Critchley and McGrath propose the proposition that Gerard showed patterns of behavior consistent with narcissistic personality disorder (NPD). How is this relevant to us? Well, beyond offering a psychological profile that helps us to understand and explain Gerard's behavior. The NPD diagnosis provides some insights into his decision making.

As I tried to show earlier, his name and reputation were of the highest importance to Gerard. Critchley and McGrath suggest Gerard exhibited the *elitest* subtype of NPD. This supports the view that his name, heritage, standing, and grandiose self-image would be central in his personality. With those things in mind, his family name and legacy would likely have been an influence on his decisions. It is not hard to explain, therefore, why he chose an area in close proximity to a Scout campground.

For those interested in further reading, the book by David Murray, *The murder of Allison Baden-Clay* is a must-read. I was particularly interested in reading about the site Gerard chose outlined in Murray's book. Gerard suggested he had no knowledge of where the creek was. This is typical of deceptive people. In trying to hide their actions, they will try to (spontaneously) negate any association with it.

I suggest Gerard most likely did know the area. The Scout campground would surely be something he recognized. He also sold and managed properties nearby, and allegedly had trysts nearby. What is of further importance is that, perhaps unknowingly, local police had realized the link to Gerard and had searched the area. It had originally fallen outside of the search zone, yet a Sergeant working the case took it upon himself to scout the area. He was so close to finding her body that I feel he should be commended on his initiative. In the future, perhaps with the improved use of Keatley's Winthropping, such locations though outside of general geographic profiling regions, may be highlighted as potential areas of interest. Reviewing the case with hindsight always allows for 20:20 vision. But this is the point of reviews. Reviews, if done properly and systematically, offer retrospective insight. Through good reviews we may learn valuable lessons, and then apply them (cautiously) moving forward.

18. Michael ATKINS*

Why the asterisk by Michael Atkins' name? Because he has been found not guilty of murder or manslaughter. His name takes the title of this chapter because it was Atkins who finally led police to where he had buried Matthew "Matt" Leveson. For the record, I will make it clear that this chapter is provided *only* in terms of my Winthropping analysis of the location Atkins chose, and then took investigators to. I make no judgment about the case beyond that. Interested readers would do well to read *Deal with the Devil* by Grace Tobin – a truly excellent account of the case.

The case of Matt Leveson is a heartbreaking one. That is not to say that every case of every victim in this book is not desperately sad and at times overwhelming. The Matt Leveson case, however, requires the reader to enter into the story of his parents and consider what we would do, if faced with the same decision. You see, Matt's parents had a difficult decision to make. They knew that Matt was dead. They knew that someone knew where he had buried Matt's body. They also knew that to find Matt, they would have to make a deal with the person who buried him: immunity from prosecution. That person was Michael Atkins. Before we get to that 'deal,' let us learn a little more about what led to it.

Matt Leveson was a happy 20-year-old, in the prime of his life and enjoying himself in the same way that many 20-somethings do. Matt spent his weekends socializing and partying with his friends – of which he had many. According to Atkins, Matt was involved in some recreational drug use. We may never know the exact cause of Matt's death, or the true sequence of events leading-up to it. As I have stated, I am not here to review the case in that way. I am only interested in the geographical decision-making, here.

The last time Matt was officially seen was 2.11am on Sunday September 23, 2007. Matt was seen leaving ARQ nightclub, NSW, with his partner, Michael Atkins. Shortly after, Matt appears to have sent a text message to a friend. Beyond this time, it is unclear what happened to Matt. Atkins finally suggested that Matt had overdosed on drugs, and in a panic, Atkins moved and buried his body. But the path to this outcome would take many years, a lot of hard work, and a deal.

Matt's body would remain hidden in a shallow grave for nearly 10 years. During that time, his parents valiantly searched for him. I have nothing but the utmost respect, admiration, and love for Matt's parents. What I offer here is in no way meant to undermine their desperate struggle or hapless helpless pursuit of finding their son. Instead, I hope that in reviewing Matt's case, we may learn lessons that save other parents, families, and loved ones the heartbreak of not having a body to properly bury.

After Matt was reported missing, a search began for both him and his car, which was also missing. On Thursday September 27, 2007, Constable Hill was conducting a routine patrol. He travelled to Waratah Oval, which is surrounded by dense bushland, situated on the edge of Sydney's Royal National Park. In the car park (parking lot) at the Oval, police found Matt's car. Before we continue with what they found inside, stop to consider what this may mean. Of course, it may mean that Matt himself drove there, and left it. He may well have known the area. Or it may mean that someone else, who also knew the area, drove it there. Of course, a final option is that it is random – but "it is just random" I think should always be our last line of explanation.

Let us consider the location is not random. It means someone knew it. Who would know it? Why was it used? In other words, for whom would it be a salient location? Why? Every time we gain a piece of geographic information, we should consider what it may tell us regarding the victim and offender. Perhaps nothing, perhaps more.

Police found another piece of geographic evidence inside Matt's car. In the trunk, police found a receipt from Bunnings Warehouse. For my international readers, Bunnings is a large store that sells a range of gardening and household equipment. The receipt was dated from the previous Sunday (September 23rd), and totaled $34.25 AUD ($22.19 USD, approximately). The sale was for tape and a mattock. For my less agriculturally aware readers, a mattock is a hand tool used for digging, prying, and chopping. It is similar to a pickaxe but has a horizontal edge on one side of the head.

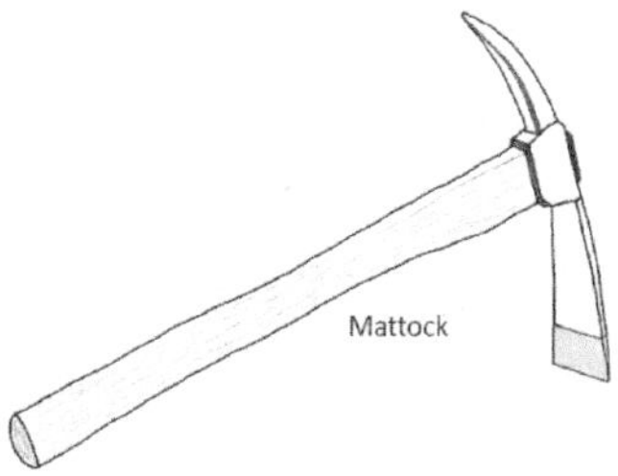

Police were quick to follow-up this lead and watched the CCTV at the Bunnings Warehouse in question. They reviewed the footage and saw a man with a striking resemblance to Michael Atkins purchasing the items. Atkins would deny this was him for a number of years. If, however, despite his denial, we were to assume it was him, we may develop the opinion that he was going to bury Matt. I am being careful in my wording of this owing to the legal complexities of the case.

The case proceeded to the best of the police investigators' abilities. Meanwhile, Matt's parents continued their desperate search for their son. Matt's father, Mark, performed some excellent deductive reasoning and geographical profiling of his own. Once Matt's car had been located, Mark studied the odometer closely. Using his skills as an accountant, he began mapping his son's journeys. Mark knew that Matt would reset the odometer every time he refueled. Based on this and bank records of when his son last filled-up, he calculated how many trips he had made and the respective distances. By the end of this process, Mark had calculated the number of unaccounted for kilometers between the car's known travelled distances and what the odometer read. The conclusion that Mark drew from his clever calculations was that *if* Matt's car had been used to transport his body, then the Royal National Park was a likely site.

Owing to our knowledge of Keatley's Winthropping, this is also a likely area. The Royal National Park offers many of the features that offenders would look for. Seclusion, ease of access, low cost, high reward, salience. It passes the bar of satisficing. It ticks most of our profiling points. Beyond this, it is also near where Matt's car was found. In terms of more classic approaches to geographical profiling, the Royal National Park also ticks the boxes. There was just one problem remaining for Mark. The Royal National Park covered approximately 15,000 hectares of thick forest.

Mark was commendable in his drive and focus. He began mapping weather charts and focusing on ways of narrowing that search down. I wholeheartedly commend Mark on this process.

I would add, with the benefit of hindsight and training, that the area could also be further narrowed down by taking Keatley's Winthropping a step further. Using my approach to Winthropping, we could consider accessible regions, and regions that may be more salient than others. But, even then, the Royal National Park is huge, and the likelihood of success quite low. There is no reason to suspect Atkins intended on returning to Matt's body, either, which affects my approach. Remember, though, even without explicit planning to return to a site, offenders are still influenced by the various factors outlined in Keatley's Winthropping, so we can still use this approach.

Without any motivation to return to a site, there is less reason to choose one that is easy to re-locate. I apologize for the seemingly callous comparison I am about to make. Imagine you are eating a snack while driving down the motorway. You finish your chocolate treat and are left with an unwanted wrapper. You absentmindedly open your window and chuck it out. Littering is awful, don't do it again. But even worse, you cannot even remember where you threw it. You never plan on going back to pick it up, so you do not pay careful attention to where you discarded it. That is the issue with cases like this. Matt was put in a place that we have no reason to suspect Atkins ever thought about returning to.

This is not to say Keatley's Winthropping cannot help, but it is a limitation worth considering. While processes may still have affected Atkins' behavior – and I think they did – it is hard to map his mental movements in the same way we might for someone who intends to return to a clandestine site.

One final moment of praise for Matt's dad, Mark, before we move on. Beyond his ingenuity of tracking the milage and weather to narrow the search. Mark also did something that I repeatedly encourage search parties and investigators to do. Perform the Keatley's Winthropping search in the same conditions as the initial process was performed. In short, Mark began searching the Royal National Park at around 2am in the mornings. This may seem obvious, but I have lost count the amount of times search parties *only* search during daylight hours, while the offender was likely there at night. I understand the practical reasons, of course. I am not suggesting daylight searches are abandoned. I am suggesting that for the purposes of Keatley's Winthropping, if we are attempting to psychologically put ourselves in the position of the offender, we should also physically and temporally put ourselves in their position, too.

Body Deposition Site

The investigation continued and in August 2008 Michael Atkins was arrested. As we know, he was found not guilty of either murder or manslaughter in 2009. And here, for many years, the case remained relatively untouched. Matt's parents, Mark and Faye Levesen, however, were not finished. They made requests to review their son's case. I have seen this parental passion so many times, but it never fails to bring a tear to my eye and lump to my throat. Never underestimate the power of parents' love for their children and their need for answers. I am once more in awe of Matt's parents. Their unwavering determination would pay off, but ultimately at a price.

In 2014, Detective Chief Inspector Gary Jubelin reviewed the case. What followed was a legal rollercoaster of criminological processes. Jubelin attempted some undercover operations to gather more evidence. These attempts revealed nothing of substantive evidentiary value to help progress the case. Atkins remained steadfast in his proclamations he was innocent. It is so easy to write these words and jump over months and years like they are nothing. Imagine the heartache and break of Matt's parents. Finally, in December 2015 a formal Inquest into Matt's case began.

What happened next was the question you may want to take a moment to consider for yourself. It is fair to say that at this point in 2015, Matt's parents felt certain that Atkins knew where Matt's body was. Despite his claims of innocence, and the jury finding him not guilty, Matt's parents likely believed otherwise. The issue was that they could not prosecute him. What options did they have left? What else could be done? The answer was not easy: a deal with Atkins. The deal was this: immunity from further prosecution for revealing where he had hidden Matt's body. As difficult as the decision was, Matt's parents did what I think many of us would at that stage, they opted to find their son and finally bring him home to bury him properly.

And if you think this is the end of the story, you are sadly mistaken. There was more legal argument about whether Atkins could or should give evidence at the inquest. Atkins attempted to maintain his right to silence, but this was ultimately dismissed, and he was made to take the stand. And so, in 2016, Atkins began his turn on the stand. During questioning he gave several responses. Atkins admitted that he had indeed been to Bunnings Warehouse. Atkins also said he thought Matt could be alive and that he thought Matt might have gone to Thailand. The questioning continued, but as the clock ticked down so too did the chances of Atkins revealing where Matt's body was. Atkins was down to his final day on the stand, with still no glimmer of hope that he would provide the information Mark and Faye so desperately wanted. The legal team had one last card to play. Prosecuting for perjury.

The original immunity deal was against charges of murder. It did not provide immunity from perjury. If there were any hope of putting enough pressure on Atkins to make him provide the information, the team needed Atkins to perjure himself. With some carefully crafted questions, they managed to do this. Atkins admitted on the stand he had lied to the court. Perjury, that is, lying in court, could incur up to 10 years in prison, and Atkins was not protected from it by the former deal. A new deal was quickly offered. Atkins would not be prosecuted for perjury, if he revealed the location of Matt's body.

I realize, by the way, I am veering off the path of Keatley's Winthropping, but this case is so interesting I hope you can agree it has been worth the detour. I have barely covered the details and the experiences, either. Tobin's book on the case is well worth the read. So, what happened next?

Atkins took the deal. Atkins maintained his innocence – claiming that Matt had overdosed. Atkins said he had then buried Matt's body out of fear of what may happen. Atkins agreed to lead the investigators and Matt's parents to where he had buried him. One of the first things Atkins did was to draw a map of where he had buried Matt. He drew this map from memory. Reconsider Chapter 4 regarding mental maps.

While Atkins' map may not have been a worthy of any cartography prizes it was the thing that Matt's parents had needed for so long. For our purposes, it also had many features that fit within a Keatley's Winthropping approach. Key features are salient in Atkins' sketch map. There is a railway line and station, a bridge, a bend on the road with a parking bay on it. Even without ever intending to return to the site, Atkins was able to recall salient features and waypoints. These waypoints are found in many MisPer and no-body homicide cases.

In a case with so many issues, you might not be surprised to hear it was still not quite so simple. Though Atkins could draw the location from his mental map. The reality of being at the site was different to what he recalled. An issue, I believe, is that he attempted to re-locate the scene during the daytime. As we know, matching conditions are important. I think this is one reason Atkins lost confidence in the first location he directed investigators to.

A wider search then began at other potential sites. Police involved The Australian Facility for Taphonomic Experimental Research (AFTER) to assist with locating Matt's body. Professor Shari Forbes stated that ground penetrating radar was unlikely to help. It seemed Atkins' memory was the best hope of finding Matt's body. I would agree.

The search continued until, after 3 days, Atkins told the police to re-search the first location. Atkins felt the landmarks he had used to initially draw his map were correct. The police, with little else to go on, returned to dig more of the initial area. And then, on May 31, 2017, nearly 10 years after Matt was taken from his parents, he was returned to them.

Matt's body was found fewer than 15 meters from the gravel car park Atkins had drawn on his sketch map. The distance also fits within the parameters we typically see in Keatley's Winthropping cases.

A timely guide to keep us on track…

I also want to use this case to serve as a timely reminder about the limits and limitations of Keatley's Winthropping. While I have hopefully made it very clear that my approach to Winthropping is not some magical wand nor silver bullet, it is also neither an indicator nor gauge of guilt. Using Keatley's Winthropping may help us to locate a body. It may correlate with the assumption we have about a suspect and their frame of mind – which we attempt to enter when performing Keatley's Winthropping. It does not, however, show guilt of the suspect.

I can show you this by offering you some examples of other situations in which an individual may know a location but be innocent of the crime. Imagine that you tell me where you have buried a body. I now have knowledge of that location. By all accounts, I could direct police (directly or indirectly, through words, actions, or maps) to the location. Does that make me the guilty party? Of course not. We cannot suggest that because Atkins took police and Matt's parents to where he had buried Matt, that he had killed Matt – that is a leap beyond the remit of Keatley's Winthropping. This is vital to remember. The person of interest, or even a suspect, may give us verbal or nonverbal clues and cues that may relate to where the body or cache is eventually found. Even then, this is not the end of the story.

Simply because someone knows the location of a cache or a body, it does not make them guilty. Consider the case of Richard Jewell, the man who found the Centennial Olympic Park bomb, but was innocent of planting it. The point is this: the goal of Keatley's Winthropping is to locate a hidden cache. The sequence and circumstances that led to the cache (body) being placed there is beyond the limits of the method. At no point would I, could I, or should I infer guilt from a 'successful' Keatley's Winthropping analysis, and nor should you.

19. Christhean RIVERA

Our next case involves the murder of Mollie Tibbets, by Christhean Rivera, in July 2018. The case is included here as it demonstrates another important aspect of Keatley's Winthropping, and why integration of classic geographic profiling approaches is important. At the risk of being painfully repetitive, I shall say again, Keatley's Winthropping is not some magical tool. It is not a silver bullet. It is best used, if at all, alongside a full and complete investigative approach. Integrate theories, data, evidence, intuitions, and hypotheses into the Keatley's Winthropping approach. If you are attempting to build a case, use every tool in the toolbox. With that in mind, let us see what happened to Mollie.

On July 18, 2018, Mollie was taking an evening jog near her home in Brooklyn, Iowa. Several witnesses reported seeing her jogging. The last eyewitness account placed her jogging at approximately 7.30pm. Beyond this final sighting, she appeared to disappear, and would not be found for nearly a month. Her last confirmed communication was to her boyfriend, who was out of town at the time. There were, initially, no clues.

The net to find her was cast far and wide. Reports of potential sightings from across several neighboring states were made – all of which turned out to be false. The efforts of police cannot be praised highly enough. From the outside looking in, it can often seem that there is a lack of movement or progress in these types of cases. This is not the case.

Police must be meticulous in their approach, cautious in their strategies, and effective in their decisions. They also need to be considerate in their communications. Too much information can be as problematic as too little. With over 2,000 tips and over 500 interviews, efforts by police in this case were commendable. Police also attempted to use newer technology to their advantage – like tracking Mollie's Fitbit, which she was thought to be wearing at the time.

In the end, video footage of a car approaching Mollie was the lead that helped police crack the case. Stemming from this piece of evidence, police tracked down Christhean Rivera – a local farmworker. He led the police to Mollie's body on August 21, 2018. She was found in a secluded location in a cornfield in Poweshiek County.

Police stated Rivera confessed to abducting and killing Mollie, and then leaving her body in the cornfield. At trial, however, Rivera changed his plea to not guilty. Part of Rivera's defense was that he had been forced by others, who had killed Mollie, to dispose of her body in the cornfield. Despite his attempt to convince the court of his innocence, he was found guilty of first-degree murder and sentenced, in 2021, to life imprisonment without parole. Rivera attempted to appeal the conviction in 2023, but the conviction was upheld by the Iowa Court of Appeals.

So, what does this have to do with Keatley's Winthropping? I'm glad you asked. To answer that, let's look at the locations in the case, and see what we can learn that may help us with other cases. First, let's begin our review from a classic geographical profiling perspective. We can see that Rivera's home is almost in the exact center of the two crime sites (abduction site and body deposition site). I say almost, because it is slightly closer to the site of attack than the deposition site. This fits with most geographical profiling approaches. An oft stated finding or heuristic is that if you have multiple crime sites, the offender lives in the middle. It is not often quite so simple, though, as we have seen previously with the serial killers. That said, beyond a small buffer around the home, many criminals do offend closer to home.

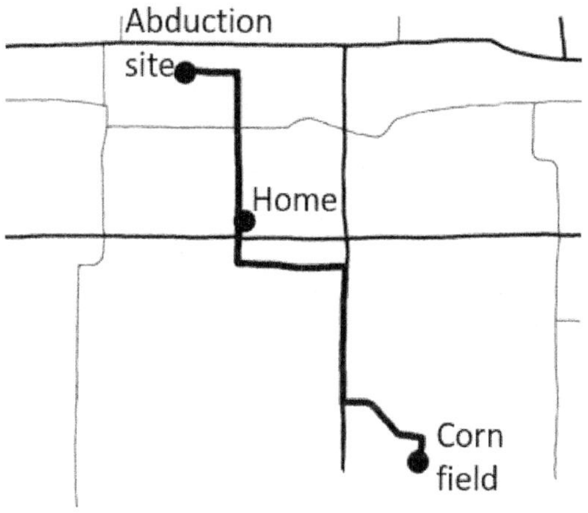

Of course, this alone does not inculpate Rivera – no more than any single piece of (statistical) evidence would. It does not exculpate him either. Of course, Rivera may claim that the real offenders also lived at the same location he did, or nearby. That would be consistent with the geographical evidence, too.

Where the body was found should also be considered. Rivera had access to a car – indeed, that was what led police to his door. Given he had access to a car, he also had access to the entirety of the USA to choose from. The question, therefore, becomes why a cornfield so close to home? We may consider practical and perhaps financial reasons (perhaps he could not afford the petrol/gasoline to travel further). I think there is another explanation, which can be found via Keatley's Winthropping.

The cornfield was local (awareness/activity space), and it was known to Rivera (comfort zone). It was easy to access – just off a main road. It was relatively isolated and offered protection from observation. Of course, an obvious issue is that this area of Iowa is replete with cornfields. Could we really narrow the search to this particular one? Perhaps not. But, with further study of the case, perhaps so.

Remember, Keatley's Winthropping is not a silver bullet. It's not a magic trick. Some cases, even with Keatley's Winthropping, may still remain unsolvable. That's just the hard and sad truth. However, I do not give-in so easily. Let us imagine Rivera had held out. Imagine he had not revealed where Mollie's body was. Could we have tried other approaches? I think so. My team and I are currently working on mind mapping exercises that may one day be useful in investigations. Do not worry, I am not naïve enough to believe that an offender who denies verbally telling us where a body is would draw a map of it for us. My question is this: what would they draw? If asked to draw a map of the local area, what would they omit? Do they miss areas on purpose? Would a criminal who has attempted to conceal a body purposefully leave out or conceal that site from their map? What would they say or leak in interviews?

Maps revisited

We dealt with this in Chapters 3 and 4, so I will not repeat it here. I will say that I do know of a concrete, criminal case involving missing information. I have anonymized and redacted parts of the case for obvious legal and investigative purposes. I have spent several years studying a MisPer case that is by all accounts likely to be a no-body homicide. A young child was taken, and for over a decade she has not been seen or heard from again. No ransom has been demanded. I hate the expression *vanished into thin air,* but it serves our purposes, here. I will not divulge the intricacies of the case for fear it would identify those involved.

In any MisPer case, we must always clear the ground beneath our feet – figuratively and literally. We must look at those closest to the victim. It is a harsh and devastating reality. I am always conflicted about this, but I know it must be done. Imagine being an innocent parent facing one of the worst moments imaginable. I believe it was a famous horror writer who said there is no story they could conjure that would compare to the terror a parent feels when their child is missing. Then along comes the police to question them as a person of interest. It must be done. It is not easy.

In this case, despite suspicion, there was no evidence. The parents continued as free people. In their defense they did not go quietly, they petitioned and promoted the search and safe return of their child. Through any means of media available, they tried to find their child. Constantly and consistently, they related the details of their daily lives, their actions, and their movements on the day their child disappeared.

Their movements? Yes. They told reporters, investigators, anyone who wanted to listen what they did, when, how, and *where*. In case that was not enough, they even drew a map of the area.

The point is this. When they spoke about their movements, they repeatedly mentioned a location. Let's call it "the hills" for simplicity and anonymity. Repeatedly in interviews and statements, the parents would mention "the hills" and their travel, trips, and hikes around "the hills." It was within range/distance of other locations on their sketch map; so, what would you expect to see on their final sketch map? The hills? Yeah, me too. Guess what was missing…

Why?

20. Robert BROWN

I fly around the world, a lot. This is not bragging. Truth told; I am a nervous flyer. More accurately, I am a nervous passenger, as I do not fly the plane, which many might consider a good thing. The 'rub' is that I put my life in someone else's hands – often for many hours. We all do this when we fly. Implicitly, we trust the pilot to take care of us, to reassure us when times are bumpy, and to be the conduit to our journey. Unfortunately, not all pilots are the superstar stalwarts of the sky that we hope for. In the case of Robert Brown, he was very far from being the model citizen that his rank, reputation, and job might infer.

On Halloween, 2010, Joanna Simpson was bludgeoned to death by being repeatedly struck over the head by her ex-husband, Robert Brown. I hate to make Joanna seem like a byline in her own life and death story. I strongly recommend readers to listen to Laura Richards' podcasts and YouTube channels on the case and on any other case Laura covers. Laura is one of my all-time favorites when it comes to care, compassion, and expertise on criminal cases – especially those regarding violence against women. For the purpose of this book, however, I must focus on the offender. In the current case, Brown would eventually lead authorities to where he had buried Joanna. The question lingers, however, what if he did not? That is the purpose of covering these solved cases. Not to claim post hoc success. But to review and learn. What can the case of Robert Brown teach us for the next offender with a similar profile? With that in mind, and with respect for Joanna and all like her, let us proceed down this path together.

Brown was an avid runner. We may, therefore, consider that placing a body outside would feel 'comfortable' to him. We might consider his running routes. Even if a suspect does not want to give this information freely, searching for apps and nearby routes might give us some insights. Given most runners prefer something scenic, and most people attempting to hide a body prefer somewhere clandestine, we could begin highlighting overlapping paths that may satisfice both these needs.

Brown was also a captain with British Airways. This is a very respectable job and one that Brown appears to have enjoyed, not least perhaps because of the sense of power and control it gave him. Reports suggest it is likely this attitude and characteristic overlapped into his relationship with Joanna. Whatever we may speculate now, Joanna and Brown were married on 13th February 1999. A pre-nuptial agreement was signed, and there is speculation this was a factor in the eventual break-up and subsequent murder of Joanna. What is known without doubt is that Joanna was a caring and devoted mother. The family moved to Ascot, UK and settled close to Heathrow Airport.

The relationship, however, was not a happy one. In January 2007, Joanna saw a solicitor about the marriage. In February, Brown told Joanna that he was having dark thoughts of familicide (of killing her, the children, and himself). Whenever such threats are made, they should always be taken with care and consideration. Whether or not Brown intended to go through with it, the fact the threat was made is a huge warning sign. As it turned out, there were other warning signs, too, including Joanna being threatened with a knife.

I am not going to get into discussions of violence against women and domestic abuse or intimate partner violence. I have studied the behavioral dynamics of these cases, with Laura Richards as one of the co-authors. For those interested in the topic, I point you once again to Laura's podcasts, channels, and training seminars.

Owing to the threats and behaviors, divorce proceedings began in Autumn 2007. Finances became a central factor. Brown claimed Joanna was hiding money and refused to accept any offers through the negotiations. This situation escalated for several years. Then, in 2010, the situation reached the critical point. After Joanna and the kids had returned from a trip to her mother's house, Joanna took them to Brown. On October 31, 2010, an argument arose between Joanna and Brown, which ended in Joanna being struck 14 times with a hammer. Brown then put Joanna in the trunk of his car.

Before Brown could leave, his and Joanna's daughters asked what was happening. Brown told them to get into the car. Alex, the elder daughter, having seen Brown put Joanna in the trunk asked if he was going to take her to the hospital. Brown did not respond to this and instead dropped the girls at his girlfriend's house. He then proceeded to Windsor Great Park, an area between the home and Heathrow Airport. He had previously dug a grave there. He then put Joanna into this grave.

The following day, November 1, 2010, Joanna's housekeeper and friend raised the alarm when he noticed her missing and some other oddities around the house. Another friend considered whether Brown might have trapped Joanna in the trunk of his car and left her in Heathrow Airport. While we know this is not entirely correct, I understand and applaud the implicit Keatley's Winthropping approach that underpins this. A known place, accessible, salient, and minimized initial risk. Of course, a body in a trunk would soon be noticeable if left there, so it is unlikely overall.

It makes sense Brown would use his car. It makes sense he would use the trunk of his car to transport his victim. I can also see the sense in Heathrow Airport being an activity space and thus a possibility. Of course, repellers to this are that leaving someone in the trunk is risky. They may raise the alarm (if they are alive) or they may begin to decompose if left for a period of time. You will often have multiple potential sites. You must systematically and structurally compare each site, perhaps by using a matrix like the one I outline later in Chapter 32.

As we know, Brown chose another location, and one that makes more sense from a Keatley's Winthropping perspective. Though Brown attempted a 'no comment' interview for several days, he eventually broke down (after the interview of his children) and admitted to burying Joanna. His version of events was that he could not clearly remember what happened after he pushed Joanna. What he remembers next is placing her in the trunk of his car and eventually hiding her in a box from a garden center and burying her in Windsor Great Park.

Through Keatley's Winthropping alone, I can neither support nor refute Brown's claims about his actions and memory. That is not really the chief aim of Keatley's Winthropping and anyone attempting to make that leap is going to find the chasm they are trying to cross falls down quickly. Keatley's Winthropping is focused on finding hidden locations. I cannot say this enough because I think it is so important expectations are managed and grandiose claims are not falsely made.

So, irrespective of pre-meditation or whether he blacked out or whether he could remember the events, or even whether he had planned it all and pre-dug the hole, let us see where Brown buried Joanna.

The approximate route from where he lived (Ascot [1]) to where he worked (Heathrow Airport [3]) would have taken him past Windsor Great Park [2]. The deposition site is thus firmly within his crime geometry. Given the proximity of Windsor Great Park and his home and his passion for running, it seems plausible he ran in this Park and knew the area. He would have felt *comfortable* there in his activity zone.

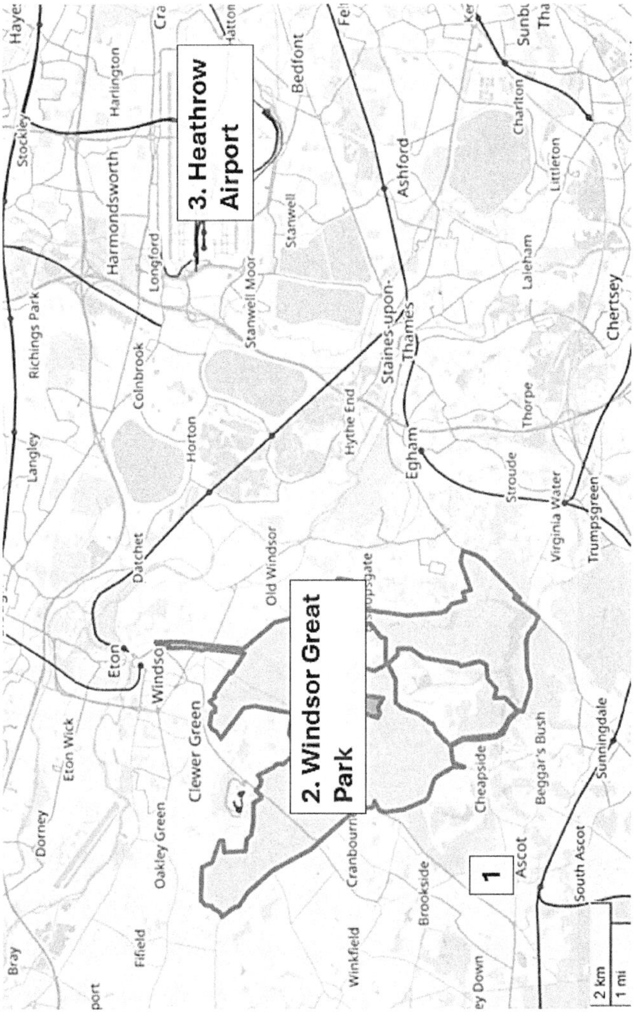

Investigating officers, when he finally revealed the deposition site, remarked on how desolate and isolated it was. Clearly, a well-chosen spot, but one that still fits within the parameters of Keatley's Winthropping. There is another aspect to this clandestine site that is worth mentioning. While it was relatively obscured and hidden from the ground, it would have been viewable from the skies. I consider it no coincidence that Brown buried Joanna in a location that was under one of his flight paths at Heathrow Airport. If we consider claims that Brown enjoyed control, narcissism, ego, and looking down on people, then perhaps the site also reflected his need to feel superior.

21. Mark REDWINE

Believe it or not, when I first started looking into criminal cases and engaging with investigators, I wanted to avoid crimes against children. I can barely mute out the haunting cries of adult victims, I just didn't want to hear children's cries alongside them. That's not how the world works though, and I soon realized that my preference to avoid such crimes was an untenable position. I raise this because sometimes students or colleagues tell me they'd love to do what I do. *It must be so exciting* they say. *It must be so rewarding* they muse. If you have ever said that to me, you have probably seen me stifle a wince and not know what to say.

How can I say that what I do is both an honor and a horror. The reality of what I do is my cross to bear. No matter how hard I work, nor how effective my methods may be, or how good I am at discerning deception from the truth; the truth is I am always too late. I guess that's why I am so obsessed with my approach to Winthropping. Perhaps, if I cannot bring a child back from their mortal grave, maybe I can bring them back from their shallow one. All that being said, here's another case of a life taken too young.

Thirteen-year-old Dylan Redwine was declared missing in November 2012. While his father was accused of Dylan's death in 2012, it would take nearly a decade before the case made it to trial. Mark Redwine was eventually sentenced to 48 years in prison for killing his son.

Mark Redwine has consistently denied his guilt. This chapter is written on the premise that Redwine is guilty. Of course, if a court or judge one day suggests that the original trial was a "sham," as Redwine suggested, then so be it. I am not suggesting that Keatley's Winthropping is infallible. I am not suggesting that at times we may have cases wherein multiple suspects fit the profile. We must proceed with caution and understand my approach to Winthropping is just another tool in the toolbox.

The case

On November 18, 2012, Dylan flew to Durango for a court-ordered visit with his father. CCTV showed Dylan and Redwine at a Walmart and McDonald's shortly after arriving. Redwine then states they returned to his home, in Bayfield – a relatively small community about 20miles (32km) east of Durango. It is unclear exactly what happened over the next 24 hours, but forensics indicated Dylan's blood in the house. This was explained by Redwine as being caused by a previous accident. A cadaver dog alerted to Redwine's truck, but from there the trail and thus the case went cold.

Dylan remained officially missing until June 2013, when searchers found parts of his body on a track approximately 8 miles from Redwine's house. While it was 8 miles by road/track the location was across a valley from where Redwine lived, thus potentially seeming much closer – perhaps somewhere he could view or look over.

There have been various statements made by Redwine's ex-wife and Dylan's half-brother about what Redwine may have said. Allegedly, Redwine said if he ever had to get rid of a body he'd leave it in the mountains – the location Dylan was found. If this is true, then it is a clear and obvious verbal indication. Of course, it may be coincidence.

Let us look into where Dylan was found to see if it matches what we might expect from a Keatley's Winthropping perspective. The goal is not to Monday-morning quarterback the investigation, but to see if our assumptions are supported.

The location Dylan was found would have been accessible to an All-Terrain Vehicle (ATV), which Redwine owned. It is, therefore, possible or even likely that Redwine knew the road and had previously visited it. Given the time it took to find Dylan's body, it is likely that it fulfilled the rational choice framework. Close enough to feel safe, isolated enough to remain hidden for some time. Indeed, it seems that animals interacted with the body, and this may have been a cause for parts of Dylan's body being found.

It should be noted, again, that Redwine consistently proclaimed his innocence. In an early interview, broadcast on KOAT-TV in 2012, Redwine gave a lengthy statement ostensibly about his innocence and his son's whereabouts. If I may dip into forensic linguistics for a moment once more, readers may be interested in a certain part of it. Redwine was given the opportunity to speak about and to his son, who was still missing at the time. The entire interview is interesting to watch and analyze, but one part in particular stuck out to me. When asked if he had anything to say to Dylan, he responded:

> "*Dylan, my prayers are with you, and I love you very much. He was the light of my life and he meant everything to me.*"

This, my friends, is one of the biggest red flags we can hear in a missing persons case. The subtle mention of prayers (associated with death) may be permissible but should not be ignored. The explicit past tense language is something that does raise red flags. "Was" and "meant" are not what we expect from a parent who is attempting to tell us that his son is missing. Past tense infers an acceptance of death. As we will see in Section 3 on linguistic leaks and Keatley's Winthropping, language is very important. Not enough to condemn, but surely enough to warrant further questioning and analyses.

22. Brett Peter COWAN

One of Australia's most infamous cases involved the abduction and murder of a young boy, Daniel Morcombe. The full story, leading to the eventual arrest of Brett Peter Cowan is worthy of a Hollywood film. However, beyond the twists, turns, and Mr. Big showdowns, remains the sad fact that an innocent young boy was snatched, and another life was taken too soon. Like all the cases I feature in this book, I wish I could spend longer talking about Daniel – telling you how his friends and family spoke and continue to speak so fondly of him. Please forgive me for moving on so quickly from him to the offender that took him. We are, however, on a pathway to understand the criminal geographical mind and the decision-making and mapping journey. So, to Cowan we shall turn.

At just past 2:10pm, on Sunday December 7, 2003, Daniel was waiting for a bus in the Woombye district of the Sunshine Coast in Queensland, Australia. Witnesses reported seeing him at an unofficial bus stop under Kiel Mountain Road overpass. Daniel wanted a haircut and to buy presents for his family. A series of events that no-one could have predicted occurred, leading to Daniel being abducted. First, the bus Daniel was meant to catch broke down. Second, the replacement bus, running behind schedule, drove past Daniel, who was patiently waiting. Then, left stranded and unsure when another bus might come, Daniel accepted the offer of a ride from a stranger.

That stranger was Brett Peter Cowan, and we only have his initial confession to go on, as Daniel was taken away, brutally killed, and put in a shallow grave. It would take nearly 8 years before Daniel was finally recovered and given a proper burial. This site discovery would come at the end of one of the most extraordinary types of police investigative tactics.

My introduction to this case was actually several years ago, while looking into a homicide case much closer to home. In Perth, Western Australia, one of the most famous cold cases involving a missing then murdered child is that of Gerard Ross. I had spent several months looking into Gerard's case, when I found that Brett Peter Cowan had been in Perth around the same time. Knowing that Cowan was arrested for the abduction and murder of Daniel Morcombe, it seemed reasonable that he may have been involved in Gerard Ross's abduction and murder. Further investigation revealed that the dates did not match, and Cowan was removed from my suspect list. As it turned out, all was not wasted, while looking at connected cases, other information came to light that I found very interesting in relation to the Gerard Ross case. At the time of writing, the case of Gerard Ross remains unsolved, though I have my hypotheses and opinions. Perhaps in a second edition there may be a chapter on that case…

For now, let's return to Daniel Morcombe. He had been reported missing and police could not find him. Through their investigation, Cowan had become a prime suspect. As it turned out, Cowan had taken Daniel some 25 miles (40 km) south of where he abducted him. This is, of course, quite a drive compared to most of the cases we have previously covered. If Keatley's Winthropping is to be useful, we have to understand

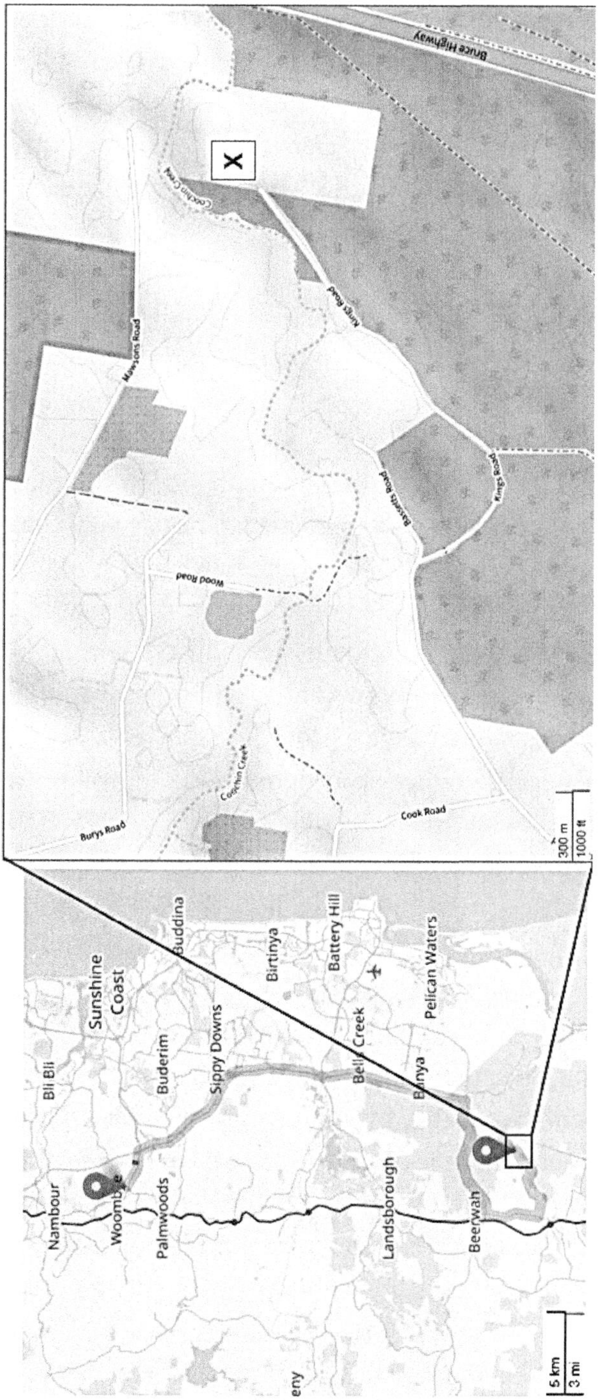

Bruce Highway
X
Coochin Creek
Kings Road
Mawsons Road
Wood Road
Burys Road
Cook Road
300 m
1000 ft
Bli Bli
Sunshine Coast
Buderim
Sippy Downs
Buddina
Birtinya
Battery Hill
Pelican Waters
Banya
Nambour
Woombye
Palmwoods
Landsborough
Beerwah
eny
5 km
3 mi

why some offenders may drive longer distances. We must provide an explanation for this extended journey. In this case, we can. But before we get there, it is worth understanding how police got there. To get to Daniel, they had to get to Cowan, to make him admit to his crime. To do that, they needed something big. They needed Mr. Big.

Mr. Big

There are cases in which the police are so sure of their suspect they will go to quite extreme lengths to pursue them. In these cases, police may have as much evidence as they can obtain, but not enough to pass the bar of the burden of proof. Some cases are so horrific that police or attorneys do not want to take the gamble of presenting a court case on circumstantial evidence alone. In these cases, very rarely, and in only a limited number of countries, police have a procedure they can use: Mr. Big.

The Mr. Big police procedure is also known as the Canadian technique owing to it being developed by the Royal Canadian Mounted Police. It is a covert operation in which undercover police officers attempt to gain a confession from a suspect through a series of elicitation pathways based on deceiving the suspect of their true identities.

There is no formal set script or sequence for a Mr. Big operation, but the basic premise is that the suspect is initially approached, casually, by an undercover officer. The undercover officer portends to be a part of an undercover criminal organization. The aim is to encourage the suspect to join the group. The suspect is given a number of tasks or deeds to commit. These tasks typically start with very mundane and easy jobs and low-harm crimes. The script escalates, with the focus on trust and commitment being repeated at each stage.

When the undercover officers feel confident that they have built a high enough level of trust with the suspect, the Mr. Big scene begins. The ruse is that the suspect needs to 'come clean' with the head of the criminal organization – the 'Mr. Big.' The suspect must be completely truthful about their criminal past. At this point, they have been led to believe that the criminal organization can make problems disappear. The important step is that the suspect must tell Mr. Big about any crimes they have been involved with. The reality is the undercover Mr. Big wants to find out about a particular crime.

In the case of Brett Peter Cowan, this ruse worked perfectly. Cowan was approached and the undercover police took their time to build his trust. At various times, through staged incidents, the undercover officers made Cowan believe they had police whom they had bought as well as other methods of getting away with crimes. The themes of trust, loyalty, and honesty were repeated like a mantra. So, when Cowan finally met Mr. Big, he had few reservations about confessing to his crimes against Daniel Morcombe.

The Confession

Cowan told Mr. Big that he had driven by the underpass and seen Daniel Morcombe. Cowan had then parked in a nearby church that he knew and walked down to the bus stop. When the bus drove past without stopping, Cowan offered to drive Daniel to the shops. Daniel had told Cowan that he wanted a haircut, so Cowan suggested to Daniel that his wife could do it. This was how Cowan said he tricked Daniel into getting into his vehicle. Sadly, Cowan actually drove Daniel to a quiet place he knew – a small hut in a farmland area.

The farm at 510 Kings Road was the perfect place in

Cowan's mind. We can understand why, from a Keatley's Winthropping perspective. As Cowan said, the area was secluded. There were also dense trees and bush, which would hide his truck and him as he did what he wanted to. Cowan suggested he did not initially intend on killing Daniel. The location of the detached farm building where Cowan said he attacked Daniel was also close to a large swamp and creek – where he would later hide Daniel. If Cowan had actually intended to kill Daniel, then he had chosen an ideal location.

We now know where Cowan put Daniel's body. The question is, could Keatley's Winthropping have helped? I think so. First, there are connections between Cowan and the property he took Daniel to. He claims to have known the area because he had been there previously. In addition, there are more subtle indicators that make sense from a Keatley's Winthropping perspective. First, when Cowan abducted Daniel, he had a wood mulcher in his truck. This cognitive association with woodland makes woodland areas 'primed' and more salient. For example, if I say "snow" you are more likely to think of white than black. If I say "hot" you are more likely to think of red than blue. If Cowan had a wood mulcher in his car, which he did, then wood is likely to be on his mind.

To support this, Cowan even says that there used to be an old timber mill down near where he took Daniel – another associative link. I admit that alone this might not seem to narrow the search areas, as there are many square miles of woodland in the area. But let's cross-reference what we have so far. Woodland areas, with isolated, secluded locations, that Cowan had a link to, that fit within his activity zones. Now, the areas narrow.

We can do better. According to Kate Kyriacou, who wrote the excellent book *The Sting*, one of Cowan's friends had bought a sandblasting business. This friend of Cowan's had intended to hand over this sandblasting business to him to manage. As it turned out, an old sand-mining site was just behind the trees where Cowan had killed Daniel. Cowan had previously looked at the area as a place he could run a sandblasting business from. How many locations in Queensland would now fit all these criteria?

Of course, hindsight is 20:20 and hardly a boast. The aim is not to show what could have been done in the Daniel Morcombe case. I think what the police did was extraordinary. The aim here is to consider the case from a different perspective. Another case may not open itself to a Mr. Big operation. So, what can we learn from Cowan that may help us moving forward. That is the goal.

One final, additional part of Cowan's Mr. Big confession that grabs my attention was that the undercover officers asked Cowan to draw a sketch map of the location he had left Daniel's body. Sadly, I do not have a copy of this. But I would be interested to see what landmarks feature in his mental map. Knowing what stuck in Cowan's memory after all those years might help us to understand more about what is salient. This is why my current research into mental maps (see Chapter 4) is so exciting to me. Any new light we can shine on this area, could pay off.

23. Additional single homicide cases

The focus of this chapter is to provide a few more case studies to help provide more examples. Experience informs me that by this point, readers/listeners are either fully on-board with my approach to Winthropping or remain doubtful. I appreciate the doubt, it is a healthy position to take. Question everything. Science ceases when the questions stop. That said, perhaps a few more case studies, sans the lengthy biographical background and sideways swerves, will help to provide more examples of the decision-making that offenders engage in. This might then help to convince you of the potential of my approach to Winthropping. I mean no less respect for the victims in this chapter than any other chapter.

Though the case outlines here are brief, I remind readers that depth of knowledge and awareness is key for Keatley's Winthropping. That is why when investigators ask me for my opinions, I typically send back a long list of questions about the case, the victim, and the persons of interest. I also prepare them to be confronted with several questions about the local geography (historical if the case is cold). Nothing is a substitute, though, for having my boots on the ground. An anecdote, a photograph, or even a video is not a substitute for the lived experience. So, if you ever call on me for my help, do not be surprised if I show up at the site before long.

Ben BLAKELEY

Our first case occurred in Oxfordshire, England. In December 2013, Jayden Parkinson, who was pregnant at the time, was reported missing. Pregnancy is often either a time of celebration and bliss, or a time of increased risk. Jayden remained missing for two weeks, until December 18, 2013. Her body was found in a disturbed grave at the local cemetery in All Saint's Church.

At the time she was reported missing, Jayden and Blakeley had been in a relationship, and Jayden was pregnant with Blakeley's child. At trial, it was discovered that Blakeley had a history of violence against women. Reports indicated he had pushed a previous girlfriend down the stairs when she was pregnant. In another book of mine, I wrote at length about patterns and sequences of behavior. Blakeley is a 'good' case study for that type of analysis. For this book, the place Jayden was found is more important.

In terms of association, the links between graves, cemeteries, and death needs no explanation. Blakeley is hardly the first criminal to use a cemetery to conduct or attempt to cover-up his crime. So, what makes this case so relevant for Keatley's Winthropping? Well, knowing that a cemetery is a salient location narrows the search net. In Blakeley's case, however, we can narrow it further. The choice of grave was definitely not random. When Jayden was finally found, she was in the disturbed grave of Alan Kennedy. I would not expect you to know the relevance of this name, so let me clarify. Kennedy was Blakeley's uncle.

Of course, I am not suggesting that every time a person is

reported missing, we all rush to the local cemetery and check for deceased relatives of the suspect. That said, I wonder what else in Blakeley's profile may have made the cemetery and the control more likely. I also read that a person close to the investigation stated Blakely had previously said "if he ever had to get rid of a body, he would put it in a family member's grave." Most criminals are not masterminds, many speak too much. The onus is on us to listen.

Also, Blakeley is not the only criminal to use a body deposition site that is influenced by his name. The convicted murderer Mitchel Quy buried parts of his wife's body in various locations. Quy then appeared on numerous television shows proclaiming his innocence. These were all taunts. This case will likely feature in a follow-up edition of this book; for now, I will simply say that his name was a major influence on his body deposition site choice. His name, for those that do not know, is pronounced as one word to rhyme with 'why' with a 'k' at the start. He buried his wife's liver under a bridge. According to Chris Kinealy in the book *More Jail Stories*, Quy referred to this as, "The Bridge over the liver Quy" (a reference to 'The bridge over the River Kwai'). Neither funny nor entertaining, but informative of how some criminals view their surroundings and some narcissists have their own name in mind.

Munawar TOHA

Coral Springs, Florida, March 23, 2010. Munawar Toha and his wife Surya Sari-Prihatin Toha woke up at 6:30am. Toha told his wife he was feeling ill and stayed in bed. Toha then called his work and said he was not going in. While Toha claimed to have stayed in bed, Surya took the kids to school around 8am (verified by CCTV at the school, at 8:11am). This is the last confirmed sighting of Surya alive.

Later that day, Toha claimed to have heard the downstairs door open and close a couple of times, but said he was unsure who was in the house. When he finally got out of bed at around 10am, Toha claimed that his wife was gone. Toha later told police he tried calling Surya's cell phone several times, but it went to voicemail. Friends and neighbors also had no information on where she was.

Allegedly not knowing where his wife was, Toha picked-up his children from school and dropped them at a friend's house. Toha then claimed he went searching for his missing wife. Finally, after hours of allegedly searching, Toha went home. The next day, he called police to report her missing. We might wonder what took him so long.

Toha told police that the day before Surya went missing, someone withdrew thousands of dollars from her bank. He claimed the money was now missing. Toha then claimed he may have heard his wife speaking to someone, too. This was likely his way of sowing the seeds of a staged script of infidelity and of his wife running away. As believable as Toha may have attempted to make this, it was not believed by anyone else that knew Surya. Surya was a devoted mother, and her friends and relatives were certain she would not have left her children. The suspicions were raised, but the location of Surya was still unknown.

Beyond dropping off the kids at the school, the leads went cold. Surya was meant to return to the school at 10am, but CCTV showed she did not come back. Attempts to track her silver Daewoo also failed to return any matches. The investigators, while still primarily focusing on finding Surya, also considered the possibility that a crime had occurred.

Toha then appeared on a television broadcast, seemingly upset and crying for his wife to return home (I will let body language analysts pick apart that video). Toha also provided police with a note he said he found, allegedly written by Surya. The letter outlined an alleged attack she had suffered, which led police to investigate a potential lead and a suspect.

During the investigation into Surya's location, police considered a geographical map of the area. Focusing on known activity spaces of their new suspect, they saw that Crystal Lake was central to several key activity zones. The police travelled to the lake and saw that it was almost completely encircled by a chain-link fence. Almost. In one section, the fence had been broken down, possibly by a car. Sometimes luck is on an investigator's side. In this case, the investigators saw a CCTV camera on a local building opposite the hole in the fence.

As it turned out, the initial suspect was not involved in this crime. In a sense, the police may have 'got lucky' here, with regards the geographic profile. I will explain later why I think the geographical approach the police took was still good.

The CCTV would eventually show that Toha had driven his wife's car, with her inside, into the lake, late at night. He was then shown riding away on a bicycle. It appeared his whole storyline was a fiction. He had almost committed the perfect crime. Almost. The CCTV was, of course, a large lead and important piece of evidence in this case. What would have happened without the CCTV, though?

I think the investigators would still have found Surya's car. Their intuition and diligent work led them to the lake. It was only a matter of time, in my mind, before they searched the lake and found the car. How they found the lake, I think, is also a good real-world example of some of the principles of Keatley's Winthropping. It is also a reminder that Keatley's Winthropping is not an evidentiary approach to profiling an individual's guilt. They examined known activity spaces of the wrong suspect (which was thus wrong) and looked for locations that would satisfice hiding a body (which was correct).

I would like to say that police are *always* suspicious of the partners of missing persons. Indeed, in the majority of cases I have assisted with, this is true. There are, however, several cases in which police appear to ignore the partner. In one case in particular that I have assisted investigators with, police appear completely blindsided to the widow. They consider her a close confidante. I would simply caution investigators to not become so fixated that you cannot hear any other suggestion.

I am delighted to say in most of the cases I have been involved with, the police are very open to new avenues being opened-up before them. The same was true in this case. Police had a suspect, but they remained open to new leads. Hats off to some fine detective work.

In other cases, please remember that even if Keatley's Winthropping successfully helps you to locate a body, it does not necessarily point to an individual's guilt. The fact that the geographic approach here found Surya, and it was based on the profile of an innocent person originally, indicates that, alone, geographic profiling is not enough to close a case.

So, in this case, were there any other indicators that would lead to the lake being a more likely location? The short answer is yes: the lake was situated next to (behind) the place that Toha worked at the Department of Transport. In terms of activity spaces, he did not have to travel far. At the time of originally focusing on the lake, the detectives had another suspect in their view; however, considering the location of the lake to others involved in the case, I think it would have then more strongly directed them to one person in particular: Toha. The CCTV and further forensic examination would then have helped to build the case. Putting ourselves in Toha's position, through my approach to Winthropping, I think would have made the body deposition site more obvious.

Tahreem Zeus RANA

On August 22, 2014, Hapeville Police were called to a secluded, desolate dumping ground in Atlanta, Georgia. Once there, they found the burning body of a murdered woman. Though her body was on fire at the time, later examination showed that she had been fatally shot. Beyond this, very little information about her identity was initially found or known. It would take a few more days before police received a MisPer report and linked that report to the body. Thus, the investigation into the murder of Vernecia Woodard began.

Vernecia Woodard was reported to use online sites to arrange dating, meet-ups, and sex work. This provided some cyber forensics opportunities, but those analyses are beyond the scope here. So, while the cyber specialists pursue that, let's return to the location she was found and see if we can help. The body has been found, so this is no longer a '*where is she?*' case, this is a '*why there*?' case. Police noted that the dumpsite was in a relatively unknown area. Put another way: only those local to the area or with detailed knowledge of the area would have known about it. We saw what this meant in the Meirhofer case (see Chapter 12).

Of course, we cannot discount the possibility of a criminal who by chance happens upon a site known mostly to locals. But to know such a hidden, tucked-away place typically takes some local knowledge. Furthermore, using a site to hide a body in the day is very risky, especially if you set the body on fire. However, if you know the site is unused and relatively unknown, you know it is lower risk to use it. But all of that knowing entails some location knowledge. What if the dumping ground were a local hangout for the kids in the area? What if there were a security patrol? Do not be so quick to dismiss the fact that a location may tell us about the knowledge of the offender.

Police investigated the possibility that the current case was linked to other murders in surrounding areas. This is diligent work and commendable. It ultimately came to no linked homicides. I am not entirely surprised by this, owing again to the place that Vernecia was found. The police noted that it was likely to reflect someone that had very local or detailed knowledge of the area. If other bodies were found in closer proximity, indicating a similar localized level of awareness, I would be more open to a serial killer being likely. What I mean is, if police found another body in the same dumpsite, then we would likely have a serial killer. But it is less likely (though not impossible) that a serial killer would have this fine-grained, detailed level of local knowledge in Hapeville and have similar knowledge of areas elsewhere. Less likely, but not impossible, for all those readers who wish to tell me about 'Serial Killer X' who exhibited those behaviors. I know they exist; I can name some, too. I am playing the probabilities here.

So, focusing again on the localized knowledge angle, police began a fresh search for all other crimes in the local area. They found a recent crime of a gun being fired at the end of the street of where Vernecia was found. Police interviewed the person who this charge was made against. I will not relate the entire interview, but several comments stood out and police were aware of this. They took their time, they questioned carefully, and they got the information they required. Turning the focus of their questioning on to the gun that the person was previously arrested for firing, he told police it actually belonged to Tahreem Rana.

Police located Rana's home and as they arrived, they noted he was just leaving. They followed him for some distance before pulling him over and asking for his identification. What Rana showed them, they did not expect. Rana's identification was a police identification card. Rana was a cop.

Hapeville
X
Airport Loop Road
Central Avenue
Digital Realty Data Center
Gresham Park
Thomasville
GA 54
Forest Park
East Point
College Park
Cooks Crossing
GA 154
GA 166

Yes, this case involves a cop. I have the utmost love and respect for police and will do all I can on my side of the blue wall to help support the thin blue line. I am not, however, unaware of the fact that some officers are bad cops. I will suggest that we, the general public, do not lose faith in the massive majority of great cops, simply because a few are bad. If someone in your workplace were caught doing something bad, would you be okay with being tarnished by the same brush? Of course not. So, let us continue to focus on Rana without generalizing to all cops.

There were multiple forensic leads and evidence that eventually led to Rana being convicted for the murder of Vernecia. I think that Keatley's Winthropping, while by no means evidentiary, could also fit in nicely alongside this evidence. The location, as we have said, indicated a highly detailed level of local knowledge. Indeed, the breakthrough came by considering who lived locally. Beyond that, investigators, taking a Keatley's Winthropping approach, might have asked: *who would have such a local knowledge?* This would narrow the suspect list, but still leave it understandably large. Large, indeed, but only as large as 'everyone in the local area,' which is still significantly smaller than 'everyone in the USA.' So, bear with me.

Police suggested that people who lived in Hapeville might not even know the site was there. So, who in the local community would? Perhaps someone that needed to. Someone who needed to know *all* the areas, including those out-of-the-way, desolate places. Someone, say, like a cop.

Next, we have the fact that the body was on fire. Why would the offender attempt to set fire to the victim? Not always, of course, but often fire is used to cover-up a crime or remove forensic evidence. Attempting to burn away forensic traces is the likely motivation in this case. So, now we are looking for someone that has very detailed local knowledge and an acute awareness of forensics and trace evidence. I know, given today's true-crime saturated world, that could still be a lot of people. As I say, no magic wands or silver bullets here. Our suspect list is narrowing though.

During an investigation, police will have multiple suspects. Often, it is not that police have no leads, it is that they have too many. So, after we have narrowed the geographical area how do we narrow the suspect list? Perhaps by being attentive and observant of each suspect's behaviors. This approach is still hardly incriminating or evidentiary, but it was not a shock to me that Rana's car, when they forensically examined it, was extremely clean. This matches the profile we have built. Rana knew he needed to clean his car to remove forensic traces in the same way he knew to burn the victim to remove traces. No magic tricks, perhaps, but good, solid police work shows that there are many more good cops than bad, and I remain in awe of them.

Wendi DAVIDSON

Lest anyone believe that Keatley's Winthropping only works on men, here is a case wherein a woman was convicted for killing, moving, and attempting to conceal her husband in a large body of water. This case is covered in detail in Dianne Fanning's book, *A poisoned passion*. On Saturday March 5, 2005, Davidson confessed to her brother that she had found her husband, Michael "Mike" Severance dead. The story, which she has largely kept to throughout the years since, was that she returned home to find her husband - deceased. According to Davidson, she panicked thinking a member of her family had killed Mike. She then took it upon herself to move and attempt to hide Mike's body.

Here, again, we are confronted with the fact that Keatley's

Winthropping may take us to the body, it may lead us to a suspect, but it cannot find the truth of the circumstances. It may very well be that Davidson returned home and found her husband already deceased. I am aware of the facts of the case; I know there is good evidence to support the state's claim that Davidson was guilty. On the whole, I would tend to side with the jury in this decision. That is not the same as saying I *know* or am certain. That is beyond the point and scope of this book. Instead, where Davidson decided to leave Mike's body is our focus.

We know that whatever the initial circumstances, Davidson used a car in her movements. She drove Mike to a ranch where she submerged his body. Once again, therefore, Davidson had the great expanse of Texas to consider as a possible deposition site. Beyond that, the USA spans many thousands of miles. To the south, the border might have loomed as either an impenetrable wall or a tempting escape from conviction, too. Of all the places that Davidson could choose from, she behaved as so many others have: within her comfort zone and activity space. The place she chose was salient with the necessary affordances.

According to Davidson, when she finally admitted to moving Mike's body, he could be found in *the* tank (a large body of water) at *Terrell's*. If we assume that Fanning is writing verbatim what Davidson said, then we may ask a few questions. Note, even if Fanning is not writing verbatim, we can still learn. First, the definite article 'the' indicates this was somewhere Davidson knew. Beyond simply knowing of it – as she had obviously been there, we could tentatively take a step further and think it was well-known to her. She does not say "a tank," which may be less clear or salient to her. There were 3 tanks at Terrell's ranch, but to Davidson, this was *the* tank. A minor point, but worth bearing in mind to see if it is consistent with further analyses. Why does one tank seem more salient to Davidson? What about it would make it stand out and become 'the' tank?

Next, 'Terrell's' is actually the first name of Terrell Sheen. Clearly, Davidson knew Sheen so well, that she as on first name terms with him. In addition, her brother, to whom she made her initial statement, also seems to be on such close terms with Sheen that he knew him by first name only, too. I will say here, there is no evidence or belief that Sheen was in any way involved in this case. He just happens to be linked to the family and had a ranch with a large body of water that Wendi Davidson knew well enough to call 'the' tank.

As it turned out, Davidson did know Terrell Sheen and his 7777 Ranch very well. First, Sheen was a long-time family acquaintance. He actually owned the building that Davidson rented for her veterinary clinic. Further, Davidson had a horse on Sheen's ranch. Sheen's ranch, therefore, would be well-known to Davidson, forming part of her activity space. Given its location and the hills surrounding it, it provides many of the features that would make it a prime location in terms of Keatley's Winthropping. Secrecy, seclusion, isolation, and for Davidson, salience and satisficing. Davidson had an innocent explanation for being there if she were caught or seen. Davidson also had a key to the ranch, so could enter and leave at her leisure. This was something Davidson would take advantage of a few days later when she returned to the site to ensure Mike was sunk to the depths of the water tank.

A short time after initially submerging Mike in the tank, Davidson became nervous about him being found. Davidson was concerned about Mike's body potentially becoming bloated and rising to the surface. Davidson took it upon herself to return to 'the' tank and use a boat to transport Mike's body, strapped with heavy blocks and weights, to the center of the tank and drop him to the depths. The boat may seem like an innocuous addition to that scenario. How else, you might ask, would she get to the center? Well, as always, let us imagine Davidson had not confessed to the crime (of moving and attempting to hide the body). Imagine she had not told us what she did or where she put Mike. Could we have used Keatley's Winthropping to find him? I think so.

For the reasons given, we know that it is likely Sheen's Ranch would have eventually been searched. That takes no special form of Keatley's Winthropping analysis. Classic geographic profiling would have taken us to his ranch. But the ranch is huge, with multiple water tanks. So, then what? Then, I believe looking more closely at Davidson's words may have helped.

First, there was one tank that could be referred to as *the* tank. So, we would expect one to stand out, to be salient. It is also likely the one with an affordance for hiding a body. This promotes one tank to be our first place to begin searching. But was there any other indicator of a tank being used? If so, what and how?

When Davidson was talking to her family about her involvement in the case, she is alleged to have said to her mother, "*No mama, if I was thinking logically, I wouldn't be in this freaking boat!*" If we trust Fanning is accurately transcribing this statement, then the choice of words becomes rather revealing. What boat was Davidson in, when considering the crime?

With that said, let us now listen to what suspects say even and perhaps especially when they don't mean to say it...

CASE STUDIES III

Linguistic Leaks

24. Karen MATTHEWS

I will begin this section with perhaps the weakest of the linguistic Keatley's Winthropping cases. I realize I may jeopardize this section if readers lose faith too soon, but I think this case is a nice entryway into the area. As with all of the applied work I do, especially in terms of investigative deception detection, I am only looking for indicators. There are no silver bullets. Every indicator is just that – an indicator. Nothing more, perhaps much less. So, if at the end of this chapter you feel a sense of, *is that it*? Good. That should always be your reaction to a statement analysis, or nonverbal analysis, or Keatley's Winthropping, or any individual piece of evidence. Remain skeptical, push back, question the questions, and question the answers. As Bernard Haisch once stated, *advances are made by answering questions, discoveries are made by questioning answers*.

In terms of questioning everything and everyone, including emotional mothers, the kidnapping of Shannon Matthews is a good place to start. Any time a child goes missing, public reaction is immediate and heartfelt. On February 19, 2008, when nine-year-old Shannon was reported missing in Dewsbury, West Yorkshire, UK, the reaction was as expected. Within a very short amount of time, large search parties were organized. A large reward was also offered in the hopes of enticing the alleged kidnappers to release her, unharmed.

Unlike so many child kidnapping cases, this one would have a happy ending, in a way. On March 14, 2008, Shannon was found alive. There was, however, a barb to this otherwise beautiful silver lining. Shannon had been kidnapped as part of a conspiracy by Shannon's mother, Karen Matthews; Craig Meehan, Karen Matthews' partner at the time; and Michael Donovan – Craig's uncle.

These three had conspired to 'kidnap' Shannon and then keep her in Donovan's house. The plan was to raise the reward money to such an extent that when Donovan eventually 'found' Shannon, the three of the co-conspirators could split the money. For better or worse, this case now rings through my mind like a lighthouse with a loud siren every time a child goes missing. There have been other cases, much closer to home, in which I have questioned whether there is a similar motive at play. The alure of reward money, infamy, or worse is not a new motive for some parents.

So, what does all of this have to do with Keatley's Winthropping and linguistics? First, of course we have the basic geographical points of awareness and activity spaces. The fact that Shannon was kept in a family member's house fits the profile of most of Keatley's Winthropping tenets. Of course, the police and investigators, diligent and unrelenting in their pursuit, found Shannon without any help from me or my methods. The point here, therefore, is not to suggest that they got lucky or did not do their job properly. I have only praise for their investigative approach and success. The point is to see whether my methods could have helped. I think they could.

For a start, I always like to begin with what the parents say. Given the stage to make their plea, let us listen carefully.

> *"Shannon, if you are out there, please darling come home. We love you so much, me and your dad, your brothers, your sisters, everybody loves you. Your dad is missing you so much Shannon, he is even out looking for you, please come home Shannon, if you're out there, come home. If anybody out there has my daughter – my beautiful princess daughter – please bring her home safe. I need her home."*

First, we have the issue of '*if*.' 'If' is a great poem by Kipling. It is also a subordinating conjunction that introduces a conditional clause. Plainly, it denotes that something may not be the case. '*If*' you understand me, places your understanding in the realm of potential possibilities, it is not a certainty. If you understand me means you may not understand me. We use the term daily, and seldom get it wrong. Because it is a high frequency word, it can slip or leak out of the mouth without us realizing. Thus, it can reveal an inner state of knowledge. In this case, we might ask why Karen entertains the thought or condition of Shannon not being 'out there.'

Remember, in Matthews' proclaimed worldview, Shannon is out there. She is missing. Wherever she is, she is not with Karen, she is not 'in here.' The statement '*if you are out there*' pushes off 'if you are in here.' But, why would Karen have this push-pull set of 'if' conditions?

Let me provide another example, because experience tells me that some people are not convinced on this point. When I say, "if I went to the shops," how certain are you that I went to the shops? If I did go, I would say so, unconditionally. So, why is Karen allowing for the possibility that Shannon is not out there? Further, why does Karen feel the need to repeat this twice? Repetition is a sign of sensitivity. It often indicates someone is not comfortable with what they are saying.

Why then change to asking, '*if anybody out there has my daughter*.' Again, repeating the *if...out there* connection. This time, adding 'anybody' – who else might have her? Perhaps somebody (known). I can understand leaving the '*if*' of abduction as an unknown, but again, we might ask what the other possibilities are. What are the conditions that 'if' is conveying?

I also note a logical issue with the "*if... then*" construction. Bear with me here. Let us see what Matthews is actually saying. 1) *If* Shannon is out there; 2) *then* come home. But, what about if Shannon is not out there? Then she cannot come home? That is a strange thing to indicate. Unless, of course, Shannon cannot 'come home' in a sense, because she is already at home – or very close to it. This is likely far beyond the mental arithmetic that went into the statement Matthews made. I am merely trying to show how we must consider word choice, sentence construction, and consider the multiple inferences and meanings from a person's statement.

Reviewing this passage, it also seems like Karen was attempting to copy typical MisPer pleas. Many parents would make pleas like, "If you're [the MisPer] seeing this..." or "If anyone has any information..." In the current example, Karen obviously could not make these pleas – she knew Shannon could not see the appeal; she knew someone had information. Karen therefore had to adapt her plea. Thus, the "if" statement she made was a leak of the knowledge she had.

A parent of a missing child is likely to plead for their safe return. That is expected. I know this because I have heard hundreds of these pleas. I am going to repeat this, because otherwise I know that critics will pick apart the fact I am focusing on one word. See, I am critiquing myself, so you do not have to. A parent pleading for the safe return of a child is expected. A parent asking for a child to come *home... home... home... home... home*. That is repetitive. In statement analysis we consider repetition as a sign of sensitivity. What, we might ask, is so sensitive about *home*? Of the 71 words Karen decides to use to make her point, one word is repeated the most, 5 times. This is even more than Shannon's name (3 times) or the word *daughter* (2 times).

If you still think I am making too much out of very little, you may be correct. All my methods should be understood as being potentially useful in a cautious investigative capacity, not evidentiary. I am more than happy to hear pushback. It reminds me, too, that I should gather more information and examples to see whether I have cherry-picked findings to suit my hypotheses. This cherry-picking leads to a risk of confirmation bias and calling ourselves Texas Sharpshooters. The advice I have, always, is to collect more information. So, let us see what else Karen said.

Karen provided further media appeals, likely in an attempt to keep the case in the public eye and increase the reward fund. She was asked, in a separate media statement, a large compound question. The question was how difficult the time had been since Shannon went missing, what her routine was, and whether she could sleep. Her response? "*Well, it's hard to sleep really, it's just... the house doesn't feel the same without, erm, them, not being there really.*" We might wonder why, even after two weeks, the *house* remained such a focal point for Matthews. She was not asked about the house. Note that she ignored the 'routine' prompt and instead tied her lack of sleeping with the house. Sleep disruption in close proximity to 'the house.' What is she conveying to us? Why ignore all of the other components of the compound question to focus solely on that link?

Clearly, mentioning 'home' repeatedly and stating 'if' is not enough to convict anyone. It is enough, however, to raise suspicion. If that is all it does, then that is more than enough at this stage. Just a small flag to follow-up on. And of course, in the early days of a MisPer case, especially one involving a child, the priority must be on searching for the child.

At the time of writing this chapter, I have been contacted by an on-going search for a missing young child. I am aware of the possibility of the parents being involved, of course. The police have yet to clear the ground beneath their feet. That said, the greater importance is on finding the child – who may very well be out in the wild. Therefore, this takes priority. There is no easy solution here. The equation is impossible to balance. Spend too long searching for the boy when a criminal act has occurred, and you may lose evidence. Spend too long treating a MisPer case as a (no-body) homicide, and you may lose the chance of finding the MisPer alive. All these things need to be accounted for. I only suggest that looking at the language with a Keatley's Winthropping lens might open further avenues of investigation – especially if the parents think they have hidden their child well.

25. Ian STEWART

If you would like to hear an emergency call that is suspicious, look no further than Ian Stewart. His lengthy though calm call to emergency services in England raises alarm bells, but not for the reasons he had hoped. The call was ostensibly to raise awareness about his wife, Helen Bailey, who he calmly claimed had been missing for some time. Given his wife is an adult, perhaps we can excuse the delay in calling emergency services. That said, how long is too long? How long before we become suspicious of the time it took? The purpose of this chapter is not emergency call analyses, *per se* – though I have multiple papers and chapters on that topic. The focus is on reminding readers that any statement a person gives may be used in the investigation.

I will not provide a full transcript of the emergency call, because it would be overly long and largely unhelpful for our current purposes. That said, it is worth listening to, if only to gain an anecdote of how strangely relaxing an emergency call can be. Let us get right into the facts of the case, and then review the call to see if we could have arrived at the clandestine location any sooner. In future chapters, I shall reverse this process. I will give you the statements and then see if you can predict the location.

For now, let us keep on learning, training, and refining our skills.

Helen Bailey was eventually found down in the cesspit (underground septic tank) underneath the garage of the house she lived in with Stewart. Good detective work helped to solve this case and find her body. My aim, when reviewing cases like this, is always on whether we could have found other pathways to the person. Were there any hints or indicators along the way that, without the beautiful benefit of hindsight, might have guided us there quicker. The aim is not to pompously and rather ridiculously claim that we are better (everyone is with hindsight), but instead, what might we learn that we can apply to the next case?

Knowing that Helen was eventually found down underground, in a small and confined space (the septic tank), let us see if we could have deduced that from statements Stewart made. We can turn first to the first interview, his emergency call. Transcribed below are excerpts from his call. I am not misleading you by only producing smaller parts. The entire call is nearly 14 minutes and transcribing and reproducing it is unnecessary for our purposes. Interested readers can access the full call online.

> Excerpts from the 999 (emergency services call)
>
> "*My partner has been missing since Monday... hasn't gone, ended up where she said she was going... she left a note, she said in the note something like 'I need space and time alone'... we've got a cottage down there, but we, people been down there with neighbors... it's a little cottage we got down there... her phone is just dead, well I say dead it just goes straight to answering machine...*

> Dispatcher: was she leaving the premises (when you last saw her)?
> *No, no, she was, I left her here... she has talked about wanting space, things just haven't been going well recently... I've spoken to the neighbor down at [*redacted*]...*
>
> Dispatcher: This may sound silly but she's definitely not at home, no?
> *No, her brother asked that, I, I, I've literally checked everywhere, we have got quite a large house, but I have literally checked everywhere...*
>
> *She did have a breakdown; I don't like to use the term breakdown...*

Believe it or not, this is a very reduced precis of the call. For now, let us focus on the comments that Stewart freely gave in his emergency call. From the outset, Stewart is keen to tell us that he does not know where Helen is. We must listen (read) carefully what he wants to tell us. As one of my favorite statement analysts says, people's words will betray them, if we listen closely. So, let's listen closely to Stewart.

Language related to directions, time, space, locations, or geography are what we are focusing on. Stewart tells us she '*hasn't gone, ended up.*' This really is cherry-picking, I know. As far as indicators go, it is barely worth noting. Except, it is a spatial or geographical reference. Moreover, Stewart is telling us she is not '*up.*' More, she has not '*ended up.*' If end is a finality, then perhaps in the end, in Helen's end, she is not up. Perhaps I am really clutching at straws, here. So, let us see if this is consistent with other leaks he may be giving that have a direction/location indication.

It does not take us long. "*Down*" and "*down there*" are mentioned multiple times throughout the call. Albeit, granted, in contexts of other things, like the cottage they own "*down there*" or that she has had a "*breakdown*." Stewart could easily make the statement about the cottage without offering "*down there*" each time. Also, there are many other ways to say that Helen suffered psychological issues. Indeed, Stewart says he does not like the term – though he repeats it.

At the very least, we have perhaps a glimmer of a pattern emerging. Imagine we are completely at a loss as to Helen's whereabouts. We have no idea where she is. Go on, say it, she could be anywhere. She appears to have vanished into thin air, as people like to say. In that circumstance, surely even a slim glimmer is worth a look.

Other indicators that may be worth noting: what does Helen need? *Time and space.* In fact, needing or wanting space is repeated twice. This is not abnormal. People in relationships may need space from time to time. That said, if we apply a linguistic Keatley's Winthropping perspective to this case based on all we have seen and heard, we have a pattern emerging. Let's join the dots.

1. Helen has not ended up.
2. Down and down there are repeated.
3. Helen needs space (x2) and time alone.

Of course, with hindsight, we can see how this overlaps with where Helen was found. In that way, it can seem almost too easy. Another way of viewing it is this: if it does seem too easy, then why can we not apply the same logic, again, in other cases? If it feels like it is intuitive or obvious, then surely a conclusion is that people do leak information that can be useful.

Finally, if a suspect tells you "*I left her here*," it is probably worth paying attention to where "*here*" is. A fourth bullet point we could add to the list above is that Stewart "*left her here*" – at the house. Where is Helen? Stewart left her at the house, which he has "literally checked everywhere" (x2). Times two? Sensitivity indicated. Time to double-down on the suspicion.

To put this another way. If Helen were still missing, today, after all this time. I would strongly suggest searching the house. That is where Stewart, who by nature of personal proximity must be a suspect, said he left her. Beyond that? Let's follow where he is verbally taking us. Not somewhere up. Not the attic. Not a crawlspace in the roof. Perhaps not even somewhere on the second floor. No, somewhere, down, down, down. But where? Somewhere that is small (she needs space x2) and somewhere that she will be for a long time.

I admit, a cellar would be a good place to start. It would also be cleared quickly. Where from there? I do not think it would take long to find the cesspit (septic tank). Not all suspects will be quite so clear in their linguistic leaks, but when we hear leaks, we should be ready to mop them up (or, in keeping with the present case, note them down).

26. Samantha WOHLFORD

I must admit, I first came across this case on one of my late-night click-a-thons on YouTube. When insomnia puts me in the position of being too tired to effectively work but too tense to sleep, I start web-crawling the darker side of the internet for cases that are interesting. This case popped up and piqued my interest owing to the statements that were made during the investigation.

Samantha Wohlford, for those who do not know, was a YouTube star of sorts. I am a bit of a dinosaur when it comes to technology and this recent trend that people have to blog or video-log (vlog) everything. It turns out Wohlford made many videos and seemed to have quite a following. Perhaps this explains why she was so talkative when police arrived and recorded her on their body worn cameras (BWC). I have studied BWC recordings extensively, and I reviewed the recording of Wohlford with growing interest. As the police arrived at the scene, Wohlford would become the star of another video, though this one would make her infamous.

Here is the story, as Wohlford would have us believe it. While it changed in several ways, I shall try and present the basics. Wohlford claimed that while she was at home with her husband, Ernie Ibarra Jr., three masked men broke into their house, tied her up, and gagged her. Following this, the men attacked her husband and abducted him. Wohlford claims she managed to dial the first number she could, which happened to be her mother, on her cell phone. How did she manage to do this while tied up? Who knows? Well, Wohlford let the investigators know that she used her nose, of course. It was her mother who then then called police.

The BWC footage showed police were immediately suspicious of the case. The scene did not appear to match the sequence of events that Wohlford was attempting to make them believe. Police continued their investigation and brought Wohlford in for a more formal interview. It is really worth watching for a great sequence of deceptive behaviors and language. For our purposes, we learn from this interview more about her. She stated that she does not go out much, is a stay-at-home mum, and spends a lot of her time making YouTube videos. In terms of her geographical awareness, we could suggest her spatial awareness is localized and limited. The only place she appears to mention, several times, is Pittsburg, Texas. This is a location some 20miles (32km) south of her home. We thus have a knowledge convex hull pointing southerly. Keep that in mind.

As the investigation progressed, it came to light that Wohlford had planned the whole crime with accomplices. One in particular would prove very enlightening in terms of the words he chose and the location his words revealed. Remember, we know now that Ernie had been killed and left in the woods near Wolford's home. We know that now, with hindsight, but the killers knew that at the time. They would have known that fact as they sat across from the interviewers.

During interviews, the biggest question hanging over the

interview, the elephant in the room: *where is Ernie Ibarra Jr.?* The suspect, John "Rebel" Sanford, knew this is what the investigators wanted to know. He knew that he knew. He knew he could not say it out loud. That's a lot of knowing without much telling. Like in so many cases, it is only so long before the distance between the brain and the mouth shortcuts and the truth comes out.

> Sanford: "*They put the guy* [Ibarra] *in the back seat. As we're going and they're telling me, like go here, go here, all while I'm driving. We go all the way out to the country. We go out to the country. Next thing I know, they walk off. So, I'm like, 'What the* [expletive]?' *So, I started walking back to the vehicle, and in my mind process, this is my neck of the woods now."*
> Officer: "*Do you know where you're at?*"
> Sanford: "*Yeah, this is my neck of the woods*"

As it turned out, Sanford directed the investigators to Ernie's location. There was no need for Keatley's Winthropping techniques, not if the suspect is going to comply and take us there. But what if Sanford had not taken police to the site? Well, we know that Wohlford had pointed her geographical hull south, to an accomplice that lived in Pittsburg. This would point us in the right direction to begin. Knowing that the accomplice then says "*my neck of the woods*" twice, would narrow the search down further still. Repetition is sensitivity, and the suspect was telling us where to look.

The phrase Sanford used tells us two things. First, the location of Ernie's body is somewhere he knows well. That is the standard meaning of "*my neck of the woods*." But note, there are many ways to express that. He could have said "my local area" or "a place I know". Instead, he said "*my neck of the woods*." Why was the word "woods" the one he used? The use of "woods" I do not think was an accident, it was a verbal leak.

I raise this case here, because had Sanford attempted to remain quiet instead, he might still have given us this verbal leak about the location. Of course, knowing that a body is possibly in some woods is still a needle in a relatively large haystack. That said, at least the haystack is reduced by some large degree. With other methods in forensics and tracking, I have every belief that based on knowing the body was in 'the woods' it would have significantly reduced the search areas and allowed the successful finding of Ernie's body.

In future books, I will turn my attention to conversation analysis and questioning protocols and styles that may assist with information gathering and narrowing Keatley's Winthropping zones.

27. Chris WATTS

Perhaps one of the most infamous of modern-day crimes was the Watts family familicide. It is infamous, but by no means unique. It is one of several such horrendous crimes to be committed. Perhaps what made it so well-known was the fact that Chris Watts was so quick to appear live on news channels, which helped to gain so much public interest. Mix in with this the fact that a loving mother and her two children were missing, and the fundamentals were there for true-crime communities to explode with theories. Between Watts' nonverbal communication on camera and his strange statements, and the fact the partner is almost always the first person of interest, many people pointed a finger of suspicion almost immediately. Notable inclusion amongst them was Watts' neighbor who made for a fine behavior analyst.

In the early hours of August 13, 2018, in Frederick, Colorado, Chris Watts, an oil field operator, killed his pregnant wife, Shanann, and two young girls, Bella (4) and Celeste (3). Most people know this story, so I shall skip the main narrative parts, and move on to a Keatley's Winthropping perspective.

Watts would eventually confess to murdering his wife,

though he initially claimed he only did this because she had murdered their daughters. He then pointed on a map to a nearby oil field, wherein he said he had hidden the bodies of his pregnant wife and two daughters. Investigators arrived at the oil field on August 16, 2018, and located the bodies. Shanann was buried in a shallow grave, very near two crude oil storage tanks. Inside one tank was the body of Bella. Celeste had been placed in the other oil tank. I do not want to wander into the territory of tabloid sensationalism. I have seen so many horrific crimes perpetrated by people that few shock me anymore. But I can safely say that this is one of those cases that haunts you long after it is solved.

We know where Shanann, Bella, and Celeste were because Watts told his father and then investigators. Obviously, with a confession and a mark on a map, Keatley's Winthropping is not needed. That said, as we know, not every suspect does confess and confer the location. So, let us not be lazy, here. Instead of taking the shortcut of Watts' confession, can we see whether he led us to their location in other ways?

Watts gave several statements to police and media. People will often leak information because the cognitive effort of keeping it hidden is overwhelming. We know that Watts was under a great deal of stress and had a lot on his mind because when police first arrived, to find him pacing the neighborhood, he told them. Consider the situation: your family are missing, and police have arrived to start the formal investigation. You are out in your neighborhood. Why are you out there? To look for your family? To ask neighbors if they have seen your family? To look for clues? Do you think this is what Watts was doing? We need not guess, he told us. Why was Watts out wandering around his neighborhood?

"To clear my head."

That was the reason Watts gave for wandering around his neighborhood. Not to look for his wife and children. Not to canvass the area; not to speak to neighbors and anyone who may be able to help find them. No. Instead, he said, "*to clear my head*." The alarms began ringing, I am sure.

A further statement Watts made, which I think is very revealing concerned his knowledge, or lack thereof, about the location of his family. No, sorry, of his wife and kids. Remember, we know now that he knew full-well where they were. We know that he knew, and we know he knew he could not reveal that. He also had to say something. So, what did he say?

> *"And I know we were having marital discord, and we had that conversation that morning and then she goes, and we have no idea where she is, or the kids."*

Negation noted. But first, let's look at the order of importance for Watts. Remember, order indicates what matters to him most. His wife and children are missing. What is his priority to tell you? "*We were having marital discord*." Not really geographically meaningful, but I cannot help but point out red flags when I see them. Next, the most important part for our purposes here: Where was his family? No, sorry, again, let me get it right. Where was "she… or the kids"?

Well, we know that to him, his 'family' is not together. How do we know this? Because he does not use the collective noun 'family' like I just did. Instead, he separates his wife ('she') from the kids. Perhaps this is simply how he normally speaks. I have heard people innocently refer to their partners and their kids separately within the same sentence. As ever, an indicator is proof of nothing more than you might want to ask a follow-up question.

In the current case, however, it may have pointed you to the fact his wife was no longer with his kids. As we know, now, he had buried his wife in one place, and the kids separately elsewhere. They were geographically separated in his mind and so they were verbally separated in his statement. Coincidence? Maybe. Worth considering? Definitely.

What is the point of this? Well, at the least it offers us a new angle to question the suspect. It might also help us to narrow down potential locations. If we follow this linguistic leak, we would be looking for a location that would allow separate placement of victims. The final body deposition site met this description.

But, of course, digging three separate holes in the ground would equally have fit the separation lead. Correct. So, did Watts offer us any other indicators? In short: yes. Let us turn to his television interview. In his interview, on his porch, he tells the reporter what he hoped would happen regarding his kids.

> *"I was hoping I was going to get ran over by the kids running through the door, just barrel rushing me."*

When he thinks about his kids, he chooses a word that I consider to be a leak. I cannot help but see 'barrel' as a leak. He knows where he put the kids, in the crude oil storage tanks. The linguistic association between oil, tanks, and barrels, I think, permeated into his mind and then leaked out of his mouth.

Of course, investigators were also aware of Watts' profession. I am sure that geographical profilers would have highlighted the fact that his job would have put the oil field he hid his family in within a search area. It fits with many of the sub-tenets of Keatley's Winthropping, too. Salience, affordance, activity space, and comfort zone, all ticked. Routine activity theory, rational choice perspective, ticks all-round. I think we can take it a step further, however, and say that it was also verbally pointed towards by Watts' own words, even before he made his full confession.

28. Scott PETERSON

On Christmas Eve, 2002, Laci Peterson was 8 months pregnant. Christmas time and close to the birth of a new child should have been a happy time for the Peterson household. Sadly, this case is another infamous one. Therefore, I assume most readers know the main details. I will not labor the details or slow the progress. The brief outline is this. December 24, 2002, Scott Peterson woke up and left his house at approximately 9.30am. What and where Peterson was going will be dissected later. According to Peterson, he called Laci and left a message for her at approximately 2:15pm. Peterson says when he returned home, Laci's car was in the driveway and the house was empty. McKenzie, the family dog, was in the backyard. After showering and washing his clothes, Peterson called Laci's mother, Sharon, to ask if Laci was with her. This led to Laci's stepfather calling the police shortly before 6pm. As we all know, now, Laci and her baby had been horrifically killed and put in the San Francisco Bay area.

The case is long, convoluted, and in many ways horrific. As much as I may want to delve into the psychology and narcissism of Scott Peterson, here is not the place. Instead, I shall focus on the geography of the case, and once more ask whether we could have found Laci sooner. At the time of writing, I am aware that Peterson has just put forward his appeal. I shall, therefore, be mindful of the fact that a court at a later date than my writing this may find him not guilty. If that happens, then we must simply ask who else, other than Scott would fit the profile of a person that knows the areas so well. Remember, Keatley's Winthropping can narrow down an area, it cannot directly reveal the suspect nor their motive.

Fishing for the truth

Remember earlier when I skipped over what Peterson was doing all day on December 24? The reason is because he appears to have changed his story. A friend who called round when Peterson returned home claimed Peterson said he'd been golfing. Other family members also said they had heard the same thing from Peterson. In the 911 call that Laci's stepfather made, we also hear support for this narrative.

> "*My son-in-law called. He'd been playing golf this morning... we just had a call from our son-in-law that he left this morning at 9:30 to play golf.*"

Perhaps there was a mistake, confusion, or assumption on behalf of everyone. However, several people all seem to have the same impression of what Peterson had been doing all day. This is important because inconsistencies can be a source of investigative breakthroughs. Alongside friends and family, one of the early investigating officers also outlined a rather strange interaction he had with Peterson at the time.

> *"I asked Mr. Peterson if he had been working all day, and Mr. Peterson stated no, that he had gone fishing in the Bay. I asked Mr. Peterson if, what, exactly what kind of fishing he was doing, what kind of fish he was fishing for today. And at that point there was a pause. He hesitated in answering me. He, he had this blank look on his face for a second or so, his eyes shifted a little bit and he kind of mumbled some stuff, but again blew off my question, didn't really give me an answer...I followed, loosely followed him at a distance, went to the front door. As he was stepping out of the front door and onto that sidewalk area, I heard what sounded like a cuss word, and if you want, I can say it in court.... Sounded like the word "f*ck," and it came through what sounded like gritted teeth."*
>
> Note: censorship added by author.

Quite a lengthy transcription, granted, but a potentially very telling one, too. This account clearly contradicts what friends and family members believed had occurred. If we were suspicious of Peterson's actual activity that day, then his reaction to having said he was fishing becomes even more dubious. Why the negative reaction? Let us imagine Peterson really is innocent. First, why would he lie about going fishing, and say golf? Second, why would he care when he admitted to the officer that he had actually been fishing?

Choosing to go fishing, though, was something that Peterson would have to explain in a formal police interview. What follows is one of those times wherein a suspect is caught in a lie and attempts to talk their way out of it.

> Det Brocchini: *"When did you realize you were going to go fishing?"*
> Peterson: *"Err, it was a morning decision; it's either go play golf at the club or go fishing – seemed too cold to go play golf at the club."*

Now, it may be true, of course, that someone could decide to go fishing instead of playing golf. It is harder to explain why he did not make that clearer to friends and family immediately. Perhaps there were more pressing things on his mind. I can almost bring myself to believe that narrative. What I find harder to understand is why, when faced with the coldness of the morning, he decided that sitting on a boat would be preferable to a golf course. This would also be labelled a need to convince, for those tracking other linguistic indicators of deception. Remember, no method nor tool should be used in isolation.

Again, this is hardly condemning information by itself. Police can hardly arrest him for making curious decisions based on warmth. That said, it does raise alarm bells about why a location is so important to him. Important enough to try and avoid it, and then appear disgruntled when he is outed. Remember what we learned about temporal (spatial) lacunas and spontaneous negations in Chapters 3 and 4. Here, I believe, is a real-world example of it. To my knowledge, Peterson never drew a map of his day's activities. I wonder, though, if he had been asked to, would he have omitted his boat and the bay area? He was certainly verbally attempting to avoid it.

For those that know the case, you will also be aware of the geographical links of the boating area and Peterson. He owned property up there; indeed, he kept his boat there. Though he was relatively reluctant to admit to it, it was well within his activity space and comfort zones. He was, therefore, in many ways a prime suspect, and it is not surprising he was found guilty.

I note that if Peterson's defense plea is successful, we will need to consider how someone else would have this level of overlap. It could be a set-up, someone staging the crime to frame Peterson (and this has been suggested, including by a retired Detective). Perhaps. This is true for all cases though. If a later trial shows that the suspect was not guilty, then we must revise our hypotheses and the analyses, so that we can improve.

29. Additional linguistic leaks cases

We have now seen multiple examples of linguistic leaks. Perhaps not enough to convince you. That is good. Skepticism keeps your minds sharp. Question everything. If the cases presented so far were all I had, I might agree that linguistic leaks are not a good indicator. As you have probably guessed, however, there are many more examples. You will just have to trust me when I say I have many more examples from my personal work that I cannot publish. I will never jeopardize a case I was involved with, nor risk the ire of investigators for releasing information they would prefer kept confidential. Know this: in the last year of looking for linguistic leak cases I have found many. Here are some more of them that that I can briefly outline, here.

James WORLEY

On July 19, 2016, at approximately 6:45pm, Sierra Joughin was riding her bicycle home from her boyfriend's house. Her boyfriend, a caring guy who was trying to ensure her safety, followed her for part of the way on his motorcycle. Tragically, he did not follow her all the way home, leaving her to ride the rest of the journey by herself. She did not make it home.

Later that evening, Sierra's parents contacted her boyfriend to ask where she was. When he could not reach her via her cellphone, the authorities were contacted.

Investigators located Sierra's bicycle within a cornfield, near where she was last seen by her boyfriend. Further investigation showed motorcycle tracks and signs of a struggle near her bicycle. Let this case be a lesson to you about connecting the dots to find the 'killer' (see Chapter 16) but not stopping with the killer dots connected. If you are thinking that her boyfriend rode a motorcycle, and motorcycle tracks were found leading to her bicycle, you would be connecting some dots. Add to this the fact that a motorcycle helmet with blood on it was found nearby, and you might have a pattern of dots to connect. Remember, you can connect some dots to find 'killer,' but are there more to point you elsewhere? Do not get tunnel vision.

Thankfully, the investigators did their job commendably. They did not stop at the potentially obvious. Instead, investigators used several technological methods to try to find Sierra, including analyzing her Fitbit activity tracker and her smartphone. Investigators also did not forget the basics. They went out and canvassed the area, face-to-face, door-to-door. Not as fancy, no clever technology, nor scientists in labs. Just good ol' fashioned policework. It paid off.

While questioning people in the neighborhood, they arrived at James Worley's door. He told them his motorbike had broken down in the area that Sierra was last seen, and the place her bicycle had been found. He then told investigators that he had found two bicycles in the cornfield, but he "*didn't steal anything or kill anyone*." Remember what we discussed in Chapter 3 about spontaneous negations? If you did not ask a suspect a question that they provide a negative response to, question why.

The investigation continued with Worley becoming an increasingly suspicious person of interest. Witnesses in the area noted a passenger van driving at speed from the location Sierra was found. The license (registration) plate was linked to Worley. Police returned to continue their investigation.

Already, we have the tenets of geographical profiling linking Worley to the scene. We have the basics of Keatley's Winthropping, too. The location was local, the area and activity space within Worley's routine activities. We can tick all of the requisite boxes.

The next 'dot' of information was the linguistically revealing part. When questioned about his activity and interaction with police, Worley attempted to explain his behavior and previous comments, "*I just didn't want to try to get myself into a f*cking hole*." Note, he did not censor his speech. *A f*cking hole*. I will ask you to think about some of the geographic locations involved in this case, based on that statement.

Worley, it turned out, had a torture chamber. Where was this chamber? A hole in the ground in his shed. Sierra was also found in a shallow grave – a shallow hole in the ground. All that remains unclear is to which hole Worley was referring. Clearly, holes in the ground were weighing heavily on his mind and with such a weight on the mind, it will soon leak out of the mouth.

Sahara ERVIN

On August 22, 2020, in Houston, Texas an Amber Alert was issued for a missing 2-year-old, Maliyah Bass. MisPer cases are always a cause for care and concern. I appreciate that most MisPers return relatively quickly and often, thankfully, unscathed. I am also aware of how underfunded and overworked police are. I am not suggesting that a full investigation is conducted instantly every time a MisPer case is called in. That said, I am also aware of the *golden hour* – the crucial early hours of an investigation in which evidence and information once lost can sometimes never be regained.

Missing children should always raise alarm bells early and receive attention. Maliyah Bass was no different. While the central focus of investigators is always primarily on finding the missing child, you cannot switch off that investigative mind. Always, you are listening for information, weighing-up possibilities, analyzing the wider dynamics of the case. In the case of Maliyah Bass, we can find our next example of a linguistic leak.

Maliyah's mother, Sahara Ervin, told investigators that her little girl was playing in the playground outside their apartment. Ervin stated that she and her partner, Travion Thomas, went inside to cook breakfast. When they returned, they claimed Maliyah was missing. Of course, leaving a 2-year-old outside in a playground, by herself, for a period of time, is questionable. It was also untrue, as would eventually be discovered. Sadly, Maliyah was killed, and her body moved by Ervin and Thomas.

I do not want to turn tragedy into some kind of game. I do not want to detract from the horror of what happened. I do want readers to learn the importance of listening carefully. The aim here is to see how your training is progressing. So, I am going to give to you Ervin's statement, which she made to television reporters.

> *"I am drained. I have been looking for her for 24 hours."*

I appreciate a missing child is a tense time. The fear must be overwhelming. Of course, Ervin would be tired, exhausted, spent, worn, weary, depleted, empty, fatigued, or weak. So many words to choose from, and which did Ervin choose? *Drained.* Knowing what you know, where do you think young Maliyah Bass was found.

Yes.

Sadly.

She was.

CASE STUDIES IV

The MisPers

30. The Missing

The worldwide numbers of missing persons (MisPer) and no-body homicides (NBH) is daunting. It is overwhelming and heartbreaking. It is a list that grows daily. I am not claiming that my approach to Winthropping will solve all these cases. If only. I am suggesting that perhaps it is a potential approach that may assist, if only as a Hail Mary pass. I also know that with every case we work, the method improves. The only slight sliver of a silver lining of being wrong is that it affords us the opportunity to learn if we are humble enough to accept it.

The following cases are ones have got under my skin for one reason or another. I could fill the next 200+ pages with even more cases. I had to draw a line somewhere, and these are the ones that have stood out to me. All information in the following cases is from OSINT. It is freely available information. While I have tried to remain as factual as possible, I note there is room for errors and misinterpretations – the first case, Suzy Lamplugh, is a textbook example of this.

Finally, let us address the obvious: where is Madeleine McCann? I have been asked this more times than I can remember. She is still, at the time of writing, a MisPer – though many would classify it more likely a no-body homicide case. In either case, the question remains: Where is she? And thus, why am I not covering her case in this book? The answer is relatively simple. There are so many authors, investigators, sleuths, and armchair detectives that have alleged to have solved the case and claimed to know where her body is, what use is one more?

I am not and have not been involved in her case. Therefore, my analyses and what I would feel comfortable writing here would be as appropriate as anyone else's. Of course, I have my suspicions about where she is. I have taken my approach and applied it to the case and come to a profile of the likely location. So, why not just come right out and say it? Mostly because I do not want to get dragged into the case and the furor surrounding it. I do not do what I do for fame or infamy. I would rather avoid that noise. Others have also stated the place I think she is, so I would not be adding new information. Already, I can feel the nerves rising as I know that this small paragraph could cause more of an issue than the entire book. So, let's move on.

Rest assured, when she is found, if the location she is found is where I think it is, the use of Keatley's Winthropping would make it an obvious choice. I appreciate some people will not be satisfied with this. Some may claim I do not have faith in my approach, that I'm scared and have run for the hills if I do not state the place etc. Fair enough. But please realize that I have given you all the tools you need, why not use everything you have learned here, compare it to your chosen location, see how it fits, or not. The aim of this book is for *you* to become proficient in using Keatley's Winthropping, too.

What follows, instead, are a number of cases I have been interested in, for various reasons. I am not offering final declarations of locations. I am simply suggesting that I think Keatley's Winthropping could be useful.

Susannah "Suzy" LAMPLUGH

Probably one of the UK's most infamous historic missing person cases is that of Susannah "Suzy" Lamplugh. A warning, dear readers, this case study will be lengthy and not entirely focused on Keatley's Winthropping. Feel free to skim this case or skip it if you are not interested. I do not want to waste your time. That said, I find this case so interesting that I am relishing the chance to write about it. It also has so many important points that are worth raising when discussing (cold) case reviews. But have no fear, the role of my approach to Winthropping will be ever present and suggested as a potential for furthering this case.

Here is the case. On Monday July 28, 1986, Suzy went to her work as an estate agent (realtor). What happened next is less clear than several authors would suggest. We know that Suzy got to work, we know that she took a phone call at some point in the morning. We know that she had an entry in her office diary for a viewing appointment that day. We know that the entry was as follows:

12 45 Mr Kipper
37, Shorrolds O/S

O/S was shorthand for "outside." This indicated that the viewing was likely to begin, at least, outside. Then, at approximately 12:30, according to her office colleague, Suzy got up and left the office. This was the last official confirmed sighting of Suzy. From this point on, the stories get confused and confusing. The eyewitness sightings get retold with different levels of certainty, and various timelines emerge.

In addition to every article and documentary I can find, I have also read six books directly related to this case.

1) *The Suzy Lamplugh Story* (1988)
   Andrew Stephen
2) *Unmasking Mr Kipper* (1995)
   Christopher Berry-Dee
3) *Prime Suspect* (2007)
   Christopher Berry-Dee & Robin Odell
4) *Searching for Suzy* (2011)
   Graham McGredy-Hunt
5) *Finding Suzy* (2021)
   David Videcette
6) *Suzy Lamplugh* (2021)
   Netta Newbound & Marcus Brown

Beyond these books, I have read hundreds of newspaper articles, sleuth-sites, and blogs. I have watched and listened to myriad documentaries, podcasts, YouTube shows, and interviews. I still would not consider myself fully informed. I have not worked officially on the case, so I am sure there is also hold-back information that was not released to the public. That is often how it goes, and for good reasons. Therefore, what follows are some of the issues I have noted with the case, or at least the semi/un-official reporting of it. I raise these issues to remind readers that details matter. The accuracy of Keatley's Winthropping may be limited to the accuracy of details, data, evidence, and input. Garbage in equals garbage out.

The key to the case?

Did you notice earlier, when I said Suzy got up and left the office, I did not say she took the keys to 37 Shorrolds Road with her. Surely, if she were going to show the house to a perspective buyer, she would take the keys to let the prospective client see inside. Let us start with the Crimewatch re-enaction that depicted Suzy's movements that morning.

Crimewatch, for my international readers, was a long-running BBC television show that reconstructed major unsolved crimes in the UK. The aim was to gain public information via call-ins. We would hope their information is accurate.

From the Crimewatch show, the following voiceover is provided while a person re-enacts the scene: "*On this Monday, she left the office at 12:40...As well as her own keys and purse, she took with her property details and keys for a house in Shorrolds Road, number 37... there's no doubt she went to Shorrolds Road.*"

Taking the keys seems intuitive and obvious. Indeed, a *Crimewatch* television re-enactment of the case showed a person, portraying Suzy, picking up the keys before she left the office. If they are portraying Suzy as having taken the keys with her, then I hope that is accurate. I am not so sure. Let us see what the authors have made of this issue.

Stephen in his book makes it clear that Suzy left the office and took the keys to 37 Shorrolds Road, "*She took some phone calls from clients as well, and had left the office just before lunchtime on a routine house-showing call – clutching the particulars and keys of 37 Shorrolds Road, a furnished, three-story terraced house that only days before had come on to the Sturgis books for £128,000.*" The front cover of Stephen's book, which shows the diary entry and the keys to 37 Shorrolds Road also indicates that they are a central part of the story. Stephen repeats several times throughout his book that Suzy took the keys, even claiming a witness corroborated this, "*he saw a young woman clutching a set of keys in her right hand, standing on her own in the gateway of number 37.*"

Berry-Dee in his first book on the case states, "*a vivacious 25-year-old blonde, she took with her the keys to 37 Shorrolds*

Road." Again, in his second book on the case, Berry-Dee and Odell repeated the claim about the keys, "*When she left the office Suzy took with her the keys to a property nearby at 37 Shorrolds Road.*" Given Berry-Dee is an author of both books, we should not technically count this as +2 for the taking-keys claim. McGredy-Hunt, however, also claimed that Suzy took the keys, "*She recorded the call in her diary and at just after 12:35pm Suzy collected the keys from Mark Gurdon and left the office.*" Where Mark Gurdon comes into the picture is unclear, as other authors do not mention this and Gurdon himself does not appear to support this when interviewed by Videcette.

David Videcette claims in his book, "*Suzy didn't have the key to 37 Shorrolds Road with her, I was now certain of it.*" Finally, Newbound and Brown, offering a brief synopsis of the case, initially make no claim of the key and later in their book reference Videcette's claim – so no independent inference can be made as to their personal views.

You might be wondering why this even matters? Surely, the bigger issue is that fact Suzy is missing. Why am I getting so hung-up on whether she had the keys or not? The answer is that details matter. Whether Suzy had the keys or not potentially changes the entire timeline of her day. If she did not have the keys, as Videcette seems so certain of, then we may conclude the Shorrolds Road viewing was a cover-up for something else she was doing. Videcette gives an account of what and where that may be. If she did have the keys, as so many sources suggest – then the house viewing seems likely.

At the end of the day, I am an academic and a nerdy one at that. It is time, I think you'll all agree, for a good ol' table of this issue.

Author	**Key taken**	**Conclusion**	**Suspect**
Crimewatch (1986)	Y	Abducted at/near 37 Shorrolds	None named
Stephen (1988)	Y	Unclear – likely abduction at/near 37 Shorrolds	None specifically highlighted
Berry-Dee (1995)	Y	Abducted at/near 37 Shorrolds	Michael SAMS
Berry-Dee & Odell (2007)	Y	Abducted at/near 37 Shorrolds	John CANNAN
McGredy-Hunt (2011)	Y	Suzy had keys but may not have gone to Shorrolds	Fred WEST John WEST
Videcette (2021)	N	Suzy likely went to Prince of Wales pub to collect items she had left there on a previous night.	None named.

What are we to make of this? The answer is that there is no clear answer, and there is unlikely to be one after all of this time. Memory fades and can be diluted or influenced by other reports. We have to wonder to what extent the *Crimewatch* re-enactment, broadcast in 1986, influenced future authors and reviewers. From what Videcette writes, the police files do not appear to add light to the issue – though I cannot weigh in on this.

In situations like this, and they occur a lot in cold cases, the only path forward that I know of is to plot hypothetical timelines. In one hypothetical 'narrative universe' Suzy has the keys and goes to 37 Shorrolds Road. In a different pathway of that timeline, she has the keys but does not necessarily go to 37 Shorrolds Road. In a completely different timeline, she has neither the keys nor the intention to go to 37 Shorrolds Road.

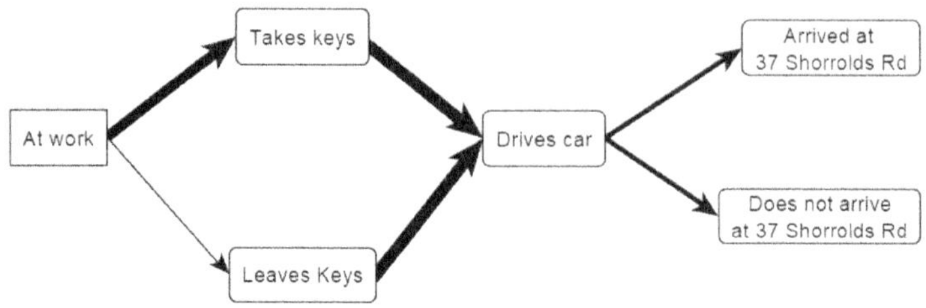

We can try to make our lives easier, perhaps, by making arrow width represent the number of sources or strength of evidence. In the above chart, it may be that we decide to weight more heavily the '*At work*' → '*Takes keys*' pathway, owing to only Videcette's interviews denying this. Or perhaps Videcette's account looms larger for us because he conducted interviews.

While the timeline flow diagram, or what I call *Crime Script Sequencing* does not give answers, *per se*, we can see what parts of the timeline converge. We know that whatever the key-viewing connection, Suzy drove her car. Perhaps more importantly are the points of divergence; for example, whether she took the keys and whether she attended 37 Shorrolds Road. At the very least, this diagram makes it very clear that the timeline so many postulated as clear is not. Did the eyewitness at number 35 Shorrolds Road actually identify Suzy or not? We can add this into the diagram and table to clarify points if we want to.

What does any of this have to do with Keatley's Winthropping? Well, in and of itself, not much. This is included here, in such detail, to show you how important it is to know a case intricately. This is the level of detail we need to ensure we are clear about the accuracy of times and locations. We should clarify what we do and do not know. Structuring case reviews may seem tedious and time consuming, but clear structure and systematic working through of evidence is vital to highlight consistencies and inconsistencies.

Once more, Keatley's Winthropping is not some magic wand that you can absentmindedly wave over case files to make a hill of evidence emerge. It should be integrated into a fuller investigation and where appropriate, help move the case forward.

To properly perform Keatley's Winthropping, you must know everything you can about the case. This is *not* to say that you must know everything possible. But the more you know, the more accurate your final analyses will be. Next, you really should work with experts in the field. That local, lived experience expertise cannot be cheated or recreated. I can show you the locations of Shorrolds Road on a map, and where Suzy's car was eventually found in relation to it. But, as we saw in Chapter 4, maps can be misleading. I want to hear from locals who lived there at the time. There is a world of difference between how far something looks on a map and how far it felt when living there. I recently went to each of the locations on the following map. Even attending them in person is not good enough, nearly 40 years later.

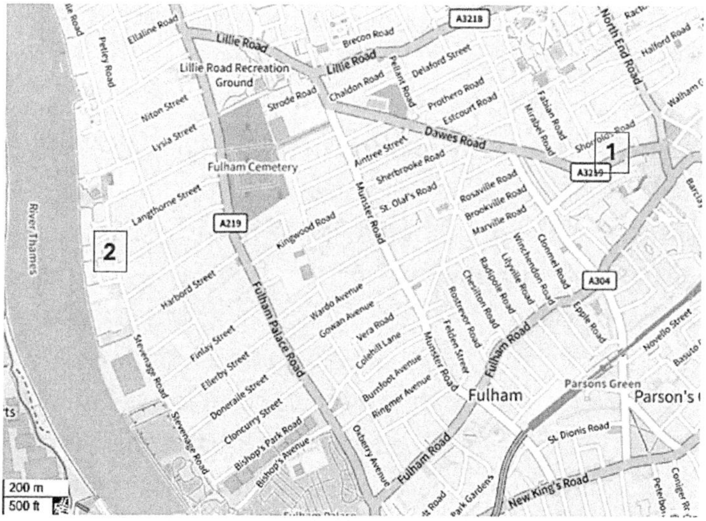

1 = 37 Shorrolds Road; 2 = Suzy's car found (Stevenage Road)

If you repeat a mistake enough times...

Of course, there may be a relatively simple explanation for the whole keys issue. Often, a piece of information is stated, and others copy it without knowing for sure. We saw this in map creation and copying (see Chapter 4). I am constantly fearful of having fallen into this trap myself while writing about cases in this book. The original mistake may be innocently made. A typo or slip. The copying of said mistake may then be naively copied. The issue is that over enough iterations, the mistakes come to sound like the truth.

This is why when I begin assisting with an investigation in real-life, I ask for all of the raw information first. I am happy and eager to hear investigators' opinions and thoughts. Their gut instincts are invaluable sources of information. But they remain only sources. They are not undeniable facts. I want to come to my own conclusions, for better or worse. That is not to say my considerations and conclusions are any more truthful, valid, or accurate than others' are. But it means that I take responsibility on my shoulders based on my analyses. Again, that is why I called it *Keatley's* Winthropping – the responsibility weighs on me.

In the case of Suzy Lamplugh and the keys, I could see how the first reporters and writers assumed she took the keys to 37 Shorrolds Road. After all, it makes intuitive sense and it is the most likely scenario, given the fact of the diary entry outlining the alleged meeting and viewing there. Once one person wrote it, another repeated it, then another seeing it written twice, added a third. The snowball begins to gain momentum. Some 30 years of retelling later, and we have repeated statements of Suzy taking the keys to 37 Shorrolds Road with her. If Videcette's interviews are correct, then he provides an important counter narrative.

This is why I do not just look for frequency of repetitions in a case. I look to evaluate the source of the information. I would like to know where all the authors gained their knowledge of Suzy taking the keys. Who else interviewed those that were there at the time compared to who read a book and repeated the key conclusions.

If you want another example of an innocent mistake regarding the Suzy Lamplugh case, I have a fun one. Nick Ross was a host of Crimewatch for many years. He was involved in helping to solve many crimes and I have the utmost respect and admiration for him. That said, he is human. We all are. We all make mistakes. Or to be more kind, whoever runs Nick Ross' website is human and open to mistakes. I was, therefore, not overly surprised to find a mistake. On the Nick Ross website, on the Suzy Lamplugh page, as of May 2024, there is information regarding the case appearing on Crimewatch. I note the following quotation next to a picture of Nick Ross and Sue Cook on Crimewatch. "Nick Ross, with Sue Cook, his co-presenter on the BBC's Crimewatch, which highlighted the Lamplugh case in 1985." That is quite some feat, considering, as we know, Suzy went missing in 1986.

It is an innocent mistake. A typo. I know. I hear you. I am not criticizing. I know I have made many more typos in this book – my students love to pick them out for me. I raise this only to remind myself and everyone else that mistakes happen. This is why we should question everything and not believe one sole source. We should also not believe sources that are predicated on a single source either. Just because a 'fact' is repeated, does not mean it is true. We know that Nick Ross (or his web manager) made a mistake. But what if there are other mistakes we cannot so easily dismiss? Remember: Question Everything.

John Cannan or John *Cannot*

There is a further, perhaps minor, area of inconsistency in the Suzy Lamplugh case that is like a splinter in my mind. In *Prime Suspect*, Berry-Dee and Odell paint a clear picture of why they agree with police views that John Cannan is the main suspect in the case. Cannan is a convicted criminal. He was charged with multiple offences, including the murder of Shirley Banks, in 1987. Part of the evidence against Cannan was the fact he had Shirley's car in his garage.

Importantly, for our purposes here, the license (registration) plate had been changed on Shirley's vehicle. The license plate was changed. But was there something more to the letters and numbers? It did not take long for police and criminologists to consider a possible link.

According to Berry-Dee and Odell in their book on the case, the new license plate, "SLP 386" had a hidden meaning. They suggested the "SLP" referred to "Suzy Lamplugh." Next, the "3" referred to 3 victims (perhaps, Shirley, Suzy, and an unknown third victim). And then, the "86" referred to Suzy's date of disappearance. SLP 386. It seemed plausible.

There is, however, just one problem that I have. One letter, really. "S." You see, when police found Shirley's car with the new license plate, it was not just "SLP 386". The license plate actually read "SLP386S." There are clear pictures of Shirley's car in the garage and the police working around it. You can see the license plate for yourself.

SLP386S

Here is my issue. When Berry-Dee and Odell comment on the license plate, in their book *Prime Suspect* they omit the final 'S.' They write, "*John claims in his letters to the authors that he chose the number, SLP 386, at random.*" They do not provide a copy of the letters, so I cannot be sure if they are quoting Cannan verbatim. But I feel they should have made it clear that in reality, 1) there is no gap between SLP and 386; 2) there is a second 'S' at the end.

I understand and can see how SLP (space) 386 paints a pretty strange and perhaps subliminal reference to Suzy. But I think it is watered down when you realize several things. First, was Suzy the third victim? Or Shirley? Given this is Shirley's license plate, who is the 3rd? Second, are we just going to ignore the final S? If Cannan were leaving some kind of encrypted cypher to taunt the police, why include that S? Third, Lamplugh is all one word. I understand there is a 'P' in there, but it is the second 'L' that breaks the word into two parts. Consider this: how many words are in 'Lamp'? One, right? Now, how many words does "Lamplight" sound like? The "L" after the "P" is what is pronounced. So, SLL might make more phonetic sense. I am nitpicking, perhaps, but details matter. Why not have SJL (Susannah Jane Lamplugh) if you wanted three letters to denote Suzy?

I am not saying that Cannan is innocent of Suzy's abduction, I am not saying he is guilty. I am saying that we have another inconsistency. "SLP 386" works well to point the finger of suspicion at Cannan – which is what Berry-Dee and Odell do in their book. McGredy-Hunt, however, who had an entirely different suspect, accurately reports the license (registration) plate: "SLP386S." I am sure that Berry-Dee and Odell are just focusing on the key parts of the plate, and perhaps they have additional knowledge not released to the public. Perhaps they are simply echoing Cannan's comments. In any case, as I have said and will say many more times, details matter.

An alternative theory for why SLP386S was used is that it refers to an Ordnance Survey grid reference. There is some speculation that the license plate digits provide a location near to where Shirley Banks's body was found. While I have not been able to support this for myself, yet I can see some logic to it. I can also see several issues. It would, of course, require Cannan to have a copy of said map, and be brazen enough to use it in such a way. Does this fit the psychological profile of Cannan? I think some would suggest it does. Herein, again, is a reminder that my approach to Winthropping may only take us so far. Input from other experts is always likely to help.

Dead Woman's Ditch

While we are discussing Cannan and his murder victim, Shirley Banks, it might be worth exploring her body deposition site. Of all the places in the United Kingdom that Cannan could have chosen, where did he go? To a place called Dead Woman's Ditch. Of course, I am not suggesting that every man who kills a woman will place her in such an aptly named ditch, but what are the chances? Is it so hard to believe that having killed a woman, Cannan would be considering where to put her body. In mentally surveying the surrounding areas for a suitable location, something in his mind stands out. Something is salient. Something that almost provides an evil irony. A location that was believed to be the site of another murdered woman (though this has since been questioned).

So, let us review a potential hypothesis. If Cannan put Shirley near Dead Woman's Ditch believing another woman had been put there many years prior. That would make two victims in that location. If Cannan did murder Suzy, and then leave grid references relating to her location, then Suzy would be the '3' victim there – or 2nd, technically. I am not convinced by this, but it is an intriguing possibility.

Keatley's Winthropping?

So, where is Suzy? Each author of each book makes a compelling argument for various killers. From Michael Sams (see Chapter 16), to John and Fred West (yes, that Fred West), to John Cannan, to someone only hinted towards. With each suspect comes a believable location. I believe that my approach to Winthropping could help with this case. To do so, the fuller case files would be needed – including those of the suspects. In the meantime, I wish the investigators luck, as it appears hard work has not yet been the key.

Phillip Island: a Murder, a MisPer, and a mystery

On Tuesday September 23, 1986, police at Cowes Police Station on Phillip Island, Australia, were confronted with two men who reported a domestic argument had occurred. What would transpire from this initial report would include a brutally murdered woman, a missing woman, and an enduring mystery that has not been solved to the present day. To most Australians, Phillip Island is famous for its Grand Prix racetrack. For some, the horrific murder of Elizabeth "Beth" Barnard is what they will know it for.

At the time of her demise, Beth was in a secret relationship with Fergus Cameron, a member of a prominent and wealthy family on the island. The Cameron family owned the Grand Prix racetrack land. Before Beth was murdered, her secret relationship with Fergus had been uncovered by Vivienne Cameron, Fergus Cameron's wife. What we know for sure, at present, is that Beth was murdered, and Vivienne is missing. How these two facts are connected remains an area of contention.

It is not clear where this series of events begins, but for the sake of providing some understanding, let us begin with the evening before Beth was found, murdered. On Monday September 22, 1986, Beth was at home. She was feeling unwell. At 8pm, Fergus visited Beth, stayed for an hour and then left at approximately 9:05pm. At approximately 9:15pm, Fergus arrived home. According to Fergus, he and Vivienne argued about his visit to see Beth. Then, Fergus claimed in his police statement that Vivienne attacked him with a broken wine glass.

Fergus suffered a significant cut to his ear and back. It was severe enough to require stitches. Fergus and Vivienne attended the local hospital in Cowes, but they did not say exactly how Fergus had been injured. Dr Powles stated Vivienne seemed tense and Vivienne suggested Fergus stay the night at the hospital. This was deemed unnecessary by Dr Powles. At around 10:10pm, Marnie Cairns (Fergus' sister) said that Vivienne called her to ask her to mind the children at their home. Marnie reported seeing blood in various rooms and signs of a struggle or fight at the Cameron house when she arrived.

Time marches on. Fergus stated he and Vivienne left the hospital around midnight. They arrived home and told Marnie she could leave and go home. Marnie told police that Vivienne said she would drop Fergus at Marnie's house after they had a chat. At around 1am, Fergus stated that Vivienne had accepted the separation and that he would be with Beth. According to Fergus, Vivienne also accepted that Fergus would leave her immediately and keep custody of the children, while she moved to Melbourne. At 2am, Vivienne dropped Fergus at Marnie and Ian Cairn's house.

At approximately 3:10am, Vivienne made a phone call to her friend Robyn Dixon. It was actually Robyn Dixon's husband, John, who took the call and stated that Vivienne said she was at the hospital (which was not the case) and had asked him to pick up her kids. John and Robyn agreed to do this. About 10 minutes later, Robyn and John arrived at the Cameron's home. Fergus and Vivienne were not present, so they picked-up the children and took them back to their own home. Robyn stated while she did not notice any blood or anything unusual, she did believe she saw Vivienne's handbag on the table inside the back door.

Beyond this point, we have no clear indication of who was where, when, or why. But, before the sun would rise: Beth Barnard would be brutally murdered, and Vivienne Cameron would be missing.

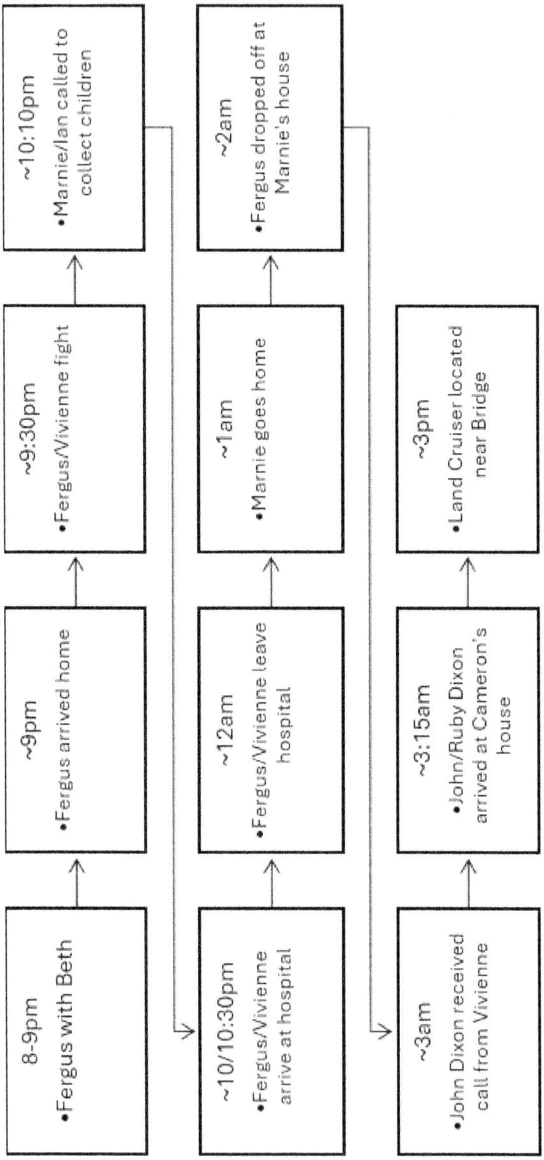
8-9pm
•Fergus with Beth
~9pm
•Fergus arrived home
~9:30pm
•Fergus/Vivienne fight
~10:10pm
•Marnie/Ian called to collect children
~10/10:30pm
•Fergus/Vivienne arrive at hospital
~12am
•Fergus/Vivienne leave hospital
~1am
•Marnie goes home
~2am
•Fergus dropped off at Marnie's house
~3am
•John Dixon received call from Vivienne
~3:15am
•John/Ruby Dixon arrived at Cameron's house
~3pm
•Land Cruiser located near Bridge

Phillip Island

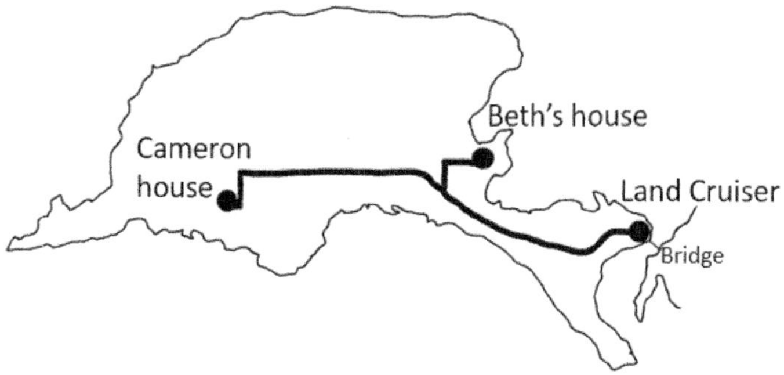

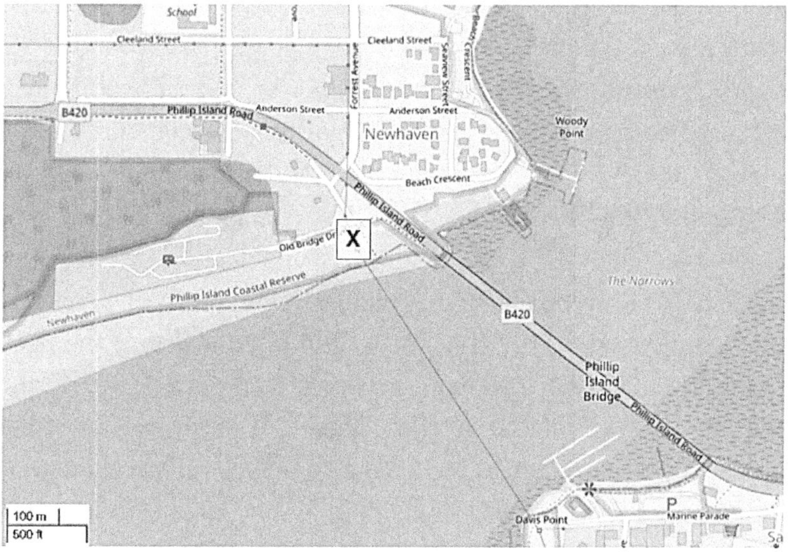

X = approximate location of Land Cruiser

It may seem easy to connect the dots between Vivienne and Beth. Indeed, inquests into the murder of Beth Barnard and the fate of Vivienne Cameron made a clear connection. While this is an easy connection, it is not to say it is the correct one. A full forensic and criminological profile of the crime is beyond the scope of this book. What is within the scope for us to consider are the circumstances surrounding Vivienne being missing. Let us look more closely at her. For, if Vivienne died by suicide, as some suggest, then she may be more likely to be the suspect.

However, there are other hypotheses.

Probably the most significant lead pointing towards Vivienne taking her own life is the Land Cruiser. The Land Cruiser that the Camerons owned was found near the San Remo Bridge, at Forrest Avenue in Newhaven. The proximity to the bridge was an easy connection to make, but again, we must not allow 'ease' to lead analyses.

You may recall, Robyn Dixon stated she saw Vivienne's handbag at the Cameron house when she arrived to collect the kids at around 3:30am. At this point Vivienne and the Land Cruiser were not there. The same handbag was later found in the Land Cruiser at San Remo Bridge. For the sake of hypothetical argument, let us assume 1) that Robyn was correct, and she did indeed see Vivienne's handbag, and 2) that the same handbag was in the Land Cruiser later that day. In this timeline, we have an issue.

What this would mean, if Vivienne did murder Beth, was that after murdering Beth, Vivienne would have had to drive back home to collect her handbag, and then backtrack again, to the bridge, to take her own life. This is not impossible, and explanations can be given to account for this. It does, however, require additional steps to explain.

An alternative explanation, of course, may be that the handbags were different. Maybe Robyn was mistaken. This means, perhaps that Vivienne did not travel approximately 7 miles (11 km) back from Beth's house to her own home, to collect her bag, before then driving a further 10 miles (16 km) to the bridge. Instead, Vivienne may have driven to Beth's, with her handbag, and then to the bridge. A lot simpler and more direct.

An alternative hypothesis entirely is that Vivienne did not take her own life. If we follow this hypothetical timeline, two further pathways emerge. First, that Vivienne may have fled and run away. In this scenario, the Land Cruiser is a form of staging, performed by Vivienne to make people believe she had taken her own life. We might wonder why other acts were not performed like a suicide note or leaving items along the bridge – though the items may have been stolen. In any case, if Vivienne had staged the Land Cruiser to lead people to believe she had then taken her own life, in some respects it appears to have worked. So, perhaps she was successful *if* this were the reality.

The second hypothetical timeline is that Vivienne did indeed lose her life, but not through her own means. In this timeline, Vivienne did not take her own life or run away because she was murdered. In this timeline, the Land Cruiser is a staged suicide by the perpetrator to conceal the murder. In this scenario, the staging of the perpetrator again seems to be successful – as the prevailing narrative is that Vivienne took her own life. This hypothetical timeline also explains why the Land Cruiser is where it is. After all, it must be considered why Vivienne would not use a simpler method of suicide. Driving back across the island to use the bridge is not necessarily the immediate or salient location.

Think about the location from my Winthropping perspective. Why there? Why jump from the bridge? There are other locations that would surely be more salient and closer to home. There are also other methods. The bridge is not the primary location for a number of reasons.

There are further issues with the bridge narrative. According to Vikki Petraitis and Paul Daley who wrote a very detailed book on this case, *The Phillip Island Murder*, there were no other suicides from the bridge. Petraitis and Daley suggest local kids used to jump from the bridge for fun during the summer months. Would Vivienne have considered the bridge a 'good' location to take her life? Added to this issue of the bridge being the location that Vivienne entered the water is the fact that extensive searches of the area did not find any trace of her. Of course, absence of evidence is not evidence of absence, but nor can we ignore this in our considerations.

There may be many more hypotheses that can be formed. Reality is seldom so simple or straightforward as television shows portray. Perhaps it is some combination of these hypothetical timelines. Perhaps Vivienne had murdered Beth and decided to flee; however, on further reflection, she was overwhelmed with guilt and so took her own life.

To even begin to attempt to solve this riddle, we must look at the broader forensic, psychological, and criminological evidence. For example, a bloodied knife at Beth's house was forensically tested and DNA evidence showed it 'matched' Vivienne. This seemed to add substantial evidence against Vivienne being the perpetrator of the murder. But I am skeptical of 'matches' until I have seen the DNA electropherograms for myself. Further investigation has also cast doubt on whether the knife was the murder weapon. Perhaps the knife is further staging. But who would want to stage the murderer as being Vivienne? Also, who called Vivienne's friend later that day?

Another important consideration is the evidence that Beth's blood was found on two sheets of paper (referred to as Item 23 in forensic/police files) found at Fergus and Vivienne's house. How can we account for this? Of course, knowing that there is blood on the pages is one thing, knowing how or when it was transferred is another.

It would take an entire book to explore this case properly, and thankfully Vikki Petraitis and Paul Daley have provided that for us. I am not suggesting that Keatley's Winthropping, alone, can solve this case. I am suggesting that using my Winthropping approach alongside the other information and evidence might shed new light into the investigation.

A serial killer calls.

The following case is, by my own admission, the most speculative of my Winthropping applications, so far. I am not entirely convinced of it myself. That said, I want to test myself and my methods. I am eager to hear feedback. If it turns out this case and my analysis of it are wildly inaccurate, then I look forward to learning why and adjusting the parameters accordingly. The following, therefore, is given as speculative opinion, no more, possibly much less.

In Perth, Western Australia, the Claremont serial killer case is infamous. Since the 1990s, when women disappeared from nightspots in the Claremont area, most people in Perth, WA, have known about this case. Originally, I was interested in the case because it involved a serial killer, and at the time I was developing temporal methods of analyzing such cases. More recently, I have returned to the case to apply a Keatley's Winthropping perspective.

The victims

To give some historical context. On January 27, 1996, Sarah Spiers left Club Bayview, in Claremont, at around 2:00am. Sarah called a taxi company at 2:06am. She was last seen on Stirling Highway by several eyewitnesses. At 2:09am, the taxi company driver arrived and claimed she was no longer there. At the time of writing, her body has never been found.

On June 9, 1996, Jane Rimmer also disappeared from the same area of Claremont. Jane and her friends had been bar hopping that night, and having arrived at Club Bayview found the waiting line was too long. Jane, however, opted to stay. Jane was last seen on security camera footage at 12:04am. Her body was found 55 days later, on August 3, 1996, approximately 44km south of where she was last seen. I recently visited the site and noted several features that I felt may have offered salient affordances. I do not consider this location to be 'random.' Though I visited the scene many years after the serial killer first did, I noted some salient features of permanence, offering me affordance as they may have to the offender.

Approximate location of Jane's body deposition site.

Then, on March 15, 1997, Ciara Glennon also disappeared from the Claremont area. Ciara had been at the Continental before attempting to make her way home. Several witnesses said they saw her walking along Stirling Highway at approximately 12:30am, eyewitnesses said she then interacted with someone in a light-colored vehicle, and then disappeared. Her body was found 19 days later, on April 3, 1997, approximately 40km north of where she was last seen.

The case, though infamous, remained cold for nearly 3 decades. Until, in 2016, police arrested Bradley Robert Edwards for the Claremont murders. Edwards eventually opted for a judge-only trial, which took several months. The judge found Edwards guilty of the murders of Jane and Ciara, but not Sarah Spiers. The judge did suggest it was "more likely" that Edwards was involved in her disappearance than not. On that basis, we can technically only speculate that Edwards murdered Spiers. Edwards is officially "not guilty" of the charge. So, this entire subsection may be a waste. Let us presume though, for the sake of opinion and debate, that Edwards was guilty of murdering Sarah Spiers and hiding her body. I am making no formal inference nor suggestion he actually was involved. This is purely hypothetical, for educational purposes – as much to see if I'm wrong and how, than if I'm right. So, while acknowledging this speculation and opinion, what can we suggest?

Where are they *vs* Why are they here?

First, let us consider the cases we do know about: Jane and Ciara. Jane was left 44km south, Ciara was left 40 km north. That may seem pretty hard to put together in terms of a geographic profile. It is indeed a large convex hull, at first glance. But it is not unheard of, of course. Other serial killers have had body deposition sites over large geographical areas.

The Birnies (see Chapter 14) were a serial killer couple also operating in Perth, Western Australia. The Birnies also changed their body deposition sites from south to north. Highway/trucker serial killers have larger distances between body deposition sites by nature of their work and lifestyle. Edwards, however, was not a highway/trucker serial killer. So, what was his 'why'?

Edwards did have a job at the time of the killings. He was employed for Telstra as a technician. He worked primarily on telephone lines. For my international readers, Telstra is one of Australia's largest telecommunications companies. Hindsight is of course always 20/20. I am not here to make comments as though I would have done any better in the 90s, if I were confronted with this case. That said, a Telstra-issued knife was found near where Jane's body was found, and this could have provided a good lead. But of course, one knife is one point, one dot, it is very hard to join a single dot to anything other than itself. How do you form a pattern from one dot? You cannot. Unless… Unless of course, there were other dots.

Why did Edwards drive Jane 44km south? He has the entirety of Western Australia to choose from and he clearly does not mind a drive. So, of all the locations he could choose and use, why there? The final place, as you can see from the image at the start, is at first glance relatively ambiguous. Nothing immediately jumps out. Nothing appears salient, right? But as you know by now, I have a hard time believing humans are as random as they think. We are influenced by our pasts. Decisions are biased by the ease with which we can think of them. Sometimes choices we feel are spontaneous or random are simply beyond our conscious awareness. So, what if I told you that Jane's body may be related to Edwards's job. In fact, in a way, his job may have pointed right to it.

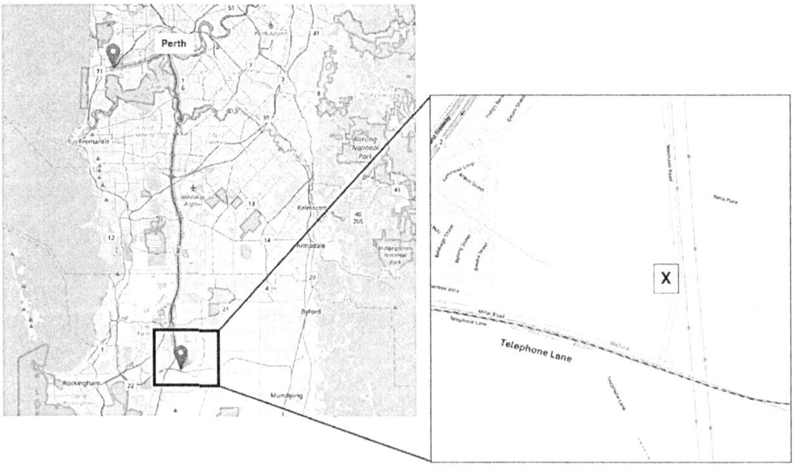

X = Body deposition site

I know, I know. It's pretty tenuous. Sure, laugh it off and dismiss it. But, then what? What else can we do to help find Sarah? Surely, after all this time and lost hope, it's worth considering something different. Think about this, of all the places in all of Western Australia, Edwards just happened to pick a quiet country lane very close to 'Telephone Lane.' If we are going to accept that SLP386S could be a covert clue from an offender, then surely, we must at least entertain the possibility that Jane's body may not have been as random as we first thought. Perhaps it was not as random as Edwards first thought.

Let me lower the level of what I am saying here. At the extreme, I could say that 'Telephone Lane' was deliberately chosen owing to its name and Edwards' job. I am happy to relax this though and suggest perhaps it was a lot less conscious. Perhaps Edwards just drove his car. Then, perhaps beyond his conscious awareness, something just felt right about this area. Something felt comfortable to him. Perhaps without thinking much about it, he noticed the name of the lane and felt right at home. Can we agree it is a possibility, however slim, at least?

If you are still not feeling confident about this, then please let me remind you of Michael Sams, whom we met in Chapter 16. If we can allow that his 'Millgate-Millgarth-Mill Gate' debacle may not have been a typo, but could have been a leak or an intentional taunt, is it so hard to believe that Edwards may have done something similar, here? I am not putting all my cards on this link, of course, I am not drawing circles around it to call myself a sharpshooter. I am, however, paying attention to locations and looking for possible meanings and links to offenders. At this stage, Sarah is still missing, what else is there to go on?

Right, are you still with me? Good. I know what you are going to ask me next, "So, what about the northern body deposition site where he left Ciara?" Good question. Sorry, no

Telephone Lanes this time. So, is my theory over? Is this the end of the road for Keatley's Winthropping? I think not.

X = Body deposition site

While there are no 'Telephone Lanes' near where Ciara was found, her location had a link to Edwards' job again. According to a book on the case, in the month prior to Ciara's body being put along this road, telephone technicians had been working there. What are the chances? Two body deposition sites, seemingly random, in opposite directions and both have a link to Edwards' profession.

My question becomes, therefore, if we posit (for opinion and argument's sake) that Edwards is responsible for Sarah's fate. Then, what else might we learn if we delve further into his work, his life, his activity (zones), and his interviews? Taking everything that we know about Keatley's Winthropping, as well as what we have seen so far in Edwards' body deposition site choices, is it worth looking at more sites related to him? I think so. The offer remains open, just pick up the telephone and give me a call.

Keli LANE

Keli Lane was a water polo player whose career looked set for great things. Lane had hopes of competing in the Olympics, which were coming to Sydney, Australia – where she lived. However, after several pregnancies, her life was spiraling out of control. The prosecution at her trial suggested she had been pregnant up to five times during the 1990s. It was the birth of Tegan Lee Lane, however, that ended with Keli Lane's arrest and eventual incarceration.

On September 12, 1996, Lane gave birth to her daughter Tegan. Lane appeared keen to leave the hospital to attend a wedding. Two days after giving birth, Lane snuck out of the hospital, leaving via an emergency exit. Between the hospital and the drive home, Tegan went missing. Keli claims she gave-up Tegan for adoption. This would be consistent with her previous behavior. Keli's other children she had given birth to were given for adoption.

In June 2005, however, a coronial inquest into the disappearance of Tegan declared that Tegan was most likely deceased. Furthermore, foul play was suspected. Following this, the New South Wales Homicide Squad was handed the case to review. Over 9,000 primary (elementary) school records across Australia were searched. After an extensive search, no leads were gained. No Tegan Lee Lanes were found. This further increased the suspicion that this was a no-body homicide case.

The police, though, not having any strong evidence to suggest homicide passed the investigation to the Director of Public Prosecutions (DPP). The DPP, on November 17, 2009, charged Keli Lane with Tegan's murder. Though Lane pleaded not guilty, she was eventually found guilty and sentenced to prison. The case remains: where is Tegan?

Given the route that Keli Lane most likely drove on her way

home, and the limited time she had, investigators soon narrowed their search to the area surrounding the Olympic grounds. The Olympic grounds were still under construction at the time. Given Lane's fixation on the Olympics and competing there, it also seems possible that this is a likely location. I am not putting all of my money on this being the case, but I am suggesting that there may be other clues in her interviews. From what we have seen in so many cases, I would be surprised if Lane did not make any leak during her interviews. Furthermore, I wonder if she were ever asked to draw a map of her drive home – I wonder what she may have included, or possibly more importantly, excluded.

Most recently, in March 2024, Keli Lane came up for parole. However, owing to the "no body, no parole" law, she was denied. It seems if Keli Lane is guilty and wants to be granted freedom, she will need to tell us where the body is. I wonder if we could find out the same information, through my approach to Winthropping. Of course, we must remain open to the possibility that Keli Lane is innocent. Finding the body of Tegan Lee Lane is important for so many reasons.

OUR NEXT STEPS

31. Additional applications

When I first started developing my approach to Winthropping I had serial killers in mind. This was largely borne out of the fact that I have a large database on serial killers, so it is relatively easy to study them. Also, believing that Winthropping was designed to help find a location that a hider intended to re-locate, I thought that serial killers fit the profile. We know that some serial killers will return to their deposition sites, so it seemed fitting to use Winthropping on them. This lasted for a couple of months, until I realized that Winthropping had so many other areas of application. My reverse engineering of the approach has allowed me so many more areas of application than serial killers. I am certain Keatley's Winthropping can be applied to further areas, still. What follows is by no means a complete and exhaustive list of applications.

Internet crawling

Here is a great example of why I love teaching. One of my postgraduate students just submitted an essay to me entitled,

"Applying Keatley's Winthropping to internet use." What the blazes is that all about, I wondered. Internet use? Winthropping was developed in the 1970s. How can it possibly be useful for the internet? I must admit, I am a human dinosaur when it comes to technology. So, I was unsure how we could possibly apply Winthropping to modern-day technology. Also, the internet is not a physical landscape, people do not physically traverse it or imagine themselves physically walking in it. 'Surfing' still seemed a stretch. I was immediately rather skeptical, but history has taught me to not be closed-minded. A few thousand words later, and the student's report received very high marks indeed. The concept was to track internet users' movements around the internet as we would track their movement in a real physical landscape. Though I had not considered it previously, I am now constantly playing with this idea to develop it. Many of the tenets of Keatley's Winthropping apply, and it may be useful in future criminal intelligence investigations. Listed below are some of the other uses that Keatley's Winthropping can/has been used on.

Arson

Recently, I was contacted by an arson investigator who had been conducting similar research investigations to those I was doing with Winthropping. Clearly, the arson investigation squad has access to a range of teachers and training. Focusing on locations, features, waypoints, markers, and landmarks is nothing new to them. That said, we did have a very engaging conversation about our approaches and how we may help each other.

Arsonists, like many criminals and people, are not as random as they may consider themselves. I am not necessarily talking about structural arson, wherein a motive is often easy to discern.

I am talking more about the fires that are set in national parks and smaller woodland areas. These can be extremely destructive, especially in Australia where the fire may go initially undetected and so grow for a period of time, which makes controlling them harder.

The arson investigator had put together something of a profiling approach to understanding why arsonists had chosen a particular location, with two aims in mind. First, to see whether the fire could be linked to any others that have occurred. Serial arsonists who enjoy setting fires will typically continually do it. Second, the investigator of course wanted to know whether the locations could be used to narrow the search area for the arsonist.

My response to both was a tentative yes. I think Keatley's Winthropping could be used to help investigators understand both issues. As we have seen, people fall into regular patterns, use what is known, and end up acting rather predictably. Second, geographic profiling is informative for narrowing search areas for suspects. I think with the additional tenets of Keatley's Winthropping, we can narrow that search further. This, of course, includes any statements made by persons of interest, locals, and people in police interviews.

Explosive Threats

One of the earliest uses of Winthrop's Winthropping was in locating Improvised Explosive Devices (IEDs). This makes sense, given what we know of Winthropping. Consider where would you place an IED, if you were the one hiding it. This Winthropping application changes the mindset question from "Where is it?" to "Where would I put it?" It can help us to see the landscape with a different lens. This was taught to military around the world and appeared in training manuals.

Moving forward from this, I have become keen to similarly localize the Winthropping process. Instead of asking where a body or cache may be in the wider world. I am interested in where an individual may hide a cache in their own home. We know that offenders sometimes keep trophies, or kits, or simply the stolen goods. I think we can take a Keatley's Winthropping approach and see if they are hiding the incriminating evidence in their own home.

On a more destructive path, I am keen to see whether bomb threats could be better investigated with the addition of Keatley's Winthropping. I think they could. Mercifully, bombings are relatively rare in the western world. However, simply because something is rare, it does not mean it is not worth investigating. Consider the following scenario: a bomb threat is made against a large shopping mall. The caller states a bomb has been placed. Could Keatley's Winthropping be used to help navigate the mall and narrow down the search areas? I believe so.

Stay at home?

This leads me to the next major development I am keen to make in Keatley's Winthropping. I would like to see if we can make hypotheses about whether a victim is more (or less) likely to have been hidden in a suspect's house. Many of the cases outlined in this book involve the movement of a victim to some other location than their home. Of course, many victims in many cases are hidden in the perpetrator's home. I am keen to see if we can begin to tease these two types apart, using my approach to Winthropping.

Recently I have been reviewing a case wherein the offender buried the victim in the cellar of his house. Through the language the person stated in various interviews, I think he gave multiple clear indicators that the victim was still in his house. Furthermore, clear indications of the victim being somewhere 'down' were also repeatedly given. This is similar to Stewart, who we covered in Chapter 25.

Of course, with forensics and linguistics, this task may be easier to do. Given what we know about the other tenets of Keatley's Winthropping, however, would it be possible to view a landscape surrounding a perpetrator's activity spaces and come to the conclusion that the victim is most likely at their house?

This may involve further psychological profiling, too. One of my postgraduate students is currently looking into the role of 'control' in homicide cases. Linked to this is whether part of the need for control links to an offender needing to control the body deposition site, continually, too. Is it possible that for a certain subset of offenders they pursue this continued control by keeping the victim in the house? I think this is a worthy line of investigation.

The Fugitives

So far, we have primarily considered those who have unintentionally gone missing and those who have gone missing through criminal means. There are, however, another group of people who go missing for themselves: fugitives. I am apprehensive about writing this section, because of the foundation from which it first occurred to me.

Recently, I was reading the book *The Betrayal of Anne Frank*, by Rosemary Sullivan. I do not want to delve into the details of that book nor the case. The book and case are very interesting from an investigative and historical perspective. The part that intrigued me, however, was whether Keatley's

Winthropping could have been used. And herein lies the issue I have with this application.

I am not comfortable with Keatley's Winthropping being used to find people who have a good cause to remain hidden. So, let us step away from Anne Frank, and instead focus on criminal fugitives.

Diane Downs, the mother that was convicted for shooting her three children, killing one and seriously harming the other two, is an infamous case in American history. After being convicted, she was incarcerated at a women's correctional center. Then, in July 1987, she escaped. She remained a fugitive for 10 days, until fine police work tracked her. However, having examined the case, the witness statements, and the final location, I am convinced Keatley's Winthropping would have helped shine a light on her movements. Remember, people are more predictable than they realize (or would like to be) and are prone to making verbal leaks. Perhaps in the second edition of this book, I shall devote a chapter to Downs.

More recently, I was asked to help track some fugitives who were wanted for a series of robberies and homicides in Europe. The process I used was largely similar to other Keatley's Winthropping approaches, though with an important difference. The fugitives could keep moving. Of course, criminals can return to graves and move bodies, or return to caches and hide them elsewhere. But in the case of a fugitive, they can continually commute and move. This provided a nuanced approach that I felt Keatley's Winthropping, in its current guise, was not well-equipped to deal with. I am very keen to develop this area and perhaps use more real-world examples. Given my work on temporal analyses and Behavior Tracking, I think we have the tools to investigate this further and improve accuracy.

I also note that many army training regimes have an escape and evasion component. I wonder how well both 'red teams' and 'blue teams' in these scenarios are trained in (Keatley's) Winthropping approaches. It could be beneficial, from both sides of the training, to learn some of my approaches. Given the history of Winthropping, I imagine there is already a certain amount of training into the concepts and approach; however, there is always room for further development.

32. The Matrix

No, not that kind of matrix. Sorry, Neo. I mean the kind that allows us to systematically synthesize, analyze, and prioritize our locations. It's basically a fancy table, but with the added benefit of a bad pop-culture joke to begin. Before I properly begin, however, please let me explain why I have waited until now to share this with you. Surely, you might think, knowing this table from the outset would have helped you process every case. Perhaps.

Many years of teaching experience, however, tells me that when I give things to students, in many cases their creative mind simply switches off and they follow rather than think. I am all for critical thinking and creativity. I learn a lot from my students and readers, and that is why I have left this until last.

I wanted you to read the cases without rigidly following a guide for how to structure the information. I wanted you to see what was salient to you, what you felt worth noting. If you made lists or notes for each case, can your lists and notes be tabulated into something like the one I am about to give you? Why not create your own. Be creative. See how it compares. If parts match and parts don't, then we have the basis for a very interesting discussion.

If parts do not match, then that is important. I am very keen to know about this, especially when it has arisen from your independent work, rather than simply attacking mine because I have said it. This happens all-too-often in academia. There is what is known as the 'Reviewer 2' phenomenon, wherein it appears certain reviewers just want to watch the world (and/or my ideas) burn. Of course, the review process is essential, but needless rejection for the sake of rejection is the antithesis to progress. Luckily, I grew a thick skin (to match my thick head) a long time ago. I am, however, getting tired of seeing the fire of ambition in early career researchers and my postgraduate students doused by ranting reviewers. So, let this be my attempt at asking us to work amicably together on this. Critique, not criticize. Let us synergistically improve rather than jump to remove.

What is the matrix?

I am tempted to say it, so I will: no one can be told what the matrix is, you have to see it for yourself. There. The point is this. I have put together an outline for ***a*** way of analyzing case file information. It is *a* way, not *the* way. You must see for yourself what fits best for your case. Let me say from the start, I do not always use the matrix I am about to show you. If and when I do, I often edit and adapt it so that it fits the case better. Again, structure and systematic reviewing is great, rigid thinking and formalities for the sake of dogmatism are not.

So, if you attempt to use this matrix and feel it does not quite do the job you need it to, then edit it. The purpose of the matrix is to make your life and review easier. If it does not make things easier, it is failing in its purpose. Do not fail in yours. Adapt it.

FACTOR	**Location A**: Name *Brief description of location*				**Location B**: Name *Brief description of location*				*… and on*
Criminological	☑	Description	Rationale	Feedback	☑	Description	Rationale	Feedback	
RAT									
RCT									
Geometry									
Activity zones									
Attractors									
Repellers									
Psychological									
ToM									
Affordances									
Salience									
Profiling									
Geographical									
Psychological									
Linguistics									
Leaks									

Note: include additional locations alongside, to the right. This will allow you to compare locations more directly. You may also include photographs and GIS data if digitized.

So, how do you fill the matrix in? Simple. First, include a brief description of your 'Location A.' This does not need to be anything fancy. In fact, keep it non-technical. What is your impression of the area? This is useful for cold case reviews many years down the line, who may not have this first-hand experience of the site.

Next, simply placing ticks in the column allows you to see which of the features you have processed in relation to the site. It forces you to systematically go through each one. We all want to jump to the quirky tree or the odd statement that may be a leak. But we must progress systematically. An empty box reminds us we need to go back and find out more.

Remember, we can add more. If you are doing this digitally, why not write out what some of the affordances are? I am in the process of developing a list, but it is many hundreds of examples long. Far too long to print here, but on a digital copy? Easy.

The *Description* column is there for you to provide a brief explanation of what the factor is in the location. For example, let's say you have ticked 'Affordance' but what does that mean? What is it you saw at or near the site? What's that? You do not know where the site is? Then think again, think about all you have learned. Look around. Remember, "they could be anywhere" is not true, so start looking for somewhere, instead of anywhere. Pick a likely location, then review it with this table.

The *Rationale* column pushes you to really be clear on why you have ticked the row and why the description makes sense. If you know the location and not the offender, then what about the location makes you think it is relevant to your offender? If you know the offender and not the location, then reverse this. Knowing what you know, both about the offender and about clandestine sites, what highlights this factor for this location?

The *Feedback* column is our constant source of development and improvement. Sooner or later, we are going to have to 'check' our answers. We are either going to have to go and look at the site or read-up and find out if we were right or wrong. If you were right, then after you've finished patting yourself on the back, check if you could have been more right more quickly. If you were wrong, then do not worry. Learn from it. Though remember, perhaps the only lesson to learn is to find another site with the same factor attributes but just another location with them.

Finally, for those interested in improving their problem-solving approaches and techniques, I highly recommend the exceptionally well-written book, *The Thinkers Toolkit* by Morgan D. Jones. Beyond creating matrices, topics such as weighting metrics and hypothesis testing are covered. Indeed, many of the concepts underpinning my approach outlined in this book owe a debt of gratitude to Jones' book.

33. The end of the road

Our final step… for now.

And so, finally, we come to our final step, the end of the road. First and foremost, my gratitude to everyone who has read this book. It has been quite an expedition, and while this is the final chapter, our journey is far from over. As the final few chapters highlight, there is still so much to unravel with this approach. I feel we are still at the very beginning in many respects. Already, Keatley's Winthropping has developed in ways that were not considered by myself or my colleagues only a few years ago. We are still, I think, developing a working model of Keatley's Winthropping. Beyond that, we then get into the minutiae of adapting it for specific cases.

Here is an example. At the time of writing, I have been loosely assisting in the case of a missing boy. The case is made more complex by the fact that the boy is autistic – which I am told is the term generally preferred by the autistic community. Straight away, an obvious alarm bell is sounded. Two actually. First, the obvious: can we put ourselves into the position of a young boy? It has been some years since I was considered young. How effectively can I get myself into his mental state?

Second, he is autistic. How effectively can I mentalize like an autistic person? Furthermore, before my readers correctly point out the caveat here. Point two suggests there is only one presentation of autism (i.e., characterized by one set of behaviors and cognitions), this is not the case. Though there are similarities between those with an autistic neurotype, individuals have unique presentations. There is a rather nice saying related to this: *if you have met one autistic person, then, you have met one autistic person*. So, what does 'putting myself in the position of an autistic person' actually mean or look like?

Of course, this issue is true of many other applications of Keatley's Winthropping. What about different genders? Different ages? Different psychological conditions? The list goes on. In each case, we have two extreme options. First, to simply give up, claim we can never know for sure, and do nothing. If that is your decision, so be it. From experience, this does not help a case, at all.

Second, we may keep ourselves aware of this limitation, and move forward tentatively. Wherever possible, we should absolutely liaise with topic, content, demographic, or geographic experts. People who can give us an insight into an individual should be listened to and the information weighed-up. Remember, it's a collaborative approach. I have called it *Keatley's* Winthropping only to ensure that any errors arising in the formulation of this version of Winthropping land squarely on my shoulders, not Winthrop's. Beyond that, I feel the method belongs to us all to develop together.

The best way of moving forward, I think, is to continue building our databases of cases. Within the last year, my database has grown a lot, it now totals over 100 cases. But as many first-year social sciences or statistics students will tell you, this is still an incredibly small sample. We should be wary, however, of falsely inflating the database to make ourselves feel more certain.

Cases need to be clearly detailed, and locations localized. Details matter. Insights into the decision processes of offenders should be added. It is not enough to plot two or three points on a map and call it a psychological or Keatley's Winthropping profile.

I believe that once the detailed database grows, we will begin to see consistent patterns across the sub-samples. Perhaps younger people make decisions and behave similarly in contrast to adults. Perhaps autistic and ADHD individuals do make certain similar patterns, irrespective of their diagnostic presentations. We simply do not know enough, yet, to make these kinds of generalizations in Keatley's Winthropping. One day, I believe we will. Even then, I would suggest extreme caution before making grandiose conclusions.

The limits of forensic science and Keatley's Winthropping

I have saved this until now because it is the section most likely to get me into trouble. As I have said many times throughout, Keatley's Winthropping is not a 'smoking gun' piece of evidence. When you use it, you will make mistakes about locations. Two responses will then be open to you.

First, you may throw Keatley's Winthropping in the bin. You may declare it a useless waste of time and ignore it. Or, second, perhaps, you may attempt to learn and improve it. As we have previously seen, sometimes investigators are more accurate than they realize. Perhaps parts of your profile were correct but your chosen location wrong. Perhaps a similar location exists nearby. Perhaps we should not expect any one method or investigative lead to be 100% accurate, 100% of the time. For example, if Redwine is eventually cleared in his case, then I would be eager to review my Winthropping approach to see how to improve it so that similar mistakes do not happen again. Again, that is why this approach is analytical, not evidentiary.

This trial-and-improvement development of forensic science and criminological theory, by the way, is normal. Science should always be seeking to improve. Hypotheses should be made with the intention of refuting or supporting them with good, unbiased evidence. If you have read ideas in this book and consider there to be something wrong or missing, then let us work together to improve this. Even DNA profiling was not perfect in the beginning – some would suggest it is still not perfect with human interpretation remaining a part of many analyses. As one leading forensic scientist puts it, if you give a mixed DNA profile to 10 different analysts, you may get 10 different interpretations back. The response is *not* to abandon it entirely. What a loss for forensics and the law that would have been. Instead, we should work together to improve Keatley's Winthropping. I know it will never be as accurate or incredible as DNA profiling, but every step forward is a step closer.

Where to from here?

Next, I suggest practicing with this method. A lot. While the premise and basis of my approach to Winthropping may seem easy, it is hard to apply in real-world situations. I have provided for you, here, over 30 cases of various types to show you some of the ways you can apply my approach to Winthropping. I have not given you a final version of my approach to Winthropping. I do not believe any such version will ever exist.

The interaction between hunter and hunted, detective and detected, investigator and investigated will always be an arms race. As we develop our methods, criminals will adapt. With the burgeoning field of popular true-crime shows, criminals are being delivered our tools piecemeal and practically. This is why guilty parents of missing children so seldom use the past tense anymore. In fact, what I hear more often now is, "he *is* such a lovely boy." The emphasis on the present tense is a reaction to the knowledge that past tense language is a guilty indicator.

Of course, not every criminal listens to podcasts, watches documentaries, or reads textbooks. Those that do may still leak information, as we have seen. Even so, enough are learning about our tools to merit the realization that our job will never be done. For every step we take forward, we must hope it is large enough, fast enough, and on a secure enough footing to ensure we stay ahead of the criminals we wish to catch.

***Keatley's* Winthropping**

To finally bookend this book, I shall explain again the use of my name. *Keatley's* Winthropping is intended only and solely to ensure that readers understand this is my approach and redevelopment of what I think Winthrop originally intended. I have no solid proof of my approach being as effective as his beyond the cases it has been applied to. I have no confirmation from Winthrop, or anyone associated with his work that I have successfully replicated his work. I could have created a new name, but this seemed disrespectful to his work and legacy. I want to acknowledge the great work Winthrop did and build upon it – as I hope others will do with my work.

I am confident that I have managed to redevelop many of the tenets that Winthrop may have envisioned. If it turns out that someone trained in the original art of Winthropping refutes my approach, then I welcome the feedback. I would be keen to see where the synergies are and more importantly where the divergences have occurred. My ego, which I have tried for a long time to stamp out, is a distant second to my desire to improve this work.

I have sat across from too many broken pieces of too many broken people who have lost a loved one. We owe it to them to be better, to do more, and to hopefully, bring their loved ones back home to them. Whether we are answering '*where are they?*' or understanding '*why are they here?*' I hope that my approach to Winthropping provides a step in the right direction.

To echo a quotation from one of my favorite criminal profiling shows: If we cannot rescue the bodies already thrown into the river, perhaps, at least, we can stop the killer before they do it again.

...And that is why I write these books...

Bibliography

Alison, L. & Eyre, M. (2009). *Killer in the shadows. The monstrous crimes of Robert Napper*. Pennant Books.

Astington, J. W., & Dack, L. A. (2016). Theory of mind. In The Curated Reference Collection in Neuroscience and Biobehavioral Psychology

Beauregard, E. (2005). *Hunting process of serial sex offenders: A rational choice approach*. In ProQuest Dissertations and Theses.

Berry-Dee, C. (1995). *Unmasking Mr Kipper. Who really killed Suzy Lamplugh?* Smith Gryphon Publishers.

Berry-Dee, C. & Odell, R. (2007). *Prime suspect. The true story of John Cannan the only man police want to investigate for the murder of Suzy Lamplugh*. John Blake Publishing Ltd.

Bettels, K., Grimstead, D., Allsop, C., Chaussée, A., Bolton-King, R. S., Sturdy Colls, C., Chapman, B., Keatley, D. A., Tilley, E., Turner, J., Spence, S., & Marquardt, A. (2022). Finding the missing and unknown: Novel educational approaches to warming up cold cases. *Science & Justice*

Berezowski, V., MacGregor, D., Ellis, J., Moffat, I., & Mallet, X. (2023). More than an offender location tool: geographic profiling and body deposition sites. *Journal of Police and Criminal Psychology.*

Berezowski, V., Moffat, I., Seckiner, D., Crebert, I., Ellis, J., & Mallet, X. (2024). The suitability of using domestic pigs (Sus spp.) as human proxies in the geophysical detection of clandestine graves. *Journal of Forensic Sciences.*

Berezowski V, Moffat I, Shendryk Y, MacGregor D, Ellis J, & Mallett X. (2002). A multidisciplinary approach to locating clandestine gravesites in cold cases: Combining geographic profiling, LiDAR, and near surface geophysics. *Forensic Science International Synergy.*

Brantingham, P. J., Brantingham, P. L., & Andresen, M. A. (2016). *The geometry of crime and crime pattern theory.* In Environmental Criminology and Crime Analysis: Second Edition

Brick. J. & Lebofsky, H. (2023). *Topic guide to cold case investigations.* The Vidocq Society.

Britton, P. (1998). *The jigsaw man.* Corgie Adult.

Canter, D. (1994). *Criminal Shadows. Inside the mind of the serial killer.* HarperCollins Press.

Canter, D. (2003). *Mapping murder. The secrets of geographical profiling.* Virgin Books.

Canter, D. (2004). Offender profiling and investigative psychology. *Journal of Investigative Psychology and Offender Profiling*

Chapman, B., Keatley, D. A., Bettels, K., Coumbaros, J., & Maker, G. (2024). Joining forces: combining police and external expertise for cold case reviews. *Forensic Science International.*

Chapman, B., Keatley, D. A., Oatley, G., Coumbaros, J., & Maker, G. (2019). A review and recommendations for the integration of forensic expertise within police cold case reviews. *Journal of Criminal Psychology*

Christian, B. (2022). *Stalking Claremont. Inside the hunt for a serial killers.* HaprerCollins Publishers.

Clarke, D. D. & Crossland, J. (1985). *Action Systems: Introduction to the analysis of complex behaviour.* Methuen Books.

Clarke, R. V. G., & Felson, M. (2004). *Routine activity and rational choice.* In Advances in criminological theory.

Cook, T. (2016). *Senior Investigating Officers' Handbook (4th Edition)*. Oxford University Press.

Conway-Grim, T. (2019). *Search and location of body deposition sites: the role of Winthropping and other innovative approaches*. Master's thesis.

Cornish, D. (1994). *The Procedural Analysis of Offending and its Relevance for Situational Prevention*. In Crime Prevention Studies

Crier, C. & Thompson, C. (2005). *A deadly game. The untold story of the Scott Peterson Investigation.* Harper

Critchley, C. & McGrath, H. (2017). *Why did they do it? Inside the mind's of Australia's most unlikely killers*. Pan Macmillan Australia.

Dalton, M. & Hill, B. H. (2005). *Presumed guilty. What the jury never knew about Laci Peterson's murder and why Scott Peterson should not be on death row*. Astria Books.

Dando, C., Gabbert, F., & Hope, L. (2020). Supporting older eyewitnesses' episodic memory: the self-administered interview and sketch reinstatement of context. *Memory.*

DiBiase, T. A. (2024). *No-body homicide cases. A practical guide to investigating, prosecuting, and winning cases when the victim is missing* (2nd Edition). CRC Press.

Donnelly, L., & Harrison, M. (2013). Geomorphological and geoforensic interpretation of maps, aerial imagery, conditions of diggability and the colour-coded RAG prioritization system in searches for criminal burials. *Geological Society Special Publication*

Donnelly, L. J., & Harrison, C. M. (2017). Ground searches for graves and buried targets related to homicide, terrorism and organised crime. *Episodes.*

Ekman, P., & Friesen, W. V. (2017). *Non-verbal leakage and clues to deception. Social Encounters: Contributions to Social Interaction*

Elms, S., Clarke, D. D., Briskey, M. & Keatley, D. A. (2024). Hanging up on emergency services: staged calls end differently. *Journal of Criminal Psychology.*

Elms, S., & Keatley, D. A. (2023). The Linguistic Disposition of Emergency Callers: Using Proximity Coefficients to Identify the Sentiments of Guilty and Innocent Emergency Callers. *Journal of Police and Criminal Psychology*

Fanning, D. (2009). *A poisoned passion.* St. Martin's Paperbacks.

Ferguson, C. (2019). Forensically aware offenders and homicide investigations: challenges, opportunities and impacts. Australian *Journal of Forensic Sciences*

Ferguson, C., & Pooley, K. (2019a). Australian no-body homicides: Exploring common features of solved cases. *Journal of Forensic and Legal Medicine*

Ferguson, C., & Pooley, K. (2019b). Comparing Solved and

Unsolved No-Body Homicides in Australia: An Exploratory Analysis. *Homicide Studies*

Franscell, R. (2022). *Shadow man. An elusive psycho killer and the birth of FBI profiling.* Penguin Random House.

Fulcher, S. (2017). *Catching a serial killer. My hunt for murderer Christopher Halliwell* . Penguin Random House UK

Gill, P., Silver, J., Horgan, J., & Corner, E. (2017). Shooting Alone: The Pre-Attack Experiences and Behaviors of U.S. Solo Mass Murderers. *Journal of Forensic Sciences*

Harpster, T. & Adams, S. (2017). *Analyzing 911 homicide calls.* CRC Press.

Harrison, P. & Wilson, D. (2008). *Hunting evil. Inside the Ipswich serial murders.* Sphere.

Havill, A. (2001). *Born evil. A true story of cannibalism and serial murder.* St. Martin's Press.

Hedges, C. (2024). *Missing: my life finding the lost and delivering justice for the living*. Seven Dials.

Houston, P., Floyd, M., & Carnicero, S. (2013). *Spy the lie. Former CIA officers teach you how to detect deception*. Icon Books LTD.

Hoysted, P. & Kidd, P. B. (2002). *Shallow Graves. The concealments of killers*. The Five Mile Press Pty Ltd.

Humphrey, N., Masters, P., & Harrison, K. (2010). *The application of Winthropping in the search and location of clandestine burials*. 8th National Crime Mapping Conference

Hyatt, P. (2014). *Wise As A Serpent; Gentle As a Dove:*

Dealing With Deception. Createspace Independent Publishing Platform

Jackaman, A. (2019). *Napper: through a glass darkly.* Waterside Press.

Jones, M. D. (1998). *The Thinkers Toolkit. 14 powerful techniques for problem solving.* Crown Business.

Keatley, D. A. (2018). *Pathways in crime: an introduction to Behaviour Sequence Analysis.* Palgrave MacMillan.

Keatley, D. A. (2020). *The Timeline Toolkit: temporal methods for crime research.* ReBSA Publications.

Keatley, D. A. (2023). *The Deception Detection Handbook.* ReBSA Publications.

Keatley, D. A. (2024). Finding the here in where: Keatley's Winthropping in missing persons and no-body homicide cases. *Forensic Science International: Synergy.*

Keatley, D. A. (2024). Investigative Deception Detection. *The Vidocq Society Journal.*

Keatley, D. A. (2024). *Behaviour Sequence Analysis in homicide investigations*. In Routledge International Handbook of Homicide Investigation.

Keatley, D. A., Arntfield, M., & Clarke, D. D. (2022). Crime Script Sequencing: an optimal forensic combination for cold cases. *Forensic Science International: Synergy.*

Keatley, D. A., & Clarke, D. D. (2020). A Timeline Toolkit for Cold Case Investigations. *Journal of Criminal Psychology*

Keatley, D. A., & O'Donnell, C. (2023). Winthropping as an

Investigative Tool in Clandestine Grave Discovery and Psychological Profiling. *Journal of Police and Criminal Psychology*

Keatley, D. A., O'Donnell, C., Chapman, B., & Clarke, D. D. (2022). The Psycho-criminology of Burial Sites: Developing the Winthropping Method for Locating Clandestine Burial Sites. *Journal of Police and Criminal Psychology*

Keppel, R. D. & Birnes, W. J. (1995). *The Riverman: Ted Bundy and I hunt for the Green River Killer.* Pocket Books.

Kidd, P. B. (2012). *Shallow Graves. The concealments of killers.* The Five Mile Press Pty Ltd.

Kinealy, C. (2019) *More Jail Stories. Altcourse Jail: Part Two.*

Kyriacou, K. (2015). *The sting: the undercover operation to that caught Daniel Morcombe's killer.* Echo Publishing

Lansley, C. (2017). *Getting to the Truth: A practical, scientific approach to behaviour analysis for professionals*. EIA Publications

Leclerc, B. & Wortley, R. (2015). *Cognition and Crime. Offender decision making and script anayses*. Routledge

López Batista, M., Rodríguez López, S., & Fieguth Batista, A. (2021). Use of GIS in Forensic Archaeology to Search Clandestine Graves in Uruguay. *Archaeological and Environmental Forensic Science*

Luther, K., Snook, B., Eastwood, J., & Fisher, R. P. (2023). Sketching: the effect of dual-modality technique on recall performance. *Journal of Police and Criminal Psychology.*

Marshall, D. (2007). *The Devil's Garden. The Claremont serial killings*. Random House Australia

McClish, M. (2001). *I know you are lying: Detecting deception through Statement Analysis*. The Marpa Group, Inc.

McGredy-Hunt, G. (2011). *Searching for Suzy.*

Moses, S. K. (2019). Forensic Archaeology and the Question of Using Geographic Profiling Methods Such as "Winthropping." *Forensic Archaeology: Multidisciplinary Perspectives*

Neldner, R. (2015). *Geographic profiling of serial murderer, Gary Ridgway, to assist law enforcement in the apprehension of future serial murderers.*

Oatley, G. C., & Ewart, B. W. (2003). *Crimes analysis software: "Pins in maps", clustering and Bayes net prediction*. In Expert Systems with Applications

OpenStreetMap contributors and available from https://www.openstreetmap.org

Petraitis, V. & Daley P. (2018). *The Phillip Island murder*. Clan Destine Press.

McClish, M. (2001). *I know you are lying. Detecting deception through Statement Analysis.* Marpa Group Inc.

McClish, M. (2012). *Don't be deceived. The definitive book on detecting deception*. Marpa Group Inc.

Monmonier, M. (2018) *How to life with maps* (3rd Edition). The University of Chicago Press.

Murphy, E. (2015). *Inside the cell: the dark side of forensic DNA*. Bold Type Books.

Murray, D. (2017). *The murder of Alison Baden-Clay*. Penguin Random House Australia.

Nickell, J. & Fischer, J. F. (1999). *Crime Science. Methods of forensic detection*. The University Press of Kentucky.

Norman, D. (2013). *The design of everyday things*. Basic Books.

Overington, C. (2020). *Missing William Tyrrell*. HarperCollins Publishers

Petteler, L. G. (2016). *Crime scene staging dynamics in homicide cases*. CRC Press.

Rocke, B., & Ruffell, A. (2022). Detection of Single Burials Using Multispectral Drone Data: Three Case Studies. *Forensic Sciences*

Schafer, J. (2019). *Psychological Narrative Analysis: A Professional Method to Detect Deception in Written and Oral Communications*. Charles C Thomas Pub Ltd

Simon, H. A. (1997). *Models of bounded rationality: Empirically Grounded Economic Reason*. MIT Press

Somma, R. (2022). Advances in Flipped Classrooms for Teaching and Learning Forensic Geology. *Education Sciences*

Somma, R. (2023). The space and time dimensions in the criminal behaviour of lust murderers. *Atti Della Accademia Peloritana Dei Pericolanti*

Somma, R. (2023b). *Tracking the Route Walked by Missing Persons and Fugitives: A Geoforensics Casework (Italy). Geosciences (Switzerland)*

Somma, R., Cascio, M., Silvestro, M., & Torre, E. (2018). A GIS-based Quantitative Approach for the Search of Clandestine Graves, Italy. *Journal of Forensic Sciences*

Somma, R., & Costa, N. (2022). Unraveling Crimes with Geology: As Geological and Geographical Evidence Related to Clandestine Graves May Assist the Judicial System. *Geosciences*

Stephen, A., (1988). *The Suzy Lamplugh story: The search for the truth.* Faber & Faber.

Sullivan, R. (2022). *The betrayal of Anne Frank. A cold case investigation*. HarperCollins Publishers.

Tobin, G. (2018). *Deal with the devil. The death of Matthew Leveson & the ten-year search for the truth*. Penguin Random House Australia.

Videcette, D. (2021). *Finding Suzy. The hung for missing estate agent Suzy Lamplugh and 'Mr Kipper.* Videcette Limited.

Wartmann, F. M. & Purves, R. S. (2017). What's (not) on the map: landscape features from participatory sketch mapping differ from local categories used in language. *Land.*

Wortley, R. & Townsley, M. (2017). *Environmental criminology and crime analysis* (2nd Edition). Routledge

Yeh, M.-H., & Ku, L.-W. (2021). *Lying Through One's Teeth: A Study on Verbal Leakage Cues*. Proceedings of the 2021 Conference on Empirical Methods in Natural Language Processing

Index

ABOUT THE AUTHOR

Professor David Keatley Ph.D. is Chair of Crime Science at Murdoch University, Australia. Prof. Keatley is also the Director of several applied research groups: Researchers in Behaviour Sequence Analysis (ReBSA); Major Crimes Review (MCR); Forensic Linguistics Analysis Group (FLAG); and a member of International Cold Case Analysis Project (ICCAP). In addition, Prof. Keatley is a full Vidocq Society Member (VSM) and co-chair of The Vidocq Society Post-Presentation Working Group. Prof. Keatley is also a member of the Pennsylvania Homicide Investigators Association (PHIA); Mid-Atlantic Cold Case Homicide Investigators Association (MACCHIA), and the International Homicide Investigators Association (IHIA). Prof. Keatley has assisted police and investigators on various cold case and major crimes around the world. Prof. Keatley has also published over 80 academic papers in peer-reviewed, leading academic journals, and written 4 books on applied forensic psychology, criminology, and behavioral forensics. Prof. Keatley has been asked to provide seminars on his methods, around the world.

If you would like Prof. Keatley to present his work at your seminar, please get in touch via his email or LinkedIn account.

Printed in Dunstable, United Kingdom

83034384R00188